THE MASTERY OF
MUSIC

THE MASTERY OF
MUSIC

Ten Pathways to True Artistry

BARRY GREEN

With a foreword by

Mark Stryker

Broadway Books   New York

Book design by Chris Welch

The Library of Congress has cataloged the hardcover edition as:
Green, Barry.
The mastery of music : ten pathways to true artistry / Barry Green.—1st ed.
p. cm.
Contents: Communication : the silent rhythm—Courage : choosing the high road—Discipline : the way of the will—Fun : the joy in music—Passion : the power of love—Tolerance : the view from the middle—Concentration : the spirit of the zone—Confidence : from bravura to integrity—Ego and humility : from fame to artistry—Creativity : the journey into the soul.
I. Music—Performance—Psychological aspects. I. Title.

ML3830 .G69 2003
781'.11—dc21   2002027815

ISBN 0-7679-1157-1

7 9 10 8 6

CONTENTS

PRELUDE

by Mark Stryker, <u>Detroit Free Press</u> music critic

Isaac Stern was on the phone, speaking in advance of an appearance with the Detroit Symphony Orchestra in which he was to play the Bruch Violin Concerto. This was the fall of 1997. The great violinist was now seventy-seven years old, and it was no secret that his once impeccable technical command of the violin, purity of tone, and intonation had all deteriorated significantly from his prime. And yet Stern's performances still often managed to startle audiences with a depth of emotion and intellect that put to shame many of the whiz kids that populate the concert scene, whippersnappers who can breeze through the entire standard literature without making any mistakes—and without making any music, either.

How, I asked Stern, did he do it? How did he manage to retain his artistry when the calendar had robbed him of his hard-won dexterity, stamina, and perhaps even some of his power of concentration? Stern, who could be as charming as a kitten or as gruff as a grouchy hound, sometimes in the same breath, paused for a moment. "Of course there's a difference from how I once played," he growled. "That's not the point. The question is how I use what I can do." Then his voice softened, as if he was about to share a secret. "Technique is not music," he continued. "Music is the thousandth of a millisecond between one note and another; how you get from one to the other—that's where the music is."

You don't have to tell Barry Green that the essence of music—and the soul of the musician—lies between the notes. That's what *The Mastery of Music: Ten Pathways to True Artistry* is all about: exploring the marrow of music and helping musicians discover and communicate the creativity and character that rest within their own hearts and souls. And while Green has specifically written his book for the practicing musician, anyone with a passion for music—from symphony subscribers to, ahem, music critics— will find that the contents open an intriguing and revealing window into the art of music making.

Remarkably, Green is exploring uncharted territory here. Countless books address the technical aspects of mastering an instrument and can help musicians learn to play faster, louder, and higher. Countless books profile great musicians, surveying the details of their lives, influences, styles, and recordings. But despite the lip service often paid to the mystical and magical realm of music beyond technique, few writers have developed a meaningful vocabulary to help focus our understanding of those qualities that separate the truly great musicians like Joshua Bell, Frederica von Stade, or Bobby McFerrin from the parade of aspirants marching behind them.

In typically generous fashion, Green believes the gap between the great and near-great isn't as wide as most of us might think. Green, whose previous book, *The Inner Game of Music*, has become a standard in the field and required reading in many music schools, is uniquely qualified to help every musician get in touch with their inner Isaac Stern. A former principal bassist of the Cincinnati Symphony, Green has also worked as a soloist, teacher, clinician, and administrator. All told, he has spent more than three decades in the trenches, and unlike some of his colleagues, Green has kept his eyes and ears open, remaining alert to those qualities that define great music making. To put it another way, *The Mastery of Music* could only have been written by an insider, and a perspicacious one at that.

This perspective is everywhere apparent—in the themes Green highlights, the musicians he interviews, the questions he asks, and the pragmatic thrust with which he, gratefully, funnels the philosophies and wisdom of his sources into the kind of everyday strategies and methods that musicians can carry with them into the practice room. Only an insider would hit upon these specific pathways to artistry—communication, courage, discipline, fun, passion, tolerance, concentration, confidence, ego and humility and creativity. And only an insider would illuminate these concepts by linking them with the instruments whose practitioners seem most to embody their spirit. Courage defines French horn players and percussionists; discipline distinguishes the woodwind section; passion animates cellists; creativity is the key to composers and improvisers: and so on down the line. It's an insightful approach, resonating on several levels. It is also witty, and so it comes as no surprise to learn that Green's own instrument, the double bass, is associated with the fun and joy in music.

It is refreshing to hear from such a catholic list of musicians—virtuoso soloists, orchestral musicians, conductors, classical players, jazz musicians, and even members of orchestra management. All have tales to tell, wisdom to share, truths to illuminate. The book takes us inside the heads of stars like Joshua Bell, Dave Brubeck, Christopher Parkening, Menahem Pressler, Frederica von Stade, Bobby McFerrin, Gunther Schuller, Evelyn Glennie, Fred Hersch, and many others. One of the book's charms, however, is that it also introduces many musicians who are widely recognized as heroes within the orchestral community but largely unknown to the general public. How marvelous it is to hear Dale Clevenger, the legendary principal horn of the Chicago Symphony, speak of overcoming a poor rehearsal at Carnegie Hall and then nailing the difficult horn part in Ravel's Piano Concerto in G during the concert. Or, to cite another example, Charles Schlueter, principal trumpet with the Boston Symphony, offers sage advice about how to stay in the moment, lower stress, and increase confidence while running the gauntlet of an audition: "There is no anxiety in the present. Anxiety is either in the past, worrying about what was just played, or in the future, worrying about what you are about to play.

Nothing can be done about either! Don't judge or evaluate while you're performing."

Aphorisms sprout on practically every page, and readers will soon find themselves underlining their favorites or marking pages with an ever-increasing number of dog-ears. A few of my picks include:

"Learn what you practice; practice what you learn" (Barry Green).

"We need to gain some perspective here; no one dies if we miss a note" (French hornist Eric Ruske).

"Without immersing yourself in a style of music, you can only play the notes" (cellist Daniel Rothmuller).

But for me, the absolute prize of the entire book is a passage by the jazz pianist Fred Hersch, a true poet at the keyboard, in which he addresses issues of creativity and spontaneity. He explains that sometimes in his practice sessions he surrenders completely to his subconscious and simply lets his hands wander on the keyboard. "I don't think," says Hersch. "Thinking is the enemy. . . . Picasso said that if you want to create art, you have to make a mess. You have to take the time to experiment. You can't get sidetracked by perfection issues if you want to be a great artist. You have to take chances—and a certain percentage of them are not going to bake . . . Sometimes in a middle of an improvisation I'll hit an absolute clam. Over the years, I have learned to say, 'Hmmm, this is interesting. I'll have to see where this goes.' "

I love this passage because it sings with a multitude of meanings. On the one hand, it echoes a truism of jazz improvisation: There is no such thing as a mistake, only a missed opportunity. But on a deeper level, Hersch has come very close to encapsulating perhaps the most profound theme of *The Mastery of Music*: In the end, one has to stop *thinking* about music and actually *make* music. This is more than a little scary because the possibility of failure is always in play; yet as Hersch says—and Green emphasizes throughout the book—one must take the leap and *dare* to make music, the fear of failure be damned. Music—indeed, all art—is less about perfection than process. Or to put it another way, great art is often defined as much by the journey as by the final destination.

Throughout *The Mastery of Music* Green identifies the tools—courage, discipline, passion, humility, et al.—that outfit musicians for the journey. These are the tools with which, as Isaac Stern might say, a musician can build a bridge between the notes. And a funny thing can happen when you start taking a few risks and building that bridge. Not only will you find the music, you just might come face to face with yourself too.

OVERTURE

Ten Pathways to True Artistry

What makes the great musicians great?

What's the quality or talent or skill that makes an Itzhak Perlman out of an already fine and talented musician? There are thousands of musically gifted eight- to eighty-year-old violin (and viola and tuba and trumpet and tympani) players out there. What's the key that makes all the difference here? What's the magic?

I believe the magic is something that we can learn from watching the great musicians, and asking ourselves about their defining characteristics. And I believe the distance between *good* and *great* that the Itzhak Perlmans of this world have traveled is a distance we all can travel, because it's the distance between being us and being ever more fully ourselves. It is what's *inside* you—whether you're in music or the fire service, business or education—that makes you unique, special, or even great.

The mastery of music doesn't stop with the mastery of musical technique. The musicians we think of as true masters of their art are the ones whose *artistry* we admire, and that goes way beyond technique, into a place that even the word "excellence" can barely touch, that almost indescribable realm of human depth which we refer to by such terms as "character" and "soul."

In this book, I propose that character or soul is something that we build over time, by a continuous process of growth that involves human "qualities" such as courage and concentration, humor and creativity. My previous book, *The Inner Game of Music*, encouraged musicianship by teaching us to avoid the pitfalls of mental interference. This book, *The Mastery of Music*, will enrich our art by teaching us the character skills which build that elusive quality we call true artistry.

FROM *THE INNER GAME* TO *THE MASTERY OF MUSIC*

Let me show you how this fits in with music education, and how this book complements my first book, *The Inner Game of Music*.

There was a time when music education was almost exclusively about technique. Over the last two decades, however, many music schools and universities have offered courses that train music students in concentration, sometimes using the principles set out in my first book, *The Inner Game of Music*, and sometimes working independently along similar lines. In this book I suggest we are entering yet another phase in the education of artists, one in which we need to address qualities within the individual: we need to explore and develop those specific qualities of the human spirit that lead to true artistry.

Music making, I propose, demands the mastery of three disciplines. First, there is the matter of technique, of being able to read and play the notes. Musicians are held to a level of accountability far beyond that found in many other professions. Music is a performance art, in which you have to play in auditions, public concerts, and sometimes competitions. You just can't afford to lose your focus on these demanding occasions. And this in turn means you need to have flawless concentration as well as technique! What this comes down to is the ability to sidestep all the ways we tend to distract ourselves: our anxieties and self-doubts, our tendency to compare ourselves with others, the tension that we feel when we're under the pressure of performance, all the issues I discussed in *The Inner Game of Music*. We need to have mastered concentration.

But there's yet another kind of mastery we need for the mastery of music. It's the third and final piece of the puzzle, and it's why I have written this book. It is where true artistry comes into the picture. We shall explore ten pathways to artistry, and be well on our way—but the road, as Tolkien said, goes ever on. . . .

Think about some really famous musicians, wonderful soloists and musicians like Joshua Bell, Bobby McFerrin, Doc Severinsen, Dave Brubeck, Cleo Laine, creative artists like Peter Schickele, and even some of the terrific people who work behind the scenes managing our orchestras. These are people who leave a mark on those whose lives they touch because of some quality they possess—passion, creativity, courage, or a sense of humor—at least as much as because of their undoubted musical skills.

It was when I started musing along these lines that a light went off in my head. Perhaps we should take a look at developing some of these qualities, as a means of making our own unique contribution in life. This doesn't mean we are all going to become world-famous virtuosi like many of those I've interviewed, but we can all develop qualities that hone and enrich our uniqueness. These are qualities of artistry that lead to the ultimate mastery of music. We shall be on a musical journey of enlightenment that has the potential to spill over into our lives as people. When we learn from watching those we admire, we gain a sense of purpose, hope, and satisfaction: an invaluable personal benefit from our journey into the personal qualities of gifted artists.

Ten Pathways to True Artistry

When I began my journey of exploration into these personal qualities among musicians, I noticed that those who play similar instruments often seem to have mastered certain specific human qualities that are closely associated with their musical roles. That was another moment when a light went off.

Which instrument can cut through the sound of a full symphony orchestra and chorus in a burst of brilliant color? The trumpet! Which musicians always seem to walk onstage with a special swagger? Trumpeters!

Trumpeters and CONFIDENCE, it seemed to me, go together—think of Doc Severinsen! The more I thought about trumpeters, the more I saw CONFIDENCE as their special quality, and the more I thought about CONFIDENCE, the more appropriate it seemed to explore it with the great jazz and classical trumpeters of the world.

The same sort of informal "matching process" seemed to take place over and over again, as different qualities of artistry and different parts of the musical spectrum fell into place. I've known for years, of course, that we bassists are a humorous bunch, usually up for a prank or a joke, and the best company at parties—we're the experts in having FUN. The composers and improvising musicians are the masters of "creativity" and the obvious choice for learning about CREATIVITY. And so on.

By the time I was through, I had ten qualities of artistry, and ten groups of musicians to represent them. These are the ten pathways to true artistry this book explores. They are also the ten qualities which I believe build up, like the layers of a watercolor, the extraordinarily rich coloration of every moment of life that is exemplified when one has truly mastered music.

Let me say here that *any* great musician, vocal or instrumental, can and perhaps will show mastery of most of these ten qualities. However, I've chosen, for my own creative journey into these ten qualities, to follow the path that links the most obvious quality with the most obvious experts.

I have chosen to order the chapters as I would order a musical program. I have tried to follow a natural pacing, to include contrast, intrigue, emotion, intellect, excitement, sensitivity, fun, celebrity gossip, spirituality, and ultimately inspiration. If you are a singer and want to jump straight to the chapter where great singers discuss (of all things) EGO and HUMILITY, then be my guest. Then come back and join us at the beginning, and work your way through the book in sequence.

In the first chapter right after this Overture, we visit chamber music groups, duos, popular combos, and conductors to explore nonverbal COMMUNICATION, a skill musicians who team together use to create rapport with each other. In Chapter 2 we explore COURAGE with percussion and horn players. We talk about DISCIPLINE with woodwind players (flute, oboe, clarinet, and bassoon) in Chapter 3. We are reminded of the Joy in music with Chapter 4 being devoted to FUN (trombone, tuba, and double bass). When it comes to PASSION in Chapter 5, we visit some of the world's great cellists. And so the journey continues, as we explore TOLERANCE (violists and management) in Chapter 6, CONCENTRATION (violin, piano, guitar, harp) in 7, CONFIDENCE (trumpet) in 8, EGO and HUMILITY (singers) in 9, and CREATIVITY (improvisers and composers) in Chapter 10.

Our Finale is dedicated to the energy and spirit that keeps us moving along on this lifelong path of developing true artistry: it features INSPIRA-TION, without which the journey itself will flag and fail, and which is also the crown of our musical experience.

As a bass teacher, as a performer and educator, and as a human being, when I began thinking about this book I felt right away that I had stumbled onto something important here. It's not about what you do or how you play but about who you are. It's about the qualities in the soul of the musicians that contribute to true artistry.

We can study these characteristics of musical mastery that are found in abundance in the soul of the very greatest musicians, we can learn from those who have them, we can build these characteristics into our own musicianship—and as we become rich in these *skills*, we'll be making a difference not just in our own music, but in our lives.

One example of this elusive quality of mastery that separates great musicians from good ones was demonstrated to me when I conducted my final interview for this book. I attended a dress rehearsal of the Marin Symphony (California) with percussion soloist Evelyn Glennie. Evelyn is a brilliant musician who happens to be hearing-impaired. While she is not totally deaf, her perspective on music and being a virtuoso percussion soloist is inspired by her hearing handicap. She explained:

When you are hearing-impaired, it changes how you perceive things. Sometimes you hear through the ear, with the eyes, with the body. But the hearing-impaired can also express subtleties in facial expressions, body movements, speed of signs, intensity of the signs, pace of speech, shouting—being rushed, angry, calm, or loved. This is why when you see Japanese Taiko drummers you can experience this enormous energy, power, and focus—you can almost see inside their bodies. The "boom" is not the climax. The true artistry is in the preparation and feeling that happens before the beater hits the drum. That is what is so exciting. That's where the mastery comes in.

Evelyn is talking about communicating all the passion, energy, confidence, concentration, and creativity within the soul of the musician. You can experience breathtaking mastery of music when Leonard Bernstein conducts. You can see this in the way Joshua Bell puts his bow on the string before he plays, you can feel this when you hear Frederica von Stade sing.

We'll be traveling the same exact road that makes the great musicians so unique and special.

THE FIRST STEP: YOURSELF AND THE MUSICIANS YOU ADMIRE

When I attend a great performance by Joshua Bell, or hear a brilliant program by the Ray Brown Trio, I leave the concert hall with a sense of these performers that's an integral part of my sense of the concert as a whole. I tell my friends, "Joshua Bell really went into the Zone—he was gone to another world, and took us with him," or "Ray Brown brought such joy to the music, and you should have seen the smile on his face—he made me feel so happy, and he still plays with such perfection and passion!"

Think about your own favorite musicians, or colleagues you feel have grown to the highest levels of artistry. How would you describe their playing, their uniqueness, or their brilliance to another person? What qualities would you mention? I don't think you'd mention their vibrato, but you might say they were daring, or polished, or creative, or just that they communicated so much feeling.

I think you would find it was their expression of artistry, of these human qualities and not the artists' technique, that you would notice.

Yo-Yo Ma and the Passion for Learning

I believe many great artists feel a special passion for developing the human spirit which goes beyond their specific disciplines. We have seen this passion at work in the diverse interest and projects of one of the world's most distinguished musicians, Yo-Yo Ma. Ma began his career as a virtuoso cellist mastering the solo repertoire, playing all the concertos with the great orchestras, and then championing the chamber music repertoire in the greatest of musical company—with the Perlmans, Zukermans, Sterns, and Axes of the world.

But this wasn't enough for Ma. His thirst to explore beyond the traditional repertoire manifested in the jazz suites with Claude Bolling. His Grammy award came from interactions with musicians like bassist Edgar Meyer, country fiddler Mark O'Connor, and banjo whiz Bela Fleck. Then came another Grammy-winning recording, *Soul of the Tango*, and a period of exploring ancient period Baroque sound and instruments, soundscapes, and collaborations with dancers, contemporary creative composers, and even popular artists like Sting. Ma's current involvement with musicians from different cultural traditions around the world is manifest through the Silk Road Ensemble.

In a recent story in *Gramophone* magazine, Ma said, *Basically everything I've learned about art has been from finding my way inside.* Ma is searching and growing through his relationships with other creative artists, with history, and with the common human spirit of all mankind. The fact that he plays the cello is secondary to his pursuit of excellence in learning and growth as a human being. This is a message that inspires me to explore these same concepts of artistry in this book. Not everyone can be like Yo-Yo Ma in the sense of virtuosic talent and the gift of communication he brings to the stage. It is not the goal here for us to become "bionic" musicians who master all ten pathways—but we can enjoy the pursuit of the same rich array of human qualities that have inspired Yo-Yo Ma, and we can only benefit and grow from such a study.

This business of inspiring and developing "artistry" is a subtle business. I certainly hope you will be inspired to explore and develop your own pathways to artistry as Yo-Yo Ma so clearly has.

After all, in the final analysis when your family, friends, and colleagues remember you after you leave this earth, it will not be *what you did* so much as the *special qualities you brought* to those around you which will be remembered. Perhaps you will be remembered for your sense of humor, or your passion. When you develop these qualities to a high level, you have achieved mastery not only of your instrument and your concentration, but of who you are and how you present yourself to others.

This is the extraordinarily worthwhile endeavor we shall be making here. *This is the Mastery of Music.*

THE SECOND JOURNEY: TEN PATHWAYS TO TRUE ARTISTRY

There are really three parts to this story. When I began this journey several years ago, my aim was to explore these ten pathways through interviews with great musicians. But a couple of things happened along the way. These great musicians kept on taking my inquiry further—revealing to me as I worked on each successive chapter what I came to think of as "a journey within the journey" or "second octave keys." They'd show me, to put it simply, how the qualities I was seeing from the outside felt on the inside, to the actual people who were living them. And that was often quite different from my initial "take" on these paths.

At the beginning of each interview, I would start with a list of questions exploring the things I thought were important in the topic. But then something very strange and exciting would happen, time after time. Behind each of these ten topics lay a glimpse of a world of artistry I really didn't know existed. As that world came into focus, I found I had to revise my questions with each interview. And gradually I came to the point that I would not ask any questions, I would just start listening—because this wasn't about what I knew, or what I wanted to hear, it was more about what the guest artist had to say.

One thing led to the next, and I learned to follow the path of discovery rather than the path of predictability. I learned to search for that moment of grace, to listen for the spontaneity of the unknown, and I also learned that this was what we all strive for in the mastery of music. And so the journey continues through all ten of the pathways to true artistry. As I explored each of these paths, I would discover a "journey within the journey."

Exploring the Ten Pathways

When I researched what happens when two performing artists COMMU-NICATE and are allowed to merge into one musical entity, I learned there is a unique nonverbal principle or force that soloists, chamber musicians, and conductors use to attune to one another. This isn't one person following the other, it is more a matter of the two artists responding to music that was within each of them—hearing it and responding to its shape, sound, rhythm, and character. That gave me a glimpse of the magic that we will discover in the first chapter exploring COMMUNICATION—the magic for which psychologists have coined the term "entrainment."

When I began to explore the concept of COURAGE, my questions were centered around overcoming terror. But when I talked to people who deal with this issue all the time, I realized that for some this wasn't about terror at all. What might appear downright scary to me may seem as simple to another artist as doing what they love. For others, it is a matter of choice: choosing to overcome fear, and embracing the courage to move forward. This chapter explains how outstanding musicians make the choice to travel the high road to courage.

At first I thought DISCIPLINE was about playing fast and accurately, but world-famous clarinetist Eddie Daniels convinces me it is about playing slow and eliminating the "garbage" between the notes. The key to discipline has a lot to do with finding your desire. I call it the Way of the Will. What gets you to the practice room? How do we learn and practice once we are there? How do we know when enough is enough?

Who would think that having FUN is one of the pathways to productivity? We explore the humor of contemporaries Peter Schickele and P.D.Q. Bach, and bassist Gary Karr explains a rich strand of musical showmanship that extends back over centuries to the time of Paganini—a man who knew that music could be playful and dramatic as well as beautiful. People who live in the low range of the bass clef have a great tradition of practical jokes. Some jokes keep everyone on their toes and actually improve their attention at work, while others have been more costly. Here we explore fun (humor included!) as a key to artistry beyond the obvious short-term punch line.

PASSION is about love and emotion. I worked on this chapter shortly after the terrorist attacks on the World Trade Center Towers and Pentagon. Many readers will recall the moving memorial service held in the National Cathedral in Washington, in which a worldwide television audience heard the mezzo-soprano and Washington native Denyce Graves sing "America the Beautiful" and the Lord's Prayer. Her performance was an expression of strength, resolve, and patriotic love. In this chapter, we explore the events and circumstances in our lives and in music that can tap into our passion. The great cellist Pablo Casals once said that passion comes from *what we learn from love—love of nature, of music, of man.*

Learning about TOLERANCE from violists and orchestral management was an eye-opener, a lesson in perspective. Violists spend their lives "in the middle"—in the middle of the orchestra, of the string quartet, and of a lot of arguments between colleagues. They have learned how to enjoy the musical and personal roles they play. There is much satisfaction that comes with their perspective.

When it comes to CONCENTRATION, our solo instrumentalists for the violin, piano, guitar, and harp are the experts. Violin soloist Joshua Bell told me that when he plays the Beethoven violin concerto, he sometimes finds himself feeling nervous during the big orchestral introduction, then moves into a state of serene concentration just as he is about to play. He enters a "sacred space" where he feels a sense of powerful guidance from the composer. When he allows himself to surrender to this guidance, his anxiety is replaced by intuitive natural playing.

The chapter on CONFIDENCE is full of helpful techniques passed along by my jazz and classical trumpet colleagues. I learned something fascinating from Doc Severinsen. He explained to me that there are *two* kinds of confidence. The first kind is based on innocence or bravura. It is un-earned confidence, and as a result it tends to be shallow and short-lived. Real confidence is the confidence that's earned by good preparation.

When we explore EGO and HUMILITY, finding humility among singers may seem like looking for a needle in a haystack, but there is another side to this story. Soul singer superstar Nnenna Freelon shatters our concept of fame when she discusses self-esteem with inner-city youths. The story of Kathleen Battle helps us understand what makes a diva a diva, as Frederica von Stade comes to Battle's defense with a convincing and compassionate perspective on the singer. What about Domingo and Pavarotti? It's a story that goes beyond lessons in humility.

CREATIVITY is the last of our ten pathways. Responding to the voice within can truly be a journey into the artist's soul. Both composers and improvisational artists live in a world of constant discovery, listening for their inner direction and following the insights it provides. Mozart was able to hear music inspired by his creative spirit and write it down without revisions, while Beethoven had to work harder to perfect his inspirations.

In the Finale (dedicated to INSPIRATION) we explore music as a forum in which to experience your growth as a human being. The great British composer Sir Peter Maxwell Davies said that if nobody remembers his music ten years after his death, it won't matter. That is not why he composes. He said that he composes because it is an ongoing process of self-refinement. Writing his own music allows him to learn things about himself. And this is an ongoing process; the learning never stops. And we can also be inspired to stay on this path through our interactions with others: teachers, mentors, even competitors. Dr. Joseph Flummerfelt, director of the Westminster Choir, believes that music allows us to tap into some kind of eternal truth, which keeps drawing us into a deeper place within ourselves. And finally, the loss of a loved one or times of great social tragedy can have a powerful and inspiring impact on our music making.

Inspiration is the engine that keeps us moving along the ten paths, and empowers our continuing mastery of music.

THE WAY OF THE MASTER MUSICIAN

We shall explore these ten pathways which together make up the difference between the good and the great, and we'll see in each case how our understanding of COURAGE or the other pathways is transformed as we read the accounts of those whose lives exemplify it. But that's not all, there is more.

As I have been exploring these ten pathways to true artistry with many of my musical colleagues, I have been surprised to find our conversations turning again and again in a direction that I can easily recognize but cannot quite name. That "quality without a name" is the third part of this message, and I trust you will pick up on it as you read along. You will find it expressed within these pages through subtle inferences and indirect suggestions in every chapter. While conducting more than 120 interviews with master musicians, I was surprised and delighted again and again at their willingness to open their hearts and souls to me—but even more amazed to see how many of them attempted to put something into words that they had never before expressed.

In one of my last interviews, Bobby McFerrin told me this is what he lives for:

> When I go to a concert, I don't want to leave the hall the same way I entered. I want TRANSCENDENCE. I want something to happen to me in there, so that when I leave the hall, I've been touched in a deep, deep way—by magic, by some holy accident. I'm singing this song, and all of a sudden I hear this voice in the balcony singing along with me. Something happens which makes people feel they have been asked to step outside themselves a little bit, to help create the musical space. That's what I want, and I think that is what everybody wants.

I have found this striving for something special, something which we can never quite control, and never quite put into words, has woven its way like a hidden theme throughout the chapters of this book, and I believe it has a great deal to do with inspiration, and with the transformation which takes place as the separate qualities we are exploring begin to meld together into that elusive thing we call mastery. Perhaps we can't explain it, but this mysterious quality seems to be something many performing artists strive for, time and time again.

OUR JOURNEY

Our journey, then, is to take a fresh look at these ten pathways to excellence which can be found in the human spirit, and which I feel so passionately contribute to the mastery of music. This list begins with the ten pathways I have named, but it will continue through your own discovery of even more pathways to artistry.

What is so remarkable is that these pathways lead to new insights and a better understanding of what we might have thought was "the right way." I encourage you to read between the lines. I invite you to spend some time thinking about the significance of what many of these great artists will say.

A true exploration of *The Mastery of Music* reveals that there is much more to learn than what appears on the surface. The process itself is endless, but within this journey lie all the marvels of discovery, spontaneity, guidance, and wisdom. What is most important is taking up the challenge and growing and developing these qualities in our lives.

The late great master violinist Isaac Stern, in *Life's Virtuoso*, the documentary about him in the American Masters Series, said:

> Composers wrote the words and the notes. You have to make your own individual sound, but you have to understand—and the understanding doesn't come out of here [pointing to his head] but out of here [pointing to his heart]. If you really know music as a professional musician, then you spend your entire life learning that you cannot learn everything. Then you learn a respect for learning from others with whom to exchange these ideas.

We learn from other master musicians, we learn from experts who have championed those qualities that have made them truly unique and special, we learn from great music, we learn from life and nature, we learn above all because we know this is one of the great reasons we are alive.

There's a popular saying that the whole is greater than the sum of its parts—and that's the way these pathways of true artistry work together to build mastery in music. May your journey enrich your life with music, and may it never end.

one

COMMUNICATION:
THE SILENT RHYTHM

(Duos, Chamber Ensembles, Popular Combos, and Conductors)

Most of the time we feel separate from one another: we call ourselves "individuals," and we know that even our disagreements are proof that each one of us is indeed a very different person. Something happens, though, when you see eye to eye with someone, and discover rich layers of agreement on the details that other people "never quite understood"—or when your body appears able to dance flawlessly with another person, with no fumbling awkwardness, just two bodies together seemingly following the same rhythm, the same lilt and sway.

At times like these, we rejoice in finding a "perfect match," a "soul mate," a "twin."

In this chapter, I am going to make the bold assumption that this feeling of togetherness—not togetherness as in some rigid lock step, but togetherness as in *dance*—is vitally important in music making, and that when a duo or combo or orchestra finds this dance, being moved as one, it communicates it to the audience, and a whole concert hall full of individuals delights in being moved as one.

Soloists, chamber musicians, jazz musicians, and symphony orchestras often have to communicate with one another without speaking—and I'm not just thinking of the notes. How will a soloist come out of the cadenza and make a seamless entrance with the orchestra? How will the ensemble stay perfectly together during a *subito* (sudden) tempo change? Jazz musicians have to communicate spontaneously as they improvise, so that two people thinking new musical thoughts at the same time can think harmoniously. And conductors and ensemble players must convey a composer's ideas and feelings to an audience with cohesion and clarity—even though the ideas come wrapped in the feelings, and the feelings in the ideas, none of which are expressed in words. All this must be expressed seamlessly by a hundred individuals breathing and bowing and striking and plucking dozens of different pieces of ebony, ivory, catgut, horsehair, iron, copper, brass, and taut animal skin!

Musicians are not the only ones who communicate like this—far from it! The operating rooms of the world would be far less able to cope with heart failures and blunt-instrument traumas if surgeons, nurses, and medical technicians weren't also performing their own intricate choreography in the heat of an emergency. But again, the musical metaphor seems to hold well: we say they are dancing to a choreography, moving to a common rhythm, working in harmony with one another.

When conductor Leonard Bernstein takes the stage, it is as if his baton is charged with lightning, and he can light up whole sections of the orchestra with his smallest gesture. Jazz bassist Ray Brown establishes a rhythmical groove when he plays with his trio, and brings his colleagues and audience there with him. Yo-Yo Ma casts a hypnotic spell over his audiences when he plays his cello—and when he plays with a piano accompanist or different musical partner, it is as though the two of them somehow miraculously blend into one musician performing in twin bodies.

It strikes us as magical, beyond coincidence, almost supernatural even, when highly individual musicians merge into a perfect synchronized whole, as though they are all parts of a greater body, as though music itself has the beat and is passing through them. How do they do it? What is this *glue* that can bind the voices of a hundred artists and the silent motions of their conductor into one profoundly moving communication?

It's easy enough to say that skilled musicians have "talent," that playing together in this way is just a skill they've acquired—but that's like explaining the drowsiness that opium causes by saying the drug contains a "dormitive principle"; it *names* the effect in question without telling us any more about it than we already knew. Some people say great conductors can communicate this way because they have charisma—but is that any different? And meanwhile, those who prefer more mundane explanations shrug their shoulders and say it's all a matter of discipline, of practice, of rehearsal.

Oddly enough, there are more sophisticated ways of talking about this kind of blending of many into one. We speak of great moments of unity as "transcendent" moments, such as the spellbinding oratory of Martin Luther King's "I Have a Dream" speech and the rhythmic cadences of black gospel preaching from which it derived. The great psychologist Carl Jung coined the term "synchronicity" to describe seemingly coincidental happenings which are bound together by what he called an "acausal connecting principle"—something other than the law of cause and effect! And words from the religious traditions of humankind like "inspiration," "spirit," "chi," and "prana" can also give us a clue that something as lofty as devotion to a higher goal, or as simple as awareness of one's breath, may be involved when people connect or merge in their communications.

There is one word, though, which to my mind tells us more than all the rest about what is happening when great artists succeed in this kind of nonverbal communication: *entrainment*.

ENTRAINMENT

Researchers have come close to explaining what happens when musicians merge their musical energies in this kind of nonverbal, rhythmic union: they call it a form of *entrainment*. The word was first used to describe the uncanny effect you'd get if you kept a roomful of old grandfather clocks ticking away. In 1665, Dutch scientist Christian Huygens first noticed that two pendulum clocks, mounted side by side on a wall, would swing together in precise rhythm; in fact, they would hold their mutual beat far beyond their maker's capacity to match them in mechanical accuracy. Author George Leonard says that this phenomenon is universal. In his book *The Silent Pulse*, Leonard explains:

> Whenever two or more oscillators in the same field are pulsing at nearly the same time, they tend to "lock in" so that they are pulsing at exactly the same time. The reason, simply stated, is that nature seeks the most efficient energy state—and it takes less energy to pulse in co-operation than in opposition.

Musicians know about entrainment and other vibratory phenomena because instruments sometimes "talk" to each other in just this kind of way—you can make a vocal or instrumental sound in rehearsal that will vibrate or rattle the snare on a snare drum clear on the other side of the room. And if parchment and metal wire can do it, why not people?

The key to this kind of communication is something way beyond following a cue, or just doing what someone says. Perhaps the idea of entrainment can help us describe this kind of group communication with a rhythm or musical ideal, an actual energy shared between us. This is the key that allows great artists to play together in perfect synchronization.

When musicians entrain, they merge and synchronize their actions. These synchronized actions in turn have the potential to reach and entrain the audience as well. And when that happens, as the final crash is heard or last long note fades at the end of a piece, the audience is one, as you can tell from the stunned silence—and thunderous applause.

Just as the pendulums of a dozen clocks can entrain each other to a common beat, a dozen violinists playing the same part find it is far more difficult to play "against" one another than it is to relax and play with the beat. And yet each musician must be sensitive to the pulse if all are to play together.

Extensive research by Dr. William S. Condon of Boston University School of Medicine provides scientific support to this principle. Dr. Condon researched micro-movements between two people engaged in verbal conversation. His startling discovery of entrainment between the two individuals—even when they were arguing fiercely—may suggest how musicians can ultimately become one with one another in sound. After watching and analyzing slow-motion videotape of people talking for many hours, Condon found:

> Listeners were observed to move in precise shared rhythm and movements with the speaker's speech. This appears to be a form of entrainment since there is no discernible lag even at ⅟₄₈ second.... Communication is thus like a dance, with everyone engaged in intricate and shared movements across many subtle dimensions.

Let's apply this kind of thinking to music. Perhaps we don't take our cues from musical partners or conductors in quite the simple action-reaction, stimulus-response way we ordinarily think we do—perhaps the truly important cues are operating at a far subtler level than we can be consciously aware of, so that we could say we are not *responding* or *reacting* to cues at all, but that as musicians we are linked together through entrainment.

Entrainment occurs in all aspects of life. For example, I have often been amused by how many people find partners and spouses who appear to have astonishingly similar facial or body characteristics. Perhaps they are synchronizing some of their speech and body mannerisms in just the same way. Perhaps it's *entrainment* at work when you notice that you eat at the same speed as your partner. When you walk side by side, you may find you are marching to the beat of the same silent drummer, and when you have a conversation with your partner, you may find yourself mirroring the crossed legs, hand positions, or the way your partner is holding his or her head slightly to one side.

Rhythmic entrainment with an opponent is critical in the martial arts. Thousands of people doing rhythmic chanting can transmit energy to the home team in a baseball or basketball game—and the energy transmitted influences the players' concentration and performance. And soldiers march together with such precision that they have to break step when they cross bridges! Not surprisingly, the marching band offers us another example of rhythmic entrainment—every aspect of movement in marching bands and drill teams is synchronized to the beat of the drum corp.

Musicians work in a subtler but similar way. They need to follow each other's tempi, dynamics, and levels of expression. When they allow themselves to entrain or merge with their partners or sections, they become a part of a greater musical unit, and speak as one musical voice.

I recently attended a concert with legendary singer/conductor Bobby McFerrin. Bobby walked into the audience, put his face within one or two inches of a complete stranger, and began feeding him pitches and gestures. In no time, Bobby would sing a phrase and the stranger would repeat what Bobby had sung. But the man was accessing a range, quality of voice, and musical ideas directly from Bobby. He even seemed to mirror Bobby's style and imagination, and his voice sounded almost as good as Bobby's! He not only sang "with Bobby" as one voice but also dialogued with Bobby. It was as if there were two Bobby McFerrins! It was phenomenal—an amazing demonstration of the power of *entrainment*.

I was amazed at how Bobby could cast this spell upon an audience. He had established an atmosphere in which everyone was willing to go wherever Bobby wanted to go. Bobby told me that before he goes out in the audience, he spends a considerable amount of time onstage establishing a level of trust. Within ten minutes everyone is singing together. Bobby described how natural it is to entrain with the audience in a concert. He said that when he attends a concert as an audience member, he is always "finding his part in the music" and beginning to sing quietly under his breath.

I have this fantasy of what it would be like to be up there onstage participating actively in whatever is happening up there. I have a feeling that everyone in the audience is going on their own journey in their own way, participating in the music. I have a sense when I'm onstage that everyone is also taking a musical journey with me in their own way. Basically, I'm inviting them to open themselves and be vulnerable and share what this musical experience really is. And believe it or not, most people are willing to do that.

Bobby believes that when people come together for a musical event, they are willing (and even striving) to be a part of a whole new community. Before the days of television, live musical events were occasions for a lot of emotional sharing and storytelling. Bobby believes that this contributes to people's willingness to merge into a musical *union*, whether it be two people or an entire audience.

This process of merging with another individual in a duo or a larger group of musicians, or with an audience, is the essence of communication. There has to be a willingness to participate that comes from trusting or letting go to the energy and spirit of the music, whether you're a performer or a member of the audience. This communication is made possible by the silent rhythm that connects everyone. This is what allows for spontaneous magic to lift people into a state of perfect synchrony where everyone can perform and experience the music as one.

Ensembles

Musicians who play in duos, chamber ensembles, combos, and large orchestras must learn to entrain with their colleagues: this is the glue that binds them together, and gives each individual the ability to play precisely in time with the others. I have often marveled at the way two percussionists, out of visual contact with each other and separated by quite a distance, can pick up the pulse and character of the music from the conductor and play *exactly* together.

What ensemble musicians are doing is tapping into a common rhythm communicated to them by the conductor. The individual percussionists, who are positioned far away from each other, somehow *internalize* this rhythm in their own bodies, *then* they respond to the flow of this common pulse or rhythm and play with it. They are *not* simply responding to the conductor's cues. Playing within this established rhythmic flow or pulse allows them to stay in perfect synch with each other and the orchestra.

The Duo Relationship

The simplest partnership in music exists between two people playing a duet together. The duo ensemble is an ideal demonstration of the principle of entrainment, which can then be applied to more complex ensembles.

For many years I enjoyed playing solo bass recitals composed of mostly original bass music with a variety of different partnering instruments: guitar, harp, flute, organ, bass, bassoon, percussion, voice, and piano. Since I was always changing accompanist, I didn't get the opportunity to develop a strong relationship with a single person. But this changed when I met James Hart—a pianist who is my current musical partner, and best friend of ten years.

Our partnership produces a musical chemistry the like of which I have never experienced with any other instrumentalist. From my first rehearsal with Jim, I have experienced something with the bass that I had never known was possible. I would play my part and Jim would be playing his part—but right from the beginning it was as though I were actually playing his part myself. He was "in my head"—our partnership feels that close! If I so much as *thought* something, it seemed Jim was already doing it.

When we rehearsed, it seemed foolish to say in words what came so naturally for us as we played. Once we learned something, it was there for good. It was as though we could tap into each other's mind, expressing the same music with two different voices, yet as one instrument and one person.

I remember re-rehearsing one of my favorite pieces, which we had not played together in over a year. It's an emotionally evocative piece of music by my teacher, François Rabbath, called *Reitba*—named for a lake in Africa. When we started to play, I stopped and said to myself, Why are we doing this? This is ridiculous—let's save it for the performance.

I had realized that this music was so much in our bones and spirit that we could follow each other through almost any musical nuance—and each know just what the other was thinking or playing. From that moment on, Jim and I agreed that unless we changed our approach to the style or tempo, we didn't have to rehearse this piece anymore.

Often when Jim plays with me, it feels to me as if we have transcended time and are lost in a fantasy world. It's as though we are riding a boat through some rapids. The thrill of the music is like the river, our bodies both respond to the musical current—and the two of us steer from the front and back of the boat in perfect synchrony. I think part of what this analogy tells me is that while we still have some power to steer the boat, we are also negotiating a current with its own rhythm, its own natural shape.

Jim and I relish this kind of special communication between us. Jim once wrote,

> After playing with Barry Green for a few months, I attached the phrase "The Vulcan Mind Meld" to our performance and rehearsal practices. This was a process that I had learned about twenty years prior, but had never identified or put into full use until I met Barry. From the beginning, playing with Barry meant total communication. During rehearsals and performances we felt our "breath" in the phrasing and nuance, and locked our minds together as if by some special magic.
>
> I realized that we were coming from the same place.

I will now try to relate where that place is, and how two or more musicians can get there.

In working in an ensemble setting with one or more musicians, I've noticed that really fine musicians never felt obliged to talk very much about the nuances of the music or the details of their performance. They tuned in to what I was trying to say through my performance of my part, then guided me through *their* performance needs in a completely nonverbal way—they showed me what they were thinking with their instruments. In a word, we were flexible to each other's musical and intellectual guidance. When you spend a lot of energy following specific visual cues, you have less attention available to pick up on nuances or directions from subtle changes in the volume, sound, speed, or character of the music. Entrainment involves relaxing and letting go to a flow or inner direction which comes from being in close proximity with your partner. Entrainment is possible because both performers are receiving their guidance from the music, while simultaneously being connected in a sensitive noncontrolling relationship with one another. Jim likes to call this the "mind meld." It is this sensitivity which allows us to unite in a state of entrainment.

Classical Chamber Ensembles:
Duos, Trios, String Quartets

The duo relationship is the simplest way to communicate through the mind meld, or entrainment—but the same kind of synchronization is what draws groups of three or more musicians together to play chamber music. As the number of musicians grows, the thrill of communicating at this level can actually increase—but when the number of performers gets very large, as in a larger ensemble, orchestra, band, or chorus, it is correspondingly more challenging to maintain a sense of intimacy and satisfaction.

Chamber musicians are notorious for playing quartets at get-togethers that last well into the night. They have the gift of an enormous body of literature written by the great masters expressing the whole gamut of feelings from triumph and joy to fury and grief. As they navigate such a wealth of music, they must pass a phrase from one to the other with the sensitivity and timing of an acrobat catching his partner on the flying trapeze.

White-water rafting is another good analogy here—and if playing in a duo is like taking rapids in a canoe, playing in a four- or five-piece chamber ensemble is like riding the rapids in a four- or five-person boat. The challenge of rafting is to negotiate the ever-changing current of the river: the people in the boat have to work together as a team to respond to the unpredictable behavior of the rapids. In playing chamber music, each member of the ensemble must respond to the flow of the music. The musical current determines what each individual must do to keep the music alive and on track. No one person can safely ignore his colleagues and act *as an individual*; each member has an equal responsibility to contribute his or her own part to the ever-changing character of the music. Communication is the essence of music.

When I was a student at Indiana University, I admired the dedication of the great musical artist and chamber musician Menahem Pressler, whose studio was next to that of my bass teacher Murray Grodner. Menahem founded the Beaux Arts Trio, which is still in existence after more than forty years. He told me how necessary it is for players in a small ensemble to get into each other's minds and bodies when playing chamber music. Musical artistry in a group has to go way beyond just playing the notes cleanly and exactly. The bonding is intense; when one of the members of the Beaux Arts Trio would make a mistake, another would often make the same mistake without thinking.

If one of us raises the left foot, the other one raises the left foot too! When you are in a group that is very intimate, every day ideas that may emanate from one of the others will refresh you and bring you back to yourself, so that you discover new things. It is a continuous search. I am a "looker": I look at their bows and know when they touch the string. I try and play so that I glide into my notes the way they do. It is by virtue of dynamics and tempo that the others understand what the feeling is on this day for this particular piece. It can be the way you look, the way your head turns. It is uncanny when we are intimate . . . we can insult one another by just making an accent in a different place.

He has learned to become alert to the way the music is played that day, because every day there are so many factors that change and require specific attention. The pianos and the acoustics of the halls are all different, the audiences are different, and the health and mood of the performers change from day to day. All these constantly changing factors have to be brought together to re-create the same music in a fresh way. It is like navigating the same river twice with the same crew and a similar raft: no matter how many times you have been down this river together, the speed and energy of the water are never the same twice. Each time, the crew has to respond to the silent rhythm within this current in a sensitive and flexible way. Menahem explained how sensitively he must listen, if he is to pick up the cues and nuances from his colleagues. He told me how subtle emphasis can be communicated in music, by comparing it to how we speak:

When I say I'm coming today for dinner I can say: I'm coming TODAY for dinner; I'm coming today for DINNER; I'M coming today for dinner;

I'm COMING today for dinner. You have all these different ways of expressing this sentence. It is the same in music. Very often we don't realize that on a given day, a player can change the accent, the meter, or he finds a new relation in the phrase. He takes it for granted that the others will understand it. But he has to react to it.

Menahem believes there's a sense in which he unites with the composer and with his colleagues to deliver a timeless message in music. The message must be much greater than any one of them, and only when the ensemble understands this message together can they communicate it to an audience. It is remarkable how music can transcend place and time through the playing of just a few musicians. Menahem conveyed this phenomenon perfectly:

I find it a miracle that I can play a Schubert trio with the same reaction in Japan, South America, Europe, all over the world. It is the love of it that envelops you and your audience, and takes you into this great moment in which you create or re-create the masterpiece.

The Kronos Quartet must surely rank among the most "closely melded" small chamber ensembles in the world. Any string quartet requires its four players to work very closely together, but the world-renowned Kronos Quartet must manage this while tackling a spectacular array of ultramodern pieces—by no means an easy task, although they pull it off with consistent mastery and grace. The sheer technical demands of playing this kind of music with ensemble precision demands a maximum of uniformity in style and execution from the players. Besides being classical virtuosos, the four members are also masterful showmen, and the Kronos is world-famous for interpretations which often integrate visual lighting, special effects, and electronics into the quartet's music. Their performances are often praised not only for their musicianship but also for their visual impact as an ensemble, and the brilliance with which they communicate and project their challenging music to the public.

When Joan Jeanrenaud, the celebrated cellist with the quartet for over twenty years, explained to me how she enjoys adapting her musical voice by "entraining" with her colleagues, I was struck by the emphasis she placed on physical entrainment, and the extensive use she makes of her body as her means of communication. Joan relies on body language and movement as much as sound in her communications with her fellow ensemble members.

Joan describes the importance of physical communication skills:

> There are two levels at work here: the physical and the intellectual. To me, that's the whole beauty of it—when you can be "in your body" with your expression, while at the same time you own the intellectual part. My goal is to know a given piece in my body. When I learn something, I feel better when it resides in my body rather than in my head. I need my body to communicate the music to my colleagues—it is difficult for them to read my mind!

Since the Kronos Quartet learns so much new music and often has to play world premieres while the music is barely dry on the score, its members rely a lot on physical movement to communicate among themselves and keep in synch. *We always had to be clear about what we were doing*, Jean told me, *so we talked things through a lot to make the music understandable. Breathing together was also very important.*

The Kronos Quartet also uses an extensive system of cueing. The members take turns starting a movement off, to explore how the group reads each person's starting cues, then decide as a group which best reflects their overall sense of the music, and they also take turns cueing parts within the music. Joan described pre-cueing by eye contact, before actually making the cue. She also looks into the center of the group, which becomes a focal point, the heart of the ensemble. She uses head cues and upper-body cues, and believes it is very important to show rhythm with her body. This allows her colleagues to adapt more quickly to her motion and follow her movement. She describes this kind of body/rhythm "entrainment" as like moving with others on the dance floor.

While many avenues of communication are important in all music making, the close-knit nature of a small chamber ensemble calls for both visual and aural uniformity of style. Ensemble members must become highly specialized in reading and interpreting each other's physical movements, just as athletes must be superb readers of their opponents' movements on the tennis court or the aikido mat.

Contemporary Ensembles: Jazz, Pop, or World Music Groups

Perhaps you know the wonderful ensemble of eclectic musicians called Oregon: they play original music, mostly written by members Ralph Towner and Paul McCandless. Oregon's music defies clear categorization, but it contains elements of improvisation, jazz, new age, and ethnic or world music sounds. I talked at length with Oregon's composer/keyboard/guitarist Ralph Towner about the communication that takes place among his colleagues, who have been playing together for better than thirty years.

Ralph and his ensemble colleagues have been able to cultivate an ability to *hear simultaneously*. In his case this is like following a musical radar scan, which moves quickly back and forth across the "eventscape" of what all the other players are doing. He told me that having this ability doesn't depend on how great a musician you are. He has played with some of the most celebrated musical giants in the business who lacked this special kind of sensory perception, and then he said:

> If it's not there, you can't force it. It's like a zen thing—as soon as you think you have it, you lose it. It takes a very delicate balance to stay in the middle of your scanning. When I'm soloing, I'm keyed into the accompaniment as much as myself. There are no secondary roles in music: everything you do affects the total music. So it is critical to be one hundred percent attentive to everything, all the time, and hear the whole as it evolves. There's no such thing as hanging back—playing in the group involves pooling your musical resources, being forgiving, respectful, and not obliterating what someone else is doing.

Great improvisation and communication involve concession and respect. When you hear a musical idea that stands out, you can counter, mock, or join in—but don't ever disregard it. This is a process of contributing to a complete product, while simultaneously listening to and shaping every moment.

Ralph has great respect for the music that is taking place. He didn't talk about what he likes to play or how he projects his own ideas, but about being a part of the big picture, and taking care to let it emerge.

My bassist colleague John Clayton recently told fellow teachers and colleagues at the Golden Gate Bass Camp, *When playing in a group—even when you're playing a solo—don't listen to yourself! You need to hear everyone else.* As musicians, we are all in service to the ever-changing kaleidoscope of musical ideas—no matter what's written on the page.

Disciplines That Support Entrainment: Reiki

Over the years I have immensely enjoyed collaborating with the English composer Tony Osborne, and have commissioned many of his works for my bass concerts. Tony has the ability to write exactly what I feel most natural playing. He also practices an Oriental healing discipline called Reiki, and has integrated its distinctive energy into his music and his professional relationships. The practice of Reiki, and how one uses this energy, is quite similar to the entrainment, synchronization, scanning, and communication principles we have been exploring in this chapter.

According to Tony, Reiki can be roughly translated as "universal life force." There are equivalent expressions in many cultures—chi, prana, élan vital, vitality, spirit, and so forth. The practitioners of Reiki believe this life force or energy is present in everything to a greater or lesser degree. This life force is within music, too—in pure sounds, in the sounds of nature, and in music as an organized or composed medium. It is within the composer and the performers.

The practice of Reiki—or yoga, qigong, or any similar mode of energy—allows you to be a vehicle for this powerful life force or energy. It can heighten consciousness in many ways. For some, it brings increased intuition; for others, it may manifest in a more peaceful, balanced state of being, or in clearer focus—freeing up the psyche and sharpening creativity. This goes hand in hand with the ability to let go, and to empathize and harmonize with others.

These feelings are fundamental to the intuitive states through which musical expression best flows. As musicians, we might benefit from an exploration of disciplines such as Reiki, yoga, aikido, meditation, and other forms of Eastern martial arts and philosophic practice, since they generally train the mind and body to open up to the powers of intuition and communication. If we can be more aware of this kind of subtle energy, we will more easily recognize it and respond to it, thereby expanding our ability to be sensitive to the ebb and flow of the music, and to communicate that flow with our colleagues.

Musicians are communicators. They have to understand the movement in the music they perform. They have to merge with their colleagues in partnerships, in small or larger numbers. Ultimately, they need to connect with their audience, so that everyone in the concert setting has the opportunity to experience the same magical experience. Entrainment is in full force when everyone is united in the experience—composer, performers, and audience.

When a performing group becomes so large that the individual musicians can no longer easily act as one interpretive soul, they can respond to the spirit and direction of a leader or conductor. In this scenario, the conductor unites the larger group of musicians with the music through his gestures, energy, and spirit. The orchestra becomes like a single body, united under the direction of its leader.

The Conductor as Master Communicator

The conductor is the *master communicator*, responsible not only for understanding the composer's intentions but for shaping them in such a way that they reach the audience via the performers. This is where the conductor can demonstrate his powers of persuasion, charisma, intuition, inspiration, and leadership, as he masterfully communicates with composer, performers, and audience.

The conductor's role is critical in heightening each individual musician's understanding of what is going on in the music, and in binding them together to communicate its meaning to the audience, so that the entire ensemble of musicians, in a sense, becomes *one*. They experience the same message, regardless of whether it is grief, suspense, anxiety, beauty, or joy.

In addition to his recent role as artistic director and conductor of the St. Paul Chamber Orchestra, Bobby McFerrin has guest-conducted orchestras all over the world, including recent engagements with the Vienna Philharmonic. He described to me that sense of perfect communication between conductor and musician:

> When you can feel everything is right, the tempo is right, the sound is right, you look at their faces and they are smiling, we are all having a good time—everyone feels, I just love this music. I just love being in the presence of Beethoven when I'm conducting Beethoven. You know it the same way you know when you are singing with someone and you are really locked together. It is the same way with an orchestra: you know when it is just right. You don't have to conduct the measures anymore, you can conduct the music, you can forget the bar lines and just really let yourself mold the phrases of the music. You can really let it go. If the musicians feel you are trying to control everything, they might as well just phone it in. But if you allow them to sense that there is mystery in the music, if you let them explore the mystery, then they really really play for you.

McFerrin was not formally schooled as a conductor, but has succeeded in mastering the art of communication. I found it interesting to study several other great conductors who possessed this gift of communication rather than a gift of conducting technique. I believe their greatness is ultimately determined by their power of communication. This goes back to one of the fundamental premises of this book: it is not the things you do (in this case, your conducting technique or accurate playing) but your character skills (in this case, the skill of communication) that make the difference between a good musician and a great artist. Here are some examples of great conductors who use their different styles of entrainment to communicate the power of music.

Daniel Barenboim: Creating Instant Music

Dale Clevenger, principal horn with the Chicago Symphony for thirty-four years, explained why his own favorite conductor is Daniel Barenboim, who became famous as a classical piano soloist and chamber musician. Dale believes Barenboim instantly communicates the evolving sounds in his head to the orchestra:

> Some conductors put all the emphasis on the melodic line, while others are fanatics about rhythm, but there are a very few conductors who are uniquely able to look at the score and hear every part before it actually happens. With the very best of conductors, it's as though there are two performances going on simultaneously.
>
> The first one is in their head: they know exactly what they want in terms of tempo, line, pacing, and connection. The second is the one they hear back from the orchestra, the one they conducted. And most of the time the two performances are not identical—but these few people are able to know exactly what they want, to hear what the orchestra plays down to every last detail . . . and then to respond instantly to fix it while it is going on, if the "played" performance isn't quite accurate to the "ideal" performance in their minds. This is the way Boulez and Barenboim conduct, and for a musician to see and hear this happening is astounding. . . .

So Barenboim has this remarkable talent of instant communication: he instantly projects what he hears "inside" as a live experience, and transmits this simultaneously to the ensemble. He negotiates the rapids with his musician crew, and gets everyone to respond instantly to what he sees, hears, and feels is important at that moment. And Barenboim believes

musicians should listen to the music for their primary source of direction—as opposed to watching for visual cues—and this in turn helps
them to be more responsive to his direction.

Thomas Schippers: Sharpening Awareness

Thomas Schippers, one of my favorite music directors with the Cincinnati Symphony, took a similar approach.

Schippers was musical director of the Cincinnati Symphony from
1971 to 1977. He came to Cincinnati from the Metropolitan Opera,
where he had earned a reputation as a matinee music idol. He was a handsome, jet-setting, high-profile, superglamorous conductor who remained
aloof from the public and his symphony players—but he was also one of
the most dramatic, electrifying, and exciting conductors for whom I have
played.

One day I was speaking with a stagehand before a concert. He told me,
"I've been working here for thirty years, and I don't claim to know a damn
thing about music—but I'll tell you one thing, I can tell you when
Schippers is conducting."

The orchestra just sounded different. The musicians felt a twinge of
anxiety as they took to the stage, and there was a sense of excitement to
the music. Schippers was very unpredictable. His baton technique was
vague, and the orchestra often didn't play very well together under his direction—but then sometimes there were magical moments beyond all ex-
planation.

I'll never forget playing the end of the slow movement of a Mahler
symphony with him. It concluded with a single pizzicato note from the
string section. When we rehearsed, it sounded as though someone had
dropped a whole bag of marbles—and since nobody came in together
with anyone else, I asked the maestro, "When are we supposed to play the
pizz? At the bottom of your beat? When your baton stops moving? At
the flick of your wrist? After the baton stops and you nod your head?
After you nod your head and then open your eyes?"

Schippers responded, "Yes, and then two seconds later!" At the concert, we waited until all signs of physical movement had stopped on the

podium—and miraculously, we then played as one! It was uncanny, almost spooky.

So how did this happen? What allowed us to play together?

I suppose that I for one simply wasn't concerned about playing with the other hundred musicians in the orchestra. My focus was riveted on Schippers, and on what he was attempting to communicate to us. This forced me to listen, think, wait, feel, trust—and be guided by my intuition. Schippers led me down a dark path and forced me to hear a little voice telling me what and when to play. And he forced every musician on the stage to find that same path. In the end, we all arrived at the same place at the same time. We may have had to work very hard to find this place, but we found it.

There is a well-known lightbulb joke about conductors. The question goes, "How many conductors does it take to change a lightbulb?" And the answer is "One—but who's really watching?" The message I learned from this experience is that the conductor does not always have to give clear visual cues. Many musical messages do not require visual cues—and on some level we already know this. Schippers taught us that the music exists somewhere, and if we are open and sensitive, we can all find it. He sharpened our awareness, put us on the edge of our seats, and made us responsive to the slightest subtleties in the silence of the rhythm.

And it worked.

Leonard Bernstein: Master of Masters

Schippers was a great friend and colleague of Leonard Bernstein's, and was often compared with him because of his charisma and ability to electrify audiences with exciting music. When the Cincinnati Symphony played Carnegie Hall and Schippers was too ill to conduct, it was Bernstein who took over the podium. This was the first time I'd had a chance to perform under Bernstein, and for me it was a truly incredible concert. It inspired me to learn more about the gift Bernstein brought to the stage—but it wasn't until later, when I had the chance to watch Bernstein conduct his own New York Philharmonic in an all-Tchaikovsky program, that I saw how a conductor truly entrains with the composer, orchestra, and audience.

This was, for me, the ultimate demonstration of a master communicator.

My first reaction going in to this concert was that I didn't need to hear my callous, reputedly "unemotional" New York Philharmonic colleagues playing one more *Romeo and Juliet* or *Pathétique* Symphony—but something told me I'd be a fool to pass up the chance to experience Leonard Bernstein conduct in the twilight of his career. So I purchased a seat in the balcony—literally above the first violin section, so my vantage point was both inside the orchestra and as part of the audience. I could watch Bernstein as the musicians saw him, and also see him with his back to the audience. I was so close that I could hear Bernstein breathe and see the perspiration drip from his face.

From the moment I saw him walk to the podium, I had a sense of what was going to happen. I already *knew* this would be the concert of a lifetime—and sure enough, it was. The experience was truly humbling, mind-blowing, way beyond what I believed possible.

Bernstein appeared possessed, as if from another world. He *became* the music he was conducting. I had of course heard Tchaikovsky's notes many times, and played the pieces more times than I care to recall. But this performance was as if I had *never* heard the music before. Bernstein says that when he conducts, he feels he is simultaneously creating or composing the music. This may be our clue to his immersion in the music when he described his experience in an interview at Tanglewood.

It happens because you identify so completely with the composer, you've studied him so intently, that it's as though you've written the piece yourself. You completely forget who you are or where you are and you write the piece right there. You just make it up as though you never heard it before. Because you become that composer. I always know when such a thing has happened because it takes me so long to come back. It takes four or five minutes to know what city I'm in, who the orchestra is, who are the people making all that noise behind me, who am I? It's a great experience and it doesn't happen often enough.

That evening the music seemed to be burning inside him, and his gestures seemed to unify orchestra and audience. We were all humbled, not so much by the conductor but by a sense of the energy that was present. The spirit of the music was so strong that orchestra and audience alike were swept up in it.

How is it that Bernstein was so effective in communicating through the orchestra?

He ruled the program, there was no doubt of that. But I never perceived him waving his baton to create a stimulus-response or action-reaction performance. While his baton beat reflected the rhythm, it was the feeling and emotion he kindled that created the *flow*. Similarly, it wasn't the greatness of the Philharmonic players that we felt, it was their collective ability to tap into the music. Every gesture, every last movement, was precisely synchronized with Bernstein's Tchaikovsky's spirit. Entrainment was in full bloom.

I have often wondered, since, why other conductors aren't as convincing as Bernstein. I believe this has to do with just what Bernstein is hearing in his head when he conducts. What separates Bernstein—and perhaps other great conductors—from the masses is that Bernstein and great conductors, I believe, hear *more* music. When Bernstein navigates an orchestra through Tchaikovsky, it sees, hears, and understands the musical current as more intense, more colorful, more beautiful, more exciting.

A gifted conductor has a deeper understanding of this musical current—and he or she communicates it to everyone.

COMMUNICATING WITH THE SILENT RHYTHM

I find it compelling and convincing that the principles of communication described by George Leonard, Dr. William S. Condon, Bobby McFerrin, James Hart, Menahem Pressler, Joan Jeanrenaud, Ralph Towner, Tony Osborne, Daniel Barenboim, Thomas Schippers, and Leonard Bernstein all suggest in their different ways that our ultimate communication experiences will be centered around a nonverbal connection with the pulse, flow, or spirit of the music. Certainly the most profound musical communications that I have experienced have been based on entrainment, imagination, and intuitive sensitivity.

The next chance you get to take part in any ensemble, notice the courage it takes to keep in tune with the ever-changing landscape of the music. We don't just play notes: music is a live current, and we navigate it. This current can be shaped and gently guided, but not pinned down. As players, we can influence its direction and add our own personalities to the mix—but the moment we interfere too much, the music's power, effectiveness, and *flow* will be disturbed.

If we are to master the power of the music as listeners and communicators, we have to be silent, attentive, and sensitive to its shape. We have to intuit a silent rhythm that has the power to unite us. We each have unique capacities to respond to music, and the better we understand, the more we feel, the closer we will come to the true spirit, and the more artistry we shall have to express.

two

COURAGE: CHOOSING
THE HIGH ROAD

(French Horn and Percussion)

Hidden way in back of the New York Philharmonic by the big brass kettledrums was a man who had never played in an orchestra before. Sure, he had played pro football with the Detroit Lions, and gone rounds in the ring with boxing legend Archie Moore. But that was then, and this was now. Now his eyes were glued to acclaimed conductor Leonard Bernstein. He was supposed to ring some sleigh bells, sometime soon. And he was terrified.

George Plimpton was by no means a regular professional musician. He could pick out a few tunes on the piano at home, but that was the extent of his musical knowledge. What he did know about was his own craft of journalism, at which he was brilliantly talented—and his specialty was taking on professional roles for a while, often in sports, and then writing about his experiences.

Maestro Leonard Bernstein had read some of George Plimpton's other writings, so when Plimpton asked if he could play with the Philharmonic for a month so he could write about the workings of a world-class orchestra, Bernstein agreed. The maestro put Plimpton in the capable hands of principal percussionist Walter Rosenberg and sent him off to what he called the "shady corner" in the back of the orchestra, where he could harmlessly hit a triangle or shake some sleigh bells. Triangles and sleigh bells are pretty simple instruments, granted—but George was still terrified playing under the fiery direction of Leonard Bernstein.

Walter Rosenberg told me how he helped Plimpton play the triangle:

During rehearsals I would lean over and point to where we were in the score, or whisper how many bars were left before he was supposed to come in. I swayed toward George at the moment of commitment as if bodily willing him to pick up the conductor's cue and perform properly. He would stare at Bernstein over the top of the triangle, metal rods gripped tightly, and look for some cue in the whirlwind of Bernstein's movements that suggested it was time for him to play. And then:

"Ping!"

Bernstein would look at him and say, "George, would you play that note for us again?"

George would pick up the triangle and play it again: "Ping."

The maestro would ask George to try it one more time.

Another, rather tentative "Ping."

"Once more," Bernstein would say as he cupped his hand behind his ear.

"Ping."

The tension in the room was mounting—the orchestra members didn't quite know where Lenny was going to take this one. Finally he said to George in a rather impatient, dissatisfied manner:

"Now, which one of those four pings do you mean? They're all different."

Poor George was obviously in shock. He stood there trembling, his face a complete blank, not knowing what he had done wrong, or what he could possibly do to play his ping any better.

One reason the usually courageous George Plimpton was so terrified was that *music doesn't have any room for mistakes.*

If you want to win at tennis, you try to make your opponent miss a shot—and missing a shot is just part of the game. In fact, in almost all sports, the errors players make go a long way toward determining the outcome. It's that way in basketball and football: half the players are trying to do something while the other half are trying to stop them doing it, so at any given time, some players are succeeding and others are fumbling and failing.

This just isn't so in music. Music has zero tolerance for error.

That's an exaggeration, I know, because there are many "correct" ways to play a piece in any case.

Imagine going to hear Yo-Yo Ma in concert—what would you think if he missed one out of every ten notes he played? If you could make nine accurate predictions out of ten about the stock market, you'd be a billionaire almost overnight, but if Yo-Yo messes up three out of the 150,000-odd notes he plays in a two-hour recital, some of the concert-goers will be muttering in the foyer that they didn't get their money's worth!

Even if you are a percussionist or a horn player, and you have only one note or a short solo to play, you get just one chance. You can't come in too early or too late, too loud or too soft, and the articulation has to be perfect. And what's more, in music the pressure is always building: once the piece starts, you can't call a time out, there are no "delays of game." You can't warm up or do a few extra dribbles before driving for the high note.

If you mess up, your mistake "happens" in a work of art—and you may not be invited back next week.

That's why getting the sleigh bells right was so terrifying. George's experience with the triangle had been daunting enough, but the sleigh bells actually open a Mahler symphony. Even George knew this was a make-or-break moment:

We got to the town of London, Ontario, where we were scheduled to play Gustav Mahler's Fourth Symphony. That symphony starts off with twenty-four strokes on the "sleigh bells"—an instrument in shape and size somewhat like a large corncob, with the bells (like the bells of a horse's harness) in rows along a center shaft. The musician holds the instrument by the handle (mine was bright red) and taps or shakes it. The Mahler score calls for the percussionist to tap the sleigh bells with the tips of his fingers the requisite number of times, diminuendo. The sleigh bells were in my charge.

Something happened in London, Ontario. To this day I have never known quite what. Mr. Bernstein walked onto the stage, a great accolade from the audience greeting him. He bowed, turned to the orchestra, nodded, and then looked across all those heads at me, poised in the Shady Corner, holding the bells out in front of me, ready to tap them and get things going. I was petrified.

A curious expression crossed his face. I have thought about it since—slightly forlorn, wistful, pleading, perhaps, as if hoping against hope that things would be all right. He raised his baton. The whites of his eyes shone as he peered up at the ceiling. His mouth went slightly ajar.

I began tapping away. Carried away in my terror, I may have hit the instrument too many times. Or not enough. Or raggedly. In any case, I knew something had gone wrong. . . .

Indeed, after the symphony ended, he appeared backstage, looking for me. In a near shout he informed me that I had "destroyed" Mahler's Fourth, that he never wanted to hear such a terrible sound emerge from the back of his orchestra ever again, and that as far as he was concerned I was finished, through!

Plimpton says he still dreams about that awful experience from time to time, and wakes up covered with sweat.

Imagine the pressure of playing an instrument for which you have little or no technique, when you can't read a note of music, surrounded by a hundred professionals who know more about what you are doing than you do yourself, and you are performing in front of thousands of paying concert-goers, not one of whom knows it's an "amateur" who is banging away on Mahler's cherished sleigh bells. Throw in arguably the world's most revered conductor, glaring at you with rage and disapproval, for good measure.

Now that, I think, takes big-time courage.

WHAT IS COURAGE?

George Plimpton ranks playing those sleigh bells with the New York Philharmonic as the scariest thing he's ever done in his capacity as an "amateur professional"—to use Bernstein's affectionate term. It may be encouraging to know that many of the orchestral professionals who play percussion instruments or French horn in our orchestras feel as though they are sitting in one of the hottest seats in the house. When I watch one of them from my comfortable seat in the double bass section, I think, Now there's a truly courageous artist. I marvel not only at what they do, but also at the spirit in which they do it. What looks like a very difficult musical challenge to me may actually be quite as challenging as I imagine to some of these artists, and entirely normal and uneventful for others. This dichotomy is what makes courage so interesting and individual.

As you can see, courage is not the easiest thing in the world to pin down. Although it's an attribute we can all recognize and admire in others, we may not be feeling particularly brave ourselves at precisely those moments when our friends would say we were being most courageous. From the outside, courage seems to be the opposite of fear. On the inside, it can at times feel like fear itself—and whether our times of fear are courageous or not seems to depend on what we do with them! Courage is far more a matter of carrying on in the face of fear than of not feeling fear in the first place.

Choosing the High Road

I find courage is really a matter of choosing between action and fear. If your desire to make music is strong enough that you will try for it despite your fear of negative consequences should you fail, I call it "choosing the high road." You might fail, you might miss a note, you might lose your job, but you have consciously decided to go for it. This choice must be made every day.

In music, fortunately, this is a very joyous choice. Many musicians who may appear courageous to others are choosing to go for the beauty of the music and the joy of playing it. Bill VerMeulen, principal horn with the Houston Symphony, explained:

> You come to a fork in the road, and one path leads to anxiety, the other leads to courage. You can allow your mind to think, I hope I don't screw up, just let me hit the right notes, let me not embarrass myself—but even though you hope you don't screw up, it's anxiety, not hope, that you're feeling. Or you can go down the road of courage—you can tell yourself, I'm going to nail this. Just listen to me! You have a split second right before that horn entrance to make that choice.

Percussionists and Horn Players

Because of the nature of their instruments, percussionists are soloists every time they play. If the "crash" comes in the wrong place, if a single note on the bells is missed or their "kitchen sink" of toys and accessories is accidentally knocked over, these players have nowhere to hide. Hazardous work of this nature attracts and demands personalities that can cope with liabilities of this kind. However, most percussionists relish the excitement of being in this position rather than fear embarrassment or mistakes. They choose to accept this challenge.

Music written for the horn can be extremely tricky, too. It is often written in a very high range, where the notes are incredibly close together—and often played while the other instruments are silent. Composers writing for this treacherous instrument seem to delight in challenging the horn player's range and flexibility! In fact, playing the horn with security and accuracy can be quite a challenge indeed—and audiences are so used to hearing "cracked" notes from horn players that this particular flaw is often quietly tolerated in performances by even the best of orchestras.

Few people play the horn unless they are prepared to dedicate themselves to its arduous technique: I and many of my colleagues think these players must have nerves of steel! But they clearly have chosen the joys over the risks, and choose to take this higher path.

Dale Clevenger is the legendary principal horn with the Chicago

Symphony Orchestra, and has been for the past thirty-four years. This is what he had to say:

> The horn has a large range, and the notes get closer as they get to the top of the range. So what? What's the big deal? In this business you just have to have the technique down. I function from the art form—that's what drives my music making. The reason I play the horn is that I like the sound of the horn. What I do is fun and enjoyable—and an incredible privilege.

His approach demonstrates the courage to move beyond the traditional fear that comes with technical difficulty. Dale loves the sound of the horn and loves to make music, so for him these benefits far outweigh the technical risks. His choice is a simple one. Dale is enjoying himself.

Scary Experiences and the Strategies to Handle Them

Playing horn or percussion can certainly appear courageous from the outside, but even the most seasoned musicians have had experiences they found downright frightening. Everyone has to get through these situations somehow; the music goes on, and the part must be played. Each and every professional musician has to make that choice to take the high road, and in my interviews and conversations with friends, I have learned that most of us draw on some kind of strategy before we choose this higher road of true artistry.

I find it fascinating that when our backs are really up against the wall, we engage our survival instincts. We may choose a particular mental strategy. We may refocus or rechannel around some of the physical blocks to our concentration. Perhaps we get a rush of adrenaline, as the flight-or-fight response kicks in. But as Bill VerMeulen says, one way or another each one of us comes to that fork in the road, and goes either to the left or the right.

At that crucial moment, successful or not, we make our courageous move.

I asked some great artists and close friends about their scariest experiences—and from the tales they have told me, we can glean a little about the strategies they use when they come to the place where one road leads to music and the other to doubt, hesitation, and paralysis.

Be Prepared

John Zirbel is the principal horn with the Montreal Symphony, and a fine musician admired by his colleagues around the world for his remarkable concentration and musicianship. His story illustrates exceptionally well the fact that "courage" may not feel like anything special or brave, but is more a matter of being prepared.

John remembers feeling all the symptoms of stage fright on one particular occasion when he knew he wasn't properly *prepared* to play. In John's opinion, it takes real courage to play when you know you *don't* know your part or when you're simply not ready. When he is prepared and knows what he has to do, playing doesn't require any special fearlessness or courage. But if he is ever unprepared . . .

> I played in a youth orchestra while I was in high school, and one time I had to play those famous high notes for horn in the Dvořák *New World* Symphony. It was very scary for me because I didn't think I could do the job well. I could only pull that passage off one time out of ten in practice—so I was scared before I began. That performance took real courage.
>
> I don't have to deal with that kind of fear now because I know the tricks. Worrying about whether or not I'll play well can be very stressful, but it is just not such a big issue. The real fear in my case is about not being ready. And there is a huge difference between worrying that you may not be playing well, and worrying that you won't be able to play the passage at all. . . .

When you doubt you have the skills or haven't properly prepared, you are in a way consciously choosing to fail. This is really choosing the low road. Rather than calling this courage, I'd call it foolishness.

Being prepared extends beyond the practice room. Celebrated English horn soloist Michael Thompson reminded me that even when you are prepared with your music, you can still experience terror on the stand because of nonmusical factors. He said making sure you are changed into the concert clothes in plenty of time and being relaxed before you play are as big a part of your preparations as having practiced and learning your music.

I've tried to think over the years about the things that unsettle me. Being taken by surprise is difficult. I don't get myself into bad situations. If I am playing in an unusual venue, then I get there in advance so I have time to warm up. Being polite and talking to people before a concert is fine but I will actually say, "You will have to excuse me, I have to have some time to myself now." In the past I wouldn't say that. I would have tea and conversations just before the moment when I have to sit down and play.

Michael is clearly telling us to keep the choice of the high road at the front of our attention. It is easy to get distracted or doubtful, and forget the real purpose of playing music.

Don't Panic; Focus on One Thing at a Time

Jack VanGeem not only heads up the percussion section with the San Francisco Symphony, he is also the backup timpani player for the orchestra. Once, he told me, his regular timpanist friend was complaining all week about how hard a particular timpani part was to play: he moaned that it was almost impossible, and he *really* didn't want to play it. Jack remembers telling himself, I hope he doesn't get sick this week!

In the end, he was right to have been concerned. On the day of the concert Jack received a call from the personnel manager telling him that his colleague had indeed called in sick, and that he would need to sight-read that tricky timpani part in that evening's performance—just twenty minutes away.

With no time to worry about the situation, Jack had no choice but to accept the assignment, step up onto the stage, and play.

I read quickly through the score and saw it wasn't so impossible, it was actually quite doable. "I can play this," I said. "I can do that. That's not too hard. And this passage looks as though it might be interesting. . . . Ah, now this could really be a challenge." I told myself it would be fun to see just how much of the part I could actually manage, playing it on such short notice.

In the concert, Jack not only played that part, he played it well.

Listening to Jack tell the story, I can see there are reasons why his calm and accepting approach contributed to his success. Jack acknowledged that he didn't panic. Instead, he approached this allegedly "impossible" task as an interesting challenge. He focused on the simple things first. He noticed what he could do, rather than what he might not be able to do. In some of the more challenging passages, he did not let his mind get involved, but trusted instinct and body wisdom to come up with the spirit and character of the music.

He talked about playing shapes and patterns, recognizable rhythms and dynamics. He wasn't focused, in other words, on playing every individual note correctly—in fact, that was the least of Jack's concerns. He allowed his sense of the music to guide him. He felt the shape of the music, he felt its flow—and that shape, that flow, in turn projected the music, carried its meaning and spirit to the other players, the conductor, and the audience.

To be sure, there are such things as wrong notes and missed notes—yet if you play a wrong note but play it with character, it usually isn't as bad as playing the right note tentatively. It is the notes you're trembling over that are likely to be missed. When you feel the sweep of the music flowing through you and trust the instincts you've established through passion and practice, you are far more likely to get the individual notes right and project the spirit of the music loud and clear. And it is that *spirit* of the music that the conductor and audience actually respond to.

Remind Yourself What Brought You to This Moment

Dale Clevenger, principal horn player with the Chicago Symphony, remembers feeling unprepared for the physical pressure of playing his first big concert with the Chicago Symphony in New York's Carnegie Hall. The Carnegie Hall appearance was to be the final concert in a month-long tour, and it was to conclude with the Ravel Piano Concerto in G— one of the most celebrated and difficult horn solos in the classical repertoire.

Dale had played the piece perhaps as many as forty times in his previous job with the Kansas City Philharmonic, but this was something else. This time it was more difficult. He had played in Carnegie Hall before, but the combination of playing in his hometown, as the new principal horn with the Chicago Symphony, and with this particular piece—let's just say it was different.

Things didn't go too well in rehearsal. I thought about it, and realized it was a combination of instrumental and musical factors. I said to my-self, I've done this before, I know I've done this. This is my orchestra, the Chicago Symphony, in my hometown, New York, in Carnegie Hall, and I've played here before, and I have played this piece many, many times. I know I can do it, because I have done it all before. So I started in, and when I got to the high F I told myself, Sing—sing it with all your heart. Whatever comes out, just go with it!

My heart was racing faster than it has at any time in my career be-fore or since—but I played the Ravel part well that night.

Dale flicked a switch in his head, remembered the past success that had gotten him there, and took the positive fork in the road, as Bill VerMeulen would say. He put himself into a state of intense concentration on what he wished to express musically, instead of allowing all the *what ifs* and thoughts of failure to take over the show. He chose the high road.

And he passed on to me some words he recalls the great maestro Sir Georg Solti once telling him before a concert. Solti was not a man who was known for kind words, a positive thought, or a therapeutic touch— but he told Dale, *This performance will neither help nor hurt your career—just go out onstage and have fun.*

Playing under a maestro with Solti's reputation for ruthlessness and perfectionism could be daunting, and perfectionism is itself one of the issues musicians have to wrestle with.

Dale has never played a piece *perfectly* in his life, and being honest with himself in this self-assessment is very important: he is a human being, therefore he is capable of making mistakes. Even if he gets all the notes, even on those wonderful occasions when everything comes together, he still feels his music making isn't perfect.

Yet here's the paradox:

> I have this philosophy I can do no wrong. My friends feel everything I do is like I'm walking on air, and when I play well, they love it. I was given the gift of a love of music and a certain talent on this instrument. It makes me happy when I play, and it pleases the audience too. Even when I don't play so well, my enemies love it—so how can I lose?

There are two things that Dale does which give him the courage to play—he reminds himself of what he is technically capable of, and perhaps more important he repeatedly reclaims and reasserts his personal reason for playing music. His courage is based on a gift of talent and his sheer love of music. Dale knows that he has something special to share. And whenever he finds that he has been temporarily sidetracked by other concerns and agendas, he only needs to remind himself *why* he is doing what he does so well.

He chooses the high road.

Believe in Yourself

Conductors aren't perfect (although you didn't read that here, and I won't be saying it out loud in rehearsal anytime soon). And one of the most terrifying things for horn and percussion soloists is to feel as though they are under extra pressure from the conductor. Sometimes a conductor is simply wrong, and picks on a musician for reasons that are not his fault. At other times a maestro may not be clear about what he wants. This puts the player in a very confusing position—and also one of confrontation. And since confrontation is not a good idea in the symphony business, it can be a test of courage and conviction for the musician to play, knowing that what he is doing may not be greeted with acceptance or approval.

John Beck, timpanist and percussionist with the Rochester Symphony, told me that just the week before I interviewed him, he was playing timpani when his conductor gave him a truly terrible look.

> I've seen that look from conductors before, but I thought about it, and came to the conclusion that at least on this occasion I was doing just fine. I had to ignore that look, and the uneasy feeling it could so easily give me, and keep on doing what I was doing. Sometimes you have to just wipe that kind of thing out of your mind.

Don Liuzzi, who had recently been appointed principal timpanist with the Philadelphia Orchestra, had his courage tested by its new music director, Wolfgang Sawallisch, during its first symphony tour. Don was playing the scherzo from Dvořák's *New World* Symphony. Like Dale Clevenger, he had played the piece many times before—but this was his first time under the orchestra's new boss. And like Maestro Solti, Maestro Sawallisch has the knack of passing out looks of glaring disapproval to the musicians under him while they are playing.

Don told me:

> After playing the passage with the three eighth notes, I got this horrible look from the conductor—like I'm worthless. The second time I played, he was even more frustrated, and I saw fire coming out of his eyes. I said to myself, What is going on here? Here comes the same passage yet another time, and this time I have to figure out what to do differently. Do I change to a harder stick? Does he want more on the first note? Am I coming in too early or too late? I did everything humanly possible with these three stupid notes, to figure out what will please this conductor. Finally, I emphasized all three notes with harder sticks—and at last, I got this nod of approval.

I find Don's story quite interesting. Rather than freezing or playing tentatively, Don *turned to the music* to explore all the possible ways he could play those three notes. In doing so, he also *noticed what he was doing*, which allowed him to reevaluate the possibilities and try something different.

It is not always easy to guess what is going on in the maestro's head. But in this case, the conductor's lack of acknowledgment promoted more self-awareness on Don's part—and this in turn may have helped him to intuit what would work best.

When the concert was over, Don went to the conductor and asked him what he really wanted. Sawallisch told him that he was glad Don had played the three notes more evenly, but what had really bothered him was that just before Don was about to play, he had put down his sticks and picked up the other sticks at the last minute. Sawallisch's real concern was that Don wasn't sure what sticks he was using and might never be able to play the notes on time!

Being a little more "steely-minded" is part of courage—there's a fine balance between being sensitive to what a conductor wants, and your commitment to what you are going to do. Indeed, Sawallisch may have been picking up on Don's lack of conviction or clarity about how he should play the notes. Believing in what you are doing for better or worse can be more important than just playing.

Evelyn Glennie is the internationally known percussion soloist who is also hearing-impaired. She is an amazing performer, and one of the things that distinguishes her playing is the conviction she brings to her music. When I asked her how she manages to find the courage to perform with this hearing handicap, she told me:

I have to *believe* and to be one hundred percent committed to that music—to what I feel at that particular moment. There is no holding back. I have to just do it consistently. It is just a way of life. I cannot let the music overwhelm me.

I know this because in recent years I have been learning how to ride a motorbike. At first it was one of the scariest things I had done in ages, and suddenly one day, I just thought, Now I'm riding the bike. I'm in control of the bike as opposed to the bike controlling me. It was something that just happened and it wasn't forced. It needs to become a part of me.

When the music becomes a part of her, she knows it so well that she can play it without thinking.

It is much better for me to *create* the sound, rather than stepping back and observing it. It is the control aspect of knowing what I want, and this is what gives me satisfaction.

I found it interesting to learn that one of the reasons Evelyn plays so courageously or fearlessly is that she is not worried about how others will receive her music. She only concerns herself with her job of being honest and convincing. She said:

I can't get them to all feel the same way. It's just like going to a restaurant and everyone ordering the same exact meal. Some may eat more quickly than others, others may mix the vegetables in a different way, and in different combinations. So the meal will not taste the same to everyone. It is the same way in a concert. They come into that hall with all different reasons as to why they are there—some coming from work, some curious, some percussionists, some friends of the composer, some who had a crisis at home—this stuff in life all affects how they digest this music. Even the sound of my drums will not register the same to the people sitting in the balcony as to those sitting close to the stage. All I can do is be *honest* . . . and serve the best dish possible.

For Evelyn, "courage" is not about overcoming fear or anxiety but about knowing that she will be giving as honest a performance as possible. There is absolutely nothing else she can do beyond that.

These three examples all show the importance of really knowing your musical intention. When you know what the music sounds like and exactly how you feel it should be played, the high road stretches before you. If you leave room for self-doubt, doubt about your understanding of the music, or doubt about what the conductor wants, you will lack courage and commitment. If you choose that higher path to the music with the conviction that Evelyn Glennie brings to her playing, you will never be questioned by conductors, teachers, or your own self.

Courage in Life

The horn and percussion sections demand strong personalities and the ability to focus under what may feel like immense pressure from within or outside. I find this character and attitude among my horn and percussionist friends refreshing, inspiring—and worthy of emulation by other instrumental colleagues, as well as those outside the profession. So I was not altogether surprised to find out that many of these individuals also have hobbies which match the courageous characteristic I have come to associate with their instruments.

Some time ago, I started noticing the various outdoor recreations and hobbies of the members of the horn section in the Cincinnati Symphony. I was fascinated to note that virtually all the members of the section were very much involved in some form of athletics—and noticing this common interest may have been what really inspired my interest in the connection between personality and choice of instruments in the first place.

Playing with the Sun Valley Idaho Summer Symphony, I noticed a similar interest in all things athletic not only among members of the horn section but also among their brass colleagues who played trumpet and trombone. They were runners, mountain climbers, rafters, and bikers! At one point the horn players invited me to jump off a ski mountain with them in a paraglider. I was just about to overcome my fear when I saw the insurance-waiver forms! I chickened out—but they didn't.

So it wasn't difficult to find another horn player, Adam Unsworth with the Philadelphia Orchestra, to talk to me about his own favorite athletic interest—marathon running. I learned that Adam runs marathons both for the thrill of competitive running itself and for the positive impact it has on his work as a horn player. Adam is an outstanding runner and places well toward the front in most of the races he enters.

I asked him about the relation between his running and his music.

I began with weight lifting, because I wanted a tight feeling in my upper body, but my teacher at Northwestern, Gale Williams, turned me on to running so that I could achieve deeper and more relaxed breathing. I usually go full blast at my hobbies—so ten years ago, I tried the

Chicago marathon. It was a wonderful, euphoric environment, and a great challenge.

I don't run to finish a race so much as to push myself faster. Many people don't ever reach their aerobic capacity. Running forces you to do that, but in a relaxed way—and short, hyperventilating breathing just isn't possible.

Now when I'm playing under stress, I am able to quiet my breathing down to a relaxed and steady rhythm, slow my heartbeat down, and play better.

Jack VanGeem is another who admits he likes to push himself. He enjoys long-distance biking for mental and physical health, and while he agrees there is pain involved, he says what makes it all worthwhile is the sense of accomplishment he gets when he finishes a long and grueling ride. Jack loves challenges and recognizes that his biking keeps him fit and ready for the physical and mental endurance (and sometimes pain) that are sometimes required of a percussionist.

Jack explained, *Pushing through resistance is worth the price of the pain*, and I think there's probably a connection between the way athletes push through pain in the hope of "hitting the wall" and experiencing the glorious rush of endorphins that kicks in on the other side, and the courage to move right on and play a supremely difficult passage under the wrathful eye of an irate conductor.

What I find so interesting here is how difficult it is to separate the musician from the person. We are talking about the characteristics of some highly adventurous people here. These master musicians embrace the challenge of performing specific musical tasks under high pressure—then seek out hobbies and outside interests that demand and develop the same kind of courage. And while their hobbies may be recreational, there does seem to be a sort of "fit" between their hobbies and their professional work.

When we practice our instruments, we practice the same *notes* we shall play in performance, but not the ways in which a performance *differs* from practice. This could be why so many musicians look for extramusical activities that offer some of the same challenges. If we were to recognize this, and practice *performance* as well as musical technique, we would have to find situations which can test the same kinds of courage and focused concentration. In this sense, hobbies like skydiving and marathon running may play their part in a great orchestral sound just as much as scales and arpeggios.

Having said that, it is still possible to practice mental toughness by rehearsing onstage and sometimes in the presence of friends or colleagues in the audience. The ultimate practice of performance comes from performance itself, and there is no substitute for the rich experience of playing in the hot seat. We need to be creative in simulating these valuable training experiences when there is less opportunity to gain actual performance experience.

CHANNELING YOUR COURAGE

In order to tap into our own courage, it's important to understand how our bodies react to stress. The body, in a state of stress, releases adrenaline. Most us have heard stories about an eighty-year-old woman who needed to rescue her grandchild from under the wheels of a car, and suddenly found the strength to lift the car up off the child. Perhaps you have heard, too, of the flight-or-fight response, which kicks in when we sense danger, sending supercharged energy to the body so we can do battle with tigers—or flee from them when discretion is the better part of valor.

The flight-or-fight response was designed originally to help us cope with the very real dangers of life in a world of predators and competitors, when running away from a rattler, bear, wolf, or jaguar was as commonplace as escaping the wrath of one's boss or conductor today. And even though it's not generally practical to fight the conductor or flee the orchestra, our bodies still release that same rush of energy in times of excitement or fear—perhaps when we're playing a solo, or taking an audition.

The dynamic horn soloist Eric Ruske described the positive side of adrenaline to me. He said:

Some of us like going to horror movies, some like to swim out too far in the ocean, and I know I get my own adrenaline highs from playing with my kids—but whatever your way of getting there, it's great to be able to get that burst of high energy. I love it.

When you walk onstage, that same nervous feeling is a great thing. If I walk out onstage and I'm not nervous, I realize something has to change, something is wrong.

So the energy can certainly be turned in a positive direction. But as Cincinnati Symphony percussionist Dick Jensen says, we also need to monitor the temptation to channel adrenaline into the music in the form of racing tempi or loud and aggressive attacks:

> Use the adrenaline when it comes to heighten your senses. Instead of running off in your own direction playing as loud as you can, use the energy to become more aware of what's going on around you. Let your energy be focused in positive, musical ways, and then you can really enjoy the extra energy of the ride!

Everyone agrees that there will be times when adrenaline floods your system. The most important thing is to have thought about it ahead of time. Do you have a plan for coping with the extra energy? Are you going to use it? Are you going to ignore or suppress it? Or will you allow it to keep you from passing through the barrier of your own fears?

It is well known that the medical community has come up with prescription drugs that combat the symptoms of both anxiety and excessive adrenaline. One such drug, which is used by a significant number of musicians, is Inderal. It was developed for people with heart problems, and it is effective in reducing symptoms of anxiety by leveling out the highs and lows. But that's what makes music musical. From the point of view of the Inner Game of Music, I believe in treating the cause of anxiety rather than the symptoms. I believe in focusing our concentration through Inner Game of Music techniques and using this energy to perform in a heightened state of awareness. To me, taking Inderal is like putting Tchaikovsky on Prozac. I need to hear the passion in music, and to feel that extra energy. . . .

Teachers and coaches need to prepare students to handle fear: while this may not be a matter of musical technique, it *is* a matter of technique that affects music. In our teaching and our studies, we need to strike a balance between musical and psychological skills.

For some people, courage is a nonissue; perhaps what they need most is not *courage* so much as *encouragement* in their love of music, reminder of their original purpose and joy in choosing to make music or to strengthen their conviction about what they are playing. At other times, however, we all need to address self-doubt and other mental distractions, stage fright and fear and the rush of adrenaline—and finding the courage and commitment to do what is called for.

Choosing the High Road Can Mean Sacrifice

I've learned that bringing forth courage to do almost anything can be a simple internal decision. All you need to do is ask yourself, *How bad do I want it?* If what you want is more important than the fear that keeps you from it, then you will take the high road to courage. It's that simple.

Playing a musical instrument is not necessarily life-threatening, to be sure, but you have to be willing to make certain sacrifices to get up on-stage and perform.

Now I'm not talking about bodily contortions here, or suggesting that you should attain your craft even at risk to your physical health, or torture yourself with difficult fingerings no matter how painful they may be. The kind of sacrifice I'm thinking of has more to do with moving through stage fright—having the willingness to do what may feel scary, along the way to artistry.

Everyone reacts differently to the challenge of live performance: some thrive on the pressure, while others get sick. Barbra Streisand gets so upset performing for live audiences she has decided to retire altogether from the concert circuit. But musicians have to be willing to deal with this pressure by some means or other. Maybe you need to take a five-mile run before a concert—or meditate! Either way, the challenge has to be accepted, and the rewards are worth the sacrifice.

Percussionist Jack VanGeem assesses potential students by placing great importance on the desire they show and how much they seem willing to sacrifice to achieve their goal. He wants to discover how deep a longing the student is tapping into, and whether the student really knows what he or she is striving for. Perhaps the student is working for the chance to win a lifetime position playing in one of the world's great orchestras. Is she aware how valuable a goal this is? If the student truly understands this ultimate goal, will it serve as an incentive to making the necessary sacrifices, and keep him or her in the line of fire for however long it takes?

Jack vividly recalls playing his first marimba solo as a kid:

> After I finished my piece, I looked up and received the enthusiastic, loving adoration of the audience. It caught me completely by surprise! "Wow . . . is that all for me?" I liked that feeling. It was great to know that playing music has these other rewards, beyond the sheer joy of just listening and learning and performing.

It takes courage to recognize your dream and follow it, through good times and rough times, under a hail of criticism and praise, from the first moment of recognition that music is a key element in your life up onto the concert platform or into the recording studio, and onward through a lifetime of making music.

And it may take countless hours of willing sacrifice—of the courageous kind.

Courage Enriches the Soul

I hope that choosing the high road of courage has become more of an option for you as you have read this chapter, and that you also realize that this is just the beginning. It has been great to explore these wonderful tips from such experienced artists. We each need to have a toolbox full of skills and techniques that can help us face and handle all the obstacles that jeopardize our freedom to play music the way we'd like.

One of the great things about techniques like these is when you have a first-rate defense, you mostly won't need to use it. The nagging voice of self-doubt somehow *knows* it will be defeated—and it doesn't usually choose to do battle unless it thinks it has a chance to win. Knowing that you have prepared yourself for any doubts or anxieties that may arise with an array of techniques may be enough to chase those fears away! Then it will be obvious that the path to choose will be the higher road to the music.

And that's as it should be. Because I firmly believe we should be focusing on our love of music, on the music itself, and on *making* music. And that's the point.

Dale Clevenger expresses his own love and dedication in such inspiring words that I would like to end this chapter with these remarks of his:

What happens in music is that composers are given the talent to write music, and we performers are given the talent to re-create it. When we do this, we make people happy! So you see, while I happen to get paid for what I'm doing, I also love it.

I had open-heart surgery for a heart murmur not so long ago. When it was all over, I tearfully thanked my surgeon for discovering I had a heart murmur in the first place, and then for saving my life. I hug and kiss the man every time I see him. And one time this same doctor whom I respect so much said to me, "Dale, we physicians deal with muscle tissue and bones . . . but what you do affects our souls."

I don't think of what I do as particularly courageous—but I do believe that what we do is deeply important: we affect the souls of those our music touches. To me, playing music is a very high calling: it is a responsibility, and a sacred trust. Making music may sometimes be difficult and sometimes fun—but for me, at least, it is first, last, and always an honor and a joy.

three

DISCIPLINE: THE WAY
OF THE WILL

(Flute, Oboe, Clarinet, and Bassoon)

An orchestra is rehearsing a difficult piece—the Overture to the Scandinavian composer Carl Nielsen's opera *Maskerade*. Nielsen has written a lot of fast consecutive and unrelated sixteenth notes which are almost impossible to sight-read: this instantly reveals who has looked at the music in advance, who has practiced, and who has not.

The maestro conducts the opening flourish with winds and strings playing the fast notes in unison, punctuated by a rather simple brass and percussion part. He stops, and begins to work first with the string section.

Let's play this a little slower and look at the notes.

He takes them through the music at a more "readable" tempo, repeating the passage a few times and gradually increasing the tempo each time, until it is clear that the only way the passage will come together is for the musicians to practice their individual parts. He instructs the strings to work on their music at home and warns them that he expects the passage to be better the next day.

Then the conductor turns to the woodwind section to repeat the rehearsal process.

They play the difficult passage once through, and it becomes evident that the wind players have practiced their individual parts and know all the notes. At the end, they go about their swabbing, blowing air out of their keys and checking their tuning, and sit prepared for the next cue.

And do some of them glance with disdain or pity at their string colleagues? Who am I, a bass player myself, to blame them?

The Difference Between Winds and Strings

I have drawn a picture of an orchestral rehearsal that's 100 percent fictional, and there are certainly many situations in which a string section will not be outshone by the advance preparations of their wind colleagues. But many orchestra musicians may nevertheless feel the scene I've portrayed is all too familiar. There are good reasons for the differences between string and wind preparations for a rehearsal—and those reasons have more to do with their instruments and their exposed roles within the orchestra than anything else.

What's more, these differences make wind players the model for us to pay attention to when it comes to matters of preparation, practice, and discipline.

As I say, wind players are used to exposed roles. For the most part, they are all soloists—each player is assigned a part which may not be "doubled" by any other musician. Thus, while there may be three flutists, each one is likely to be playing a separate part. And the conductor could ask any flutist to play his part in front of the orchestra at any time, to check for note accuracy or coach the flutist's musical style.

Contrast this kind of perpetual vulnerability and exposure to the way the members of the first violin section feel. First violin parts are usually played by as many as ten to eighteen players together—and the resulting group accountability hardly compares with the pressures on a solo wind player. When violinists, violists, and cellists are not playing in the orchestra, they play their inspiring solo literature and chamber music, all of which demand their best musicianship and preparation. However, when they are playing in the orchestra as part of a large section with many other string players performing the same exact notes, they are not as motivated to learn the disjointed sixteenth notes of Carl Nielsen's *Maskerade* Overture, say, as they are their part in a Beethoven string quartet. By contrast, the solo wind players are still soloists, whether playing in the orchestra or in smaller groups.

What I'm suggesting here is that the demands of the job often dictate styles of preparation. Woodwind players not only have to practice their music, their instruments demand constant maintenance. Oboists are notorious for needing to spend countless hours making reeds—which may fail or succeed in concert regardless of the meticulousness of the preparations. Woodwind players are commonly surrounded by their boxes of reeds, screwdrivers, knives, tuners, towels, water, paper, swabs, schedules, conductor's scores, and clocks. When the string players arrive at a rehearsal, the woodwinds will already be there practicing, adjusting their instruments and rehearsing with their partners. They are often the first to arrive and the last to leave.

DISCIPLINE MEANS FOCUSING

Discipline grows from the wish to do something. When you very much want to accomplish something, your ambition will call forth the strength and commitment you need to do *whatever is necessary to realize your goal*. Discipline flows from and follows your ambition and your passion.

My mentor Timothy Gallwey described the skill of discipline in his most recent book, *The Inner Game of Work*, as "focusing." He writes:

> If there is one thing that excellence in sports and excellence in work/life have in common, it can be summed up in a single phrase: focus of attention. Focus is the quintessential component of superior performance in every activity, no matter what the level of skill or age of the performer.

Having clear focus and discipline is essential. When we lose our focus, we lose our intention and our will. We no longer practice and prepare, and ultimately stop being productive.

In this chapter, we will look at the many wonderful incentives to discipline suggested by great wind players who have themselves mastered these principles, and we will explore the art of a disciplined practice session. But first, let's examine where discipline comes from.

Inner Game Basics: Self 1 vs. Self 2

Natalie wants to learn the flute, practice her scales, long tones, and études, play well during her lessons, learn her music and come well prepared for rehearsals and concerts, please her parents and get good grades. She also wants to play on the soccer team, watch her favorite TV show, talk with her friends, go to the mall, and finish her science project.

One voice in her head tells her, *I need to practice. My last lesson was terrible, I wasn't prepared and played out of tune. Mom wants me to clean my room. My science project is due in two days, and my teacher didn't like my proposal. And there's the soccer tournament tomorrow afternoon . . . English homework . . . math homework . . . phone calls to return—and I'm going crazy! How can I possibly manage to do all this? It's hopeless! I give up!*

Meet what Tim Gallwey calls Self 1. This is the voice that tells you what you *should* do. It's also an expert on how well you did or didn't do in the past, and what you hope and fear, and in general *how to get you flustered.* That's the key part, that's what it's always driving at. Even when Self 1 tells you that you were brilliant, it's setting you up.

There is another voice in Natalie's head, but she won't hear it unless she listens. This voice says, *I have forty-five minutes before dinner, I can put in some practice time. I can do my homework after dinner. I'll call Jenny tomorrow. Let's get started.*

Meet Self 2—the artistic part of Jenny that taps into the flow of what works and what's possible, that isn't concerned with constant assessment and judgment, the part that simply knows what is possible and the part that learns in the most effortless way.

When both Self 1 and Self 2 have made their cases, who do you listen to? Who do you believe? That's the question the Inner Game of Music poses to us: which voice shall we listen to, whose game shall we play? The voice that's worried about musical success, or the voice that pays attention to the music?

The first step to playing and winning the Inner Game is to recognize the difference between Self 1 and Self 2. Self 1 doesn't go anywhere, it doesn't accomplish anything. It doesn't help you one bit. It's Self 2 that has the good stuff, Self 2 that you can rely on. It's like tuning a car radio when there's a lot of static: Self 2 is the music you want to listen to, Self 1 is the interference. When you make this choice, when you ignore the interference from Self 1 and choose to go with Self 2, you are exercising will and discipline.

Start with a Goal

Setting goals is the first step toward developing discipline and choosing the way of your will. What do you really want?

Goals come in different sizes, long-term, medium-term, and short-term—and they need to fit together inside one another, the short-term goals within the medium-term goals within the long-term ones, like those Russian dolls that fit within themselves. Long-term goals include career goals that might happen over five to ten years:

> to make a living playing music in a professional orchestra
> to be the best musician I am capable of being
> to be able to play jazz or chamber music with great colleagues
> to be a technical and musical master of my instrument or voice

Or perhaps even

> to be a professional concert soloist in my field.

Your medium-term goals, the things you aim to accomplish within the year, follow naturally from your long-term goals. These are naturally less dreamlike and more concrete. They may include such things as completing a degree, learning specific pieces, playing a concerto, or reaching a particular level of proficiency on your instrument/voice.

And short-term goals are your specific goals for this week, or today, or this practice session. They track your medium-term goals and turn them into practicable, doable details. Your short-term goals may include finding technical solutions to one movement of a classical sonata, or learning how to phrase or interpret another piece.

I suggest that you write down all three kinds of goals in a handbook or journal, which will soon become a powerful and constant reminder of your progress. But remember that your goals—and even your dreams— may shift over time. There's no need to become a prisoner of old goals: it's better to revise your goals and work efficiently than to be paralyzed or overwhelmed by nonfunctional goals. Remember, it's the clarity of your focus on your goals in the long, medium, and short term which will give direction and discipline to your work.

Are you clear on what you want to accomplish? Let's do some serious soul searching here: are these your own goals, or did they come from your teachers, your colleagues, your parents or friends? Have you created them on your own, or are they obligations, burdens you've taken on, and not really things *you* wish to accomplish at all? There are Self 1 and Self 2 wishes, you see, and once again, it's important to know the difference, and choose Self 2.

As Jeff Zook, flutist and piccolo player with the Detroit Symphony and professor at the University of Michigan, would say, *It's your dreams we're talking about.*

Jeff believes that our goals change throughout our professional life, and that bringing them into focus is one of the most important things we can do. He often tries to nudge his students into greater clarity about what they really want:

> The first thing I do with my students is to access what their dreams are. You shouldn't be afraid to dream about what you really want. Sometimes the dream may not be big enough. If you just want to play a good audition, that's not really going to cut it. On the other hand, if you say, "I'm doing this because I want to play this concerto from memory next year in front of a live audience," your dream has greater immediate and future consequences.

"What is your dream, what is your purpose, what do you want to do?"

I ask my students to answer these questions in writing. I tell them, "This is where your goals come from." And after they see their goals in writing, they can focus on achieving them.

FOUR MOTIVATING FACTORS

It is difficult to make ourselves or our students want to practice when the motivation doesn't come from within. Motivation or the will to practice should not be something you have to fight for when playing great music. The music should be the inspiration. But often this isn't enough. External motivators are often used by teachers, parents, and even ourselves. If you practice, you get a gold star, money, rewards, a vacation, an instrument, or a special meal. But this becomes a problem when the prizes or bribes are no longer offered. These external motivators have little to do with making, learning, or performing music.

As we explore four types of motivation that can improve will and discipline, your task is to identify the motives that suit you, and go with them. In each case, it is important to use these motivators in an honest and effective way. In some situations, these motivations can be powerful tools. In other situations, they can be destructive distractions from the necessary work of discipline in your practice.

1. Competition

Celia Nicklin, who is head of the oboe department at London's Royal College of Music and a distinguished English oboist with the Academy of St. Martin in the Fields under Maestro Neville Marriner, explained to me that the academy doesn't offer its players contracts for an entire season: every engagement is only for that one specific date. She also told me that this lack of job security in the orchestra keeps everyone on alert: *Neville Marriner's attitude is to keep the musicians on their toes by making them feel there is always someone else around the corner,* she told me. Yet despite this formidable policy, Celia has been there for every recording session the orchestra has played in thirty years.

Personally, I'm no great fan of the concept of competition for motivation, probably because Self 1 is so adept at using it to make crippling judgments and instill self-doubt. I have, however, learned to respect the simple fact that being held accountable for something can and does produce results. Competition can inspire hard work and great performances. It works best when it serves as an incentive for learning, performance, and concentration rather than as an external reward or goal that produces tension, anxiety, or an inflated ego. Our job is to look at competition in this more positive, constructive way, as an inspiration to discipline.

2. Required Performances

In the highly structured British school system, there are so many demands, required performances, examinations, and standards that students don't have time to think about *not* practicing. At very early ages, they must play required scales and solo pieces several times a year, and they cannot advance until these examinations are successfully completed. They play in youth orchestras and consequently have to learn orchestral music while competing for their chairs. All these requirements demand so much preparation that practicing just happens—without anyone noticing that it really was not a choice.

While the academic demands in different countries may vary, there is great value in holding regular class recitals, music festivals, informal and structured performances, and periodic reviews. These deadlines remind performers that a standard has to be met within a specified time, and will call forth the desire and commitment to do what is necessary to play—namely, practice!

So often one can perform or recall memorized information in the comfort of your private practice or office space. Expressing this knowledge in public or on demand may require a higher level of mastery.

3. Pride

Over the many years I played in the Cincinnati Symphony, I always admired my colleague principal bassoonist William Winstead. I don't ever recall hearing him mess up a solo: his consistency, mastery, and dedication are exemplary. His students come from all over the country, and always play at a high artistic level.

Winstead explained that keeping up with his teaching load at the university and playing principal bassoon with the symphony forces him to be well organized—and the motivating factor that keeps him on track is pride. He has felt this internal motivation since he was quite young, and speculates that some of it comes from praise he received from his parents when he'd accomplished some task well as a child. But he also spoke of having a lack of personal satisfaction at times, of feeling he has to prove something to himself. As a result, he often puts his work before his personal life.

> The most important thing for me is producing music. The most embarrassing thing would be to go to a rehearsal and find myself not sounding good in front of my colleagues, not knowing what I am doing, or sounding like a klutz. For whatever reason, I must find the time to be prepared. And it's not just with music. The same goes for teaching—and it's the same with my cooking.

In order to prevent embarrassment and maintain your pride, it may become necessary to overlearn or overprepare, then when the heat is applied to the kettle, the water is cool enough so it doesn't boil over.

4. Fear

While it is pride that helps William Winstead ward off embarrassment through focus and discipline, when I asked the world-famous jazz/classical clarinet soloist Eddie Daniels what motivates him to self-discipline, *Fear!* was his one-word reply.

While we all love music, it is not always easy to maintain one's "personal best" level of play all through the year. When he's on tour, Eddie gets in a real groove playing concerts every night—but when he returns home to Santa Fe, New Mexico, he may have several weeks off, then need to go out onstage again for one single performance. At the recent dedication of the new concert hall in his hometown, he was onstage for only twelve minutes after a long vacation from touring. Fearful that he wouldn't know how to get back into his "touring groove," Eddie embraced his anxiety as though it was an old friend.

> Anxiety motivates me to get my act together. My guru has a saying: "Trust in God—but first tie your camel." God will take care of you if you make reasonable preparation. So I take care of my reeds and do my preparation—and I still don't know what's going to happen, but I know I've done my part.

Whether we are motivated by competition, required performances, pride, or fear, the presence of motivation helps inspire your will to do your best. You have to want to do well. With this desire, you can embrace these motivators as keys to improving your will.

GETTING TO THE PRACTICE ROOM

Now that we've explored the meaning of discipline, let's take a look at the place where discipline and focus take center stage: the practice room. There's a saying I'd like to pass on to you: *Amateurs practice until they play it right; professionals practice until they can't play it wrong.*

Discipline in music is synonymous with practicing. Some people don't find themselves attracted to the idea of practice, while others find joy in it and treat it as a ritual, a sacred experience. Like it or not, however, most disciplined and well-prepared musicians *do* practice.

Most of us know the eventual value we'll get from practice. The challenge here is to increase our desire for that end result to the point where the means to help us reach that end become goals in and of themselves.

Bassoonist Yoshi Ishikawa inspires his students to practice by inviting them to focus on interpreting the music. He might play for them, to show them the beauty of the music and thus motivate them, or he might encourage them to listen to recordings for the same kind of inspiration. For Yoshi himself, the most inspiring experience is to listen to Mozart's piano concertos and operas.

Paul McCandless, the wonderful reed player with the popular ensemble Oregon, likes to practice because it energizes him and gives him pleasure—but also because it keeps him prepared and in shape. He recognizes there is a physical component of preparation that makes practice essential. He must be prepared to deal with whatever comes up in the world of improvisation, and the only way to relax and have a good time is to be ready for anything.

> The oboe requires the most time. It is like being a marathoner; it's no fun unless you can go the distance. The only way to enjoy this instrument is to be really strong.

For Eddie Daniels, discipline and practice should make technique a nonissue. When he gets to a performance, he wants to be able to enjoy himself and the instrument without any interference:

> For me, practicing leads to a place where you are onstage and there isn't this reed, there isn't this technique, there is just music happening and it feels good.

Fernaud Gillet, former oboist of the Boston Symphony, feels that practicing is an art in itself—he believes that practicing should be a perfectly tailored expression of the individual concerned, and should always be done at the highest possible level.

Although famous oboist Robert Bloom prided himself on *not* practicing much (he said he wanted the words *If only he had practiced* inscribed on his tombstone), he believed that when he did practice, he should do so with the utmost concentration, as if he were playing a concert.

Finally, Allan Vogel, principal oboist of the Los Angeles Chamber

Orchestra, believes that disciplined practice sessions are an art form in themselves:

> It is something worth doing for its own sake. If you don't have a gig to practice for, you can still practice as experience of your art. For me, it is a matter of practicing with discipline while also being flexible about it.

While practicing may or may not be an enjoyable experience, it remains the means to an end that we all know is essential. If the musician chooses to have discipline, then the way to discipline includes dedication and commitment to the process, and the process is one of learning the skills that will be responsible for your ultimate joy in making music. But that joy can really be there in the journey as well. Acquiring skills and experiencing your own improvement is a joy in itself. While practicing may not always be fun, it can be a valued and pleasurable experience. Any skill that is worth acquiring is worth working for.

Preparing for the Practice Session

Getting to the practice room involves both mental and physical preparation.

In Monopoly, there's a card that says *Go directly to jail. Do not pass Go. Do not collect $200.* If you're on your way to the practice room and you're already feeling bad about it, you've already picked up your *Go directly to jail* card—but you can switch it to a *Get out of jail free* card anytime by taking a deep breath and giving yourself a change of attitude.

That's the mental preparation. But we also need to address the space and environment we practice in, and the time we devote to practice.

Some people find it helps them to have a regular time in the day that they devote to practicing—but students, professionals, and amateurs alike all have to juggle personal life, work obligations, school, sports, and family commitments, and even shared space, and keeping that many things straight can make it very difficult to have a set practice time each day.

Perhaps the most important thing is to make a commitment to finding a certain amount of time to practice each week, with some degree of regularity.

As you schedule time to practice, remember that most teachers and professionals believe that taking at least one day off a week allows both mind and body to assimilate what they are learning. Some teachers may recommend you take more than one day of rest a week—perhaps spacing them one every three or four days. There is no magic formula that's right for every instrument or voice—except consistency. And that's crucial.

The Warm-up

How will you organize your practice session? Most teachers and professionals engage in some kind of warm-up exercise before practice, for a variety of reasons. Some instruments need to be played for a certain time before they actually function properly: keys, resin, valves, and the lubrication in all the joints can be sluggish when any instrument is played right out of the box. What's more, the muscles we use in playing or breathing likely need to go through a period of movement before they respond fluently and quickly to signals from the brain.

Paula Robison, internationally celebrated flute soloist, asks her students to pay attention to the ways marathon runners, ballet dancers, and figure skaters take care of their bodies: they all take great care to warm up very carefully. Paula used to study ballet, and she learned the value of this kind of discipline with the ballet warm-up known as the barre.

It was the dancers' discipline which really brought this home to me. You'd never see a dancer run out onto the center of the floor and make a tour jeté without running through a full barre first. That would be complete insanity, because the muscles wouldn't be ready for that amount of movement. You can hurt yourself pretty badly if you aren't properly warmed up. But the warm-up is also a kind of blessing, a spiritual thing, and if you go through the same routine every day, you are prepping yourself internally as well. To me, playing scales and arpeggios should be done with the greatest of reverence and gratitude: it is the process by which we prepare for something sacred.

Paula explained that for playing the flute, the muscles need to be warmed up slowly and gently at first, with slow long tones. Then the fingers need to be warmed up—and through this process, the mind sharpens and becomes ready for concentration.

Mastering the Good Stuff

The next component of the practice session, learning or mastering some of the music, is the beating heart of the whole process. And here again we have the opportunity to make our practice efficient, enjoyable, and productive.

This is an area that I've researched deeply and personally, in my own practicing and playing, and in talking with Edwin Gordon and Richard Grunow, two of the most highly respected researchers in this area. What I'd like to do is to show you the way I used to practice, and then introduce you to a profound and simple new approach to the learning of music.

The old-style Barry Green liked to work hard. At times he even *liked* to sweat, suffer, and get frustrated—because when he finally reached his goal, he felt as though he had accomplished something. In fact, this Barry used to worry that if his practicing was effortless and free of tension, he might not feel inspired to work—and if he didn't have any major problems with his music, then there would be nothing left to fix, and consequently no need to practice or suffer!

To give you an idea of how this worked . . .

The Ten-Week Practice Crunch

In week one, I get my music—and my first impulse is to try to play the whole piece through *with no mistakes whatsoever* that very first day! That's not the advice Self 2 would give—that's a Self 1 idea—but Self 1 is the only self I listen to, so I begin, and of course it sounds terrible, and I stop! I don't even know what the pitches or harmonies sound like, but I'm telling myself I've got to play it all today! So I start again and plow ahead, hoping that by the end of the day I will have made it through most of the notes.

And another thing: I *hate* playing slow when I practice. There's no challenge to it, and besides, I will never *play* the music slow, so why *practice* slow?

During that first week, it may take me two hours to get through the piece—but I slave away at it.

After a few weeks, I can make it through the piece in a quarter of that time. I am still working out fingerings and bowings, I'm still making changes with stuff that doesn't work.

I play the piece over and over, and you know—I notice the same trouble spots every day.

The hard parts are still hard, but I think it's fair to say things are improving, slowly, slowly. Hey, I have spent a lot of time on this piece now, and some passages are finally beginning to feel reliable.

In week eight—only two weeks to go—it's time to arrange a meeting with the accompanist. I think I have this thing sounding pretty good. But when I play it with the piano, it feels like it did after that first week—terrible! Some passages I thought were passable suddenly sound very weak and exposed. So I have to restructure the way I understand the music, practice different passages in a new way, change fingerings, sweat, cry, worry, get mad at the family—but *keep working*.

In weeks nine and ten, everything *has* to come together—and indeed, it is sounding a lot better. I'm playing pretty well, in fact—but once in a while I forget which version I was supposed to play, because I have changed so many things at the last minute.

Okay, I have spent nine weeks slaving away at this music, stopping and starting, trying first this fingering, then that—and now, under the worst kind of pressure, with people listening, I must forget all those other habits, and play exactly the way I did in practice yesterday.

I start the concert. I forget if I was supposed to start with a down-bow or an up-bow, but luckily my body remembers for me. The performance is so-so. I get through the really difficult section that I practiced so hard without a mistake, but then I goof up on some passages that have never given me any problems before. That's when I come to the one section where I always make the same mistake. I've been making that mistake in practice for ten weeks now—and I make it again!

Overall, I give myself a B-minus. I could certainly have done better, but considering the pressure I've been under, it wasn't really that bad. And you know, I'm never really satisfied; I *always* think I could have done better.

I only wish I'd had a little more time to practice.

I have changed since those days—and I owe Timothy Gallwey a great deal for illuminating the difference between Self 1 and Self 2 practicing for me, and giving me permission to choose between the two. I have learned more than I'd care to remember from my own mistakes, taught myself to learn and practice music in an entirely different manner, fine-tuned my understanding while talking with Edwin Gordon and Richard Grunow—and articulated my new approach in greater detail in a series of Inner Game of Music workbooks, published by GIA Music in separate books for most orchestra instruments, keyboard, and voice.

The essence of the new approach can be summed up in two simple principles: learn what you practice, and practice what you learn.

LEARN WHAT YOU PRACTICE, PRACTICE WHAT YOU LEARN

When we make mistakes in practice, we tend to behave as though we can just rewind the tape to a point before we made the error and "record over it" with our next attempt. But suppose it doesn't work like that; suppose the mind remembers each of our mistakes as well as our eventual successful phrasings. Science tells us this is the way things work. What then?

If you play a passage with the same mistake five times, then once with the mistake corrected, *you've just practiced your error five times and the correct version once.*

We spend far too much time practicing our mistakes.

In the ten-week ordeal I described, for instance, I may have spent as much as ninety percent of my time practicing my mistakes—and then expected, in performance, in the heat of the moment, to retrieve only that ten percent when I played correctly.

Does this sound just a little crazy? I believe it is. And also I believe this is precisely why, as much as ninety percent of the time, most people feel they could have done better in their performances.

Can we learn another way to prepare our music? A way that allows us to come to a performance with 90 percent error-free practice memories? That certainly sounds as though it might help things go a whole lot better under the stress of performance. Here are some simple rules to follow.

1. Don't Practice Mistakes

The world-famous flutist and teacher Julius Baker is quoted as saying, *You'll never make a mistake if you never make a mistake.* But how can we manage that?

There is a way. The key to greater accuracy in your playing is to realize that unconscious mistakes don't count. We use this simple fact to change the way we learn our music. We can focus in on one aspect of the music at a time—and practice just that one aspect. If you are learning a melody, it doesn't matter what tempo you play at while you're learning it—the melody is what you are focusing on, and you can learn it at any tempo. Start playing slow enough so that you can get the melodic line right, and you'll be practicing the correct melody—at an altered tempo. I like to tease my violin colleagues and boast that I can play the Mendelssohn violin concerto perfectly on the double bass. It's true—it's just that I need about four days to get through it!

What do I mean by "unconscious mistakes"? If your mind is consciously focusing on melody, it is not paying attention to your tempo, dynamics, expression, or articulations—and any mistakes you make in these areas simply aren't highlighted. To use the computer analogy again, they don't become a part of your program.

Do you see what a huge difference this makes? If you instruct yourself to focus *only* on the rhythm, then you can make mistakes with the notes and it doesn't matter. If you are practicing for tone quality, that's your only focus, and you don't have to play perfectly in rhythm. Whatever you are practicing *consciously* is what your memory will retain.

That is how you can practice without spending most of your time practicing mistakes. If you are practicing for the notes, don't play so fast that you make mistakes. It's that simple.

So we need to follow a routine that makes sure that each time we play, we choose what we want to focus our attention on, and learn it—and only after we've learned it, move on to rehearsing what we want our minds to remember. It is very important to get into the habit of separating that first stage, in which we are learning, from the second and quite different stage in which we practice.

2. Learn First, Then Practice What You Learned

Learning takes place before practice.

Does that sound strange? First you learn the different parts of a piece you want to practice—its melody, rhythm, best fingerings, and so forth—and then you use practice to reinforce what you have learned.

But how can you learn something before you practice it?

Learning implies study. In order to practice what you have first learned, you need to get the music in your head *before* you put it to work. There are many ways to do this. You can study a recording, a teacher can play the piece for you, or you can play the piece very slowly yourself with the sole purpose of learning the sound, line, rhythm, or harmony—*not* to master the piece or play it perfectly. If you are careful to play it this way—being very clear in your own mind that you're not trying to "play" it, just to acquaint yourself with it—you are not practicing the piece, just checking it out.

You should spend a good percentage of your time listening to or studying the music before you ever attempt to play the piece. Once you have really internalized what the melody sounds like, even if you do make a small mistake, your ear will immediately tell you and you will tune the error out. But if you haven't learned what the melody should sound like, and don't recognize incorrect notes when you play them, you are likely to practice the wrong notes until you are corrected—and then you will need to unlearn whole passages before you can learn them again and practice them correctly.

3. Practice Away from Your Instrument

Sometimes our bodies and fingers fall into old habits and inappropriate patterns when we are at the instrument. Running through parts of a piece in your head, imagining how your arms or hands or lips will move without actually playing, may allow you to organize some of your movements and phrasings in a larger and sometimes more musical perspective. You will find you can figure out many important aspects of the music *before* you actually explore these ideas with your instrument or voice—and one of the values of practicing away from your instrument is the likelihood that you will make far fewer mistakes!

Once again, the secret here is to do this one part at a time, in a simple, nonjudgmental way—so that you can input all this new information into your nervous system, the central processor of your body-computer, accurately. Then, when the time comes to perform, you will find your body-computer has the music, not the mistakes, in its memory.

4. The STOP Tool: For Focusing

I've found that truly outstanding professional players and teachers all believe very strongly in practicing with great concentration and efficiency. When you leave the comfort days of being a music student, pressures on your time will likely increase, and you won't have the luxury of "wasting" valuable practice time—indeed, you may complain that you don't even have time to maintain your technique and learn all the music you must play. The result, in any case, is that you cannot afford to work inefficiently.

The pressure of learning and practicing can leave little room for creative thinking and finding musical solutions. When you find yourself plagued by boredom, stress, or anxiety, you must begin to recognize that you learn more and perform better when you are free of these obstacles.

One way to do this is to use the tool Tim Gallwey calls STOP.

Tim breaks the technique down into four steps:

S—Stop. Take a break, refresh yourself.

T—Think. Reevaluate what you are doing. Remember your goals—not just your music goals, but your goals in terms of learning and enjoyment, too. What do you want to do? What do you need to do? What do you have to do?

O—Organize. Are you on track? Are you practicing mistakes? Have you learned the music you are practicing?

P—Proceed. Go back to work. Do you feel any different? How about your experience of the music?

The goal is to practice efficiently.

Franklin Cohen feels the most valuable support you can have when you're practicing is the sense that you're doing good work.

> Some days you'll feel inspired, and some days not. The composer John Adams told me, "People think composers sit around waiting for an inspired moment and then rush for the manuscript paper—but that's not the way it is. If I had to wait for inspiration, I might never write another note!" So just do good solid work. Don't set your goals where you won't meet them—that just leads to frustration. Take joy in your work—and don't worry about the performance, the concert is another day!

Paula Robison believes in the STOP tool, but she also believes in pushing herself to a place where she gets her best work done:

> If you notice you are watching the clock, it's time to take a break and go outside, get something to drink, do something that will restart your engine. The goal is to lose track of all time. After the warm-up period

when you are just starting out and the session isn't really working yet, there's a period where you can maintain what you know—get beyond the first wall, and you're there. And there's another wall, usually after about two hours: if you get past that one into the third and fourth hours, you can really improve and move ahead. Sometimes it is a challenge to make it past that two-hour mark to the place where the passion and excitement can really come in, and this is where the voice of discipline can tell you to stay with it!

Bassoonist professor/soloist Yoshi Ishikawa believes that if you overorganize your schedule, you may not have time to complete your goals to your satisfaction. He suggests it is best not to put a time limit on what you intend to accomplish:

It is important to work with real concentration, but you can never know exactly how long it will take to realize your intentions. After a concert, it's easy to say you didn't have enough time to practice—but I believe this expression is overused. I have made it a personal goal never to use that excuse.

5. Practice Slow

I first heard about practicing slow from my esteemed bass colleague Edgar Meyer. I had just attended a workshop at which he had played so flawlessly that I felt compelled to ask him the simple question: *Edgar, how do you do it?* His response was the one word: *Slowly.*

When Edgar plays a Bach cello suite on the bass, it can take him hours just to get through the first prelude. He demonstrated the first few notes for me, holding on to each note for at least eight seconds, and making a seamless connection to the next note. I was impressed with his skill and what was for me his novel approach—but it wasn't until I began to hear the same idea from Paul McCandless, Eddie Daniels, Allan Vogel, and others that I realized what Edgar's "slowly" was all about.

Paul McCandless said Leon Goosens once told him that it was most important to *eliminate the garbage between the notes so there is no noise*. Paul says he uses *legato* as a doorway to velocity. Think about it. When you increase your tempo, you may find you're speeding up the notes themselves, but not necessarily the transitions between them—or at least, not to the same extent. This means that any lack of clarity in your transitions is occupying a greater and greater percentage of the total playing time—and as computer scientists would say, your signal-to-noise ratio is going way down.

So the *legato* is the first step toward mastering a passage. The mastering of slurs comes next, according to Paul:

Discovering a way to do something really well is a highly creative activity, and if I can get really psyched about one thing, the energy and enthusiasm will echo through my entire practice session—like getting one slur from a C to a D-flat. And the secret is in your quality of attention and movement.

Eddie Daniels is another believer in practicing slowly—really slowly, like Edgar Meyer:

I don't have a system as such, and when I practice I don't just practice slowly. I have a way of going from a note to the flow. When people want to be able to go faster, they often take things just a little bit slower—but I slow things down so much, it's maybe to the point where I'm playing sixteenth notes as though they were whole notes, and I listen intently to each individual note.

You may think, Well, gee, I should be playing fast—but your finger is now holding down that note. A lot of times when people play fast, they think it is the movement between notes that really makes the difference, but it's not, it's arriving and being at the right place that really creates accuracy in playing a fast passage. When you are sitting on a note, you are getting to know what it feels like to play that exact note, you are familiarizing yourself with its position. Let yourself experience the sound and feeling of the note, by playing very, very slow.

Oboist Allan Vogel tells me he doesn't practice anything faster than it should be played, and he feels he can only improve a piece by slowing it down:

> I don't work up from my metronome markings, I work down from them. When I slow my playing down, I can be more musical, I can be more aware of my posture, breathing, and tone quality, or vary my rhythms. I believe practice should be on the slow side in general. It is rare for me to practice at performance tempi. At a slower tempo, you can interpret the markings better and play with more energy.
>
> Confidence comes from not making mistakes, and avoiding mistakes is a matter of picking the right speed.

What an amazing concept! I used to think being prepared meant I should be able to play the music much faster, and that's how I practiced. Now I have come to recognize that if I play faster, I cannot clean up my problems—and will only have more of Goosens's "garbage" between the notes. Now I understand why I hear those trumpet players playing all those long tones! After practicing slow and passing some of these exercises on to my students, I can hear and feel the difference.

6. The Beautiful Voice Inside

The first human instrument is the voice. When we hear great violinists, flutists, or even pianists, we often say they are "singing through their instruments." Just as jazz can't swing without the beat, music cannot communicate unless it sings.

Celia Nicklin tells her students (and reminds herself) that all the music she makes must sound vocal. She goes to great lengths to get her pupils and herself to work with their voices.

> We do a lot of singing. In the beginning, the kids hate doing it, and can find it quite embarrassing, but eventually they get used to it. And I try to find ways to make it interesting, because it's so hard at first. I ask

fantasy questions: Does the composer have long hair, red hair, is he short, and fat, did she live on a mountain? Does this piece sound as if it is written in shades of purple, or yellow perhaps? Could you paint a picture of this piece? Would the sea be in the picture? Why did Dvořák write this utterly impossible second oboe part in the cello concerto? Was he mad at his wife for having an affair with the second oboist?

I ask my students to listen to birds. Birds always sing in a clear, deep voice that can carry for great distances. It's not croaky, it doesn't rattle, it is the most sensationally wonderful sound. I tell them that this is the clarity of sound we have to create.

Franklin Cohen feels he is singing with his inner voice when he plays his clarinet. He told me a wonderful story about Maestro Casals. Apparently the maestro once gave a master class in which he was singing really terribly to his students, while telling them how beautiful it was to hear the singing voice—and then he smiled and pointed to his head, and said, *I'm not talking about what I just sang for you, I'm talking about the beautiful voice inside.*

You will find techniques which involve singing with your instrument one way or another scattered throughout this book, and I believe they are very important. It all comes down to that indefinable something we call true artistry. The mastery of music and this kind of "internal singing" are closely interwoven, perhaps even inseparable. That's why these different kinds of voice work are so profound and important to achieving artistry of the voice or of any instrument.

KNOWING WHEN YOU ARE READY

Predicting the future is a risky business. You can practice, prepare, rehearse, or pray—but the end result of all your conscious efforts is really out of your hands. You might be able to say you are playing a piece as well as you can, but what does that mean? What you are really preparing for when you practice is building a body of experience that you can take with you into the heat of battle! It's not a classroom situation, it becomes an adventure! Paula Robison explained why she loves the uncertainty of performing:

> That's what makes performing such a total blast—anything can happen. You always need to be available for something new, some other thing; the audience may be different, your colleagues may do unexpected things in performance—you have to be constantly on your toes. And this in turn allows you to approach things fresh. It has to be a new adventure every time. Have your bags packed—that's the greatest feeling.
>
> I do know what it feels like when I'm not ready. That's why I practice so much. It's a matter of being ready to take a chance. The Greeks used to say that the muse might come down and kiss you, or some god like Apollo might want to play with you—and you need to be ready to pick up that challenge from another world! Mozart will play a trick on you—and you don't want to miss it.

This is what the discipline of preparation is all about—having the confidence and comfort with the music to be ready for the moment to move and inspire in performance. This is where the artistry comes in.

It all comes down to motivation.

The Way of the Will

Eddie Daniels could not easily tell me the source of his motivation or will. He doesn't believe it is self-manufactured, it just happens to be there.

> I used to say at clinics that anybody can be as good as me—all they have to do is practice. And yet I don't think it's really as simple as that. It's not easy to get someone to practice the way I practice, it's not easy to get someone as excited about a piece as I am. That inner motivation I have is hard for others to manufacture.

In my view, it all comes back to the idea that playing music on the stage is a very godly thing; it comes from God, it is the most communicative, nonverbal, direct line to the heart. So you can deal with learning all the notes and technique, but if you haven't learned the direct line to your heart yet, most probably you won't manage to do it tomorrow onstage. My idea of the true artist is someone who has all the technique at his disposal, but who also has a depth of being that comes through when he plays.

Along somewhat similar lines, Paula says:

We live in a generous, freedom-loving country, and we have the opportunity to develop a personal gift, the love of music, and we should be thankful. But there's a responsibility that comes with it, the responsibility to develop and share it. It is our gift—let's make it our gift to others.

You know, sometimes I wonder how we ever manage to make music, given the terrible influence Self 1 exerts on us when we practice! We need personal development as well as technical advances. To get beyond where we are, we have to figure out the cause of a given problem or articulation, so we can teach the muscles so they will perform for us. This makes it imperative to practice accurately!

Let me put it simply. This is the way of the will. Self 2 choices can overcome Self 1 interference. The tools we need are to be found in discipline—and within discipline lies our freedom to express ourselves, to transcend, to experience the joys and realities of life.

four

FUN: THE JOY IN MUSIC

(Trombone, Tuba, and Double Bass)

We might have known a low-note bassoonist would cause nothing but trouble:

In 1954 bassoonist professor Peter Schickele, rummaging around a Bavarian castle in search of rare musical scores, happened instead upon the original manuscript of *Sanka Cantata* by one P.D.Q. Bach, being employed as a strainer in the caretaker's percolator. A cursory examination of the music immediately revealed the reason for the atrocious taste of the coffee; and when the work was finally performed the Professor realized too late that he had released a monster on the musical world.

Unable to restrain himself, Prof. Peter Schickele has since discovered more than a hundred of P.D.Q. Bach's scores, each one more jaw-dropping than the last, each one another brick in the wall which will someday seal the doom of Musical Culture.

That's the official story—and Peter Schickele, together with P.D.Q. Bach, the previously unknown member of the already enormous (and enormously musical) Bach clan that he invented, have been bringing delight to concert audiences, NPR listeners, recording players, and book lovers for almost half a century now. And yet, even though I'd like to pin all that fun on a bassoonist, the fact is that Peter himself was inspired by a trio of string players. . . .

As a student at the Juilliard School, Peter attended chamber music parties where Itzhak Perlman, Pinchas Zuckerman, and Emanuel Ax played Mozart quartets into the wee hours of the morning. The music itself was serious, but the young musicians were having tremendous fun.

> They weren't goofing around with the music itself, making musical puns or wrong notes or anything, but they were certainly having a jovial time playing together. They would make up jokes to complement the music: "Remember, this passage is mezzo-fortissimo," one of them would say, mocking the dynamic markings—for nonmusicians, that means a little less loud than the roar of a jet engine.

Their humor was infectious, and when Peter was asked to write a serious piece for eight flutes at the 1959 Aspen Music Festival, he chose to call it *Tutti Flutie*. Peter soon began to introduce musical jokes and surprise juxtapositions of Beatles melodies with Bach themes into his music making, and the Spike Jones in his character began to emerge.

Since 1965 the tireless professor has kept audiences in stitches with his presentation of P.D.Q. Bach's uniquely typical music. In addition to his annual concerts in New York City, he has appeared as a soloist, conductor, and host with all the great orchestras of the world. Even the titles of Peter's pieces offer a prelude to the fun and humor in the music itself: *The Abduction of Figaro, Concerto for Bassoon versus Orchestra, Erotica Variations, Fanfare for the Common Cold, Hansel & Gretel & Ted & Alice, A Little Nightmare Music,* and *Prelude to "Einstein on the Fritz."*

Classical music is often presented in a "serious" atmosphere, adorned with white tie and tails. Schickele, anything but stuffy, reminds us that there are probably as many jokes about musicians as there are blonde jokes or lawyer jokes. On a more serious note, he also points out that in

Mozart's day concerts were considered social events and opportunities for celebrity spotting, with audiences applauding in the middle of movements as we do after jazz solos today. There was a lot more conversation during the music at church services in Bach's time than we might feel comfortable with, and some masses went on for so long that people came and went during the course of the service. Some great chess games were played by audience members at nineteenth-century operas. In short, classical music hasn't always been quite so classical as it now appears.

Any serious enterprise will need its share of buffoonery and clowning, and human beings will seek to balance intellectual discipline with spontaneity and surprise in almost any endeavor. This is no doubt why we have jokesters among our orchestra colleagues. Rehearsals can be tense, as a conductor can put pressure on the musicians to play exactly as he or she directs. Recording sessions can raise the blood pressure beyond healthy levels. Ensemble tours can be unbearably restrictive. Humor and character onstage, on the other hand, can highlight the vitality of music, heighten the alertness of performers, and relax the musician from criticism and tension. Psychologists and educators tell us that we learn and perform best when we are having fun—so let's explore some opportunities to facilitate optimal performance!

A lot of musical humor comes from the need to create a balance—and what seems to tip the scales is living at either end of the acoustic spectrum. What are known as "character parts" in music are often reserved for those who play the lowest (or highest) instruments: as a bassist, I am one of them. Those of us who play the orchestral "extremes" are deprived of the great wealth of literature that's available to solo instruments such as the violin or piano, so perhaps we have more idle time to get into mischief. Okay, some people might claim my bass-clef colleagues sometimes get carried away with the lighter side of their artistry, but in all fairness, those playing low-pitched instruments don't hold an exclusive franchise on fun.

Music making doesn't have to be all high seriousness and clenched teeth: fun times can be enjoyed by instrumentalists and singers of all types! So if we explore the profile of humor as I've found it among those who play those heavy, low-pitched instruments, perhaps we can also see how to apply it best to both our musical and nonmusical lives.

STORIES WITH BASS-CLEF COLLEAGUES

My own glimpse into the special talents of low-voiced instrumentalists began at an early age when I joined the Cincinnati Symphony and embarked on our first long international tour. This experience confirmed for me that low-pitched instrumentalists really know how to have fun.

It was 1969, just two years after I'd joined the Cincinnati Symphony. I was an inexperienced, twenty-three-year-old principal bassist, and I was away on my first European orchestral tour. As you might guess, it was very exciting for a kid fresh out of college to find himself playing with such a wonderful group of musicians, and performing in many of the world's greatest concert halls. Imagine getting to tour Europe, staying in first-class hotels with all the travel arrangements taken care of—and *getting paid to do it!* The orchestra members were treated to receptions at fabulous restaurants, wine-tasting parties, and plenty of days off when we could visit the sights, take tours, and have a great time.

When orchestras go on tour, the basses are transported in shipping trunks, and they travel by truck except when we're actually crossing an ocean. Because of these shipping arrangements, bassists and tuba players can't take their instruments back to their rooms to practice when they are on tour, as the clarinetists and violinists can, so those of us who play these big low-pitched instruments have learned to deal with not practicing on tour, especially on free days.

We use a simple coping technique: go have a good time!

During this first European tour, it wasn't long before I experienced a "touring phenomenon" with my bass colleagues. On one of our first days off in Germany, I found what looked like an incredibly fun thing to do. A local travel agent handed me a brochure describing an all-day tour of the Rhine River, including stops at various castles, a wine tasting, and other entertainment. I thought it would be great to get away from some of the other orchestra members and spend the day on this boat excursion, *all by myself*.

I bought my ticket and boarded the vessel. It was very sunny on the top deck, but the passengers were very quiet and polite—not the place for me. I could hear a band playing on the lower back deck, and people making a lot of noise. And there was a bar with food service—that's where I wanted to be! I moved to the "fun" deck, and felt more at home at once. I bought a drink, went out to the sunny area of the back of the boat, and took a chair. The next thing I knew, someone was asking me, "Barry, what's happening?"

I turned around—and found myself grinning at six of the orchestra's bass players plus the tuba player! Two of the bassists had come together, but the other four had each discovered the tour boat independently. And there were no other musicians from the orchestra on the boat besides us bassists and the tuba man! Not one!

I know, we're the ones that don't have our instruments with us to practice, so we're the only ones who are more or less forced to have a good time—scientifically, I'm not proving anything. But it hit me then, as it has hit me many times since, that my bass colleagues are a bunch of people who know how to have fun and intend to do it.

Scientific or not, these experiences gave me my first indication about the kinds of people who are attracted to playing low-pitched instruments. In general, they are a fun-loving bunch. The nature of their job requires them to sit in the back of the orchestra and spend a lot of time listening to the conductor talking to everyone else. When the conductor does speak to the bass section, he often makes less than bright comments such as "You sound like you're moving furniture," or "Basses, you are too loud, out of tune, and too heavy." After hearing these comments for years, bassists tend to acquire a rather laid-back attitude. Our instruments are heavy, moving them around is a lot like moving furniture, and we wear back braces under our cummerbunds! Give us a break!

Most bass and low brass players have a great sense of humor both on and off the stage, perhaps because they need it. Musically speaking, they are specialists in playing the characters of the elephant, bear, cow, rhinoceros, clown, villain, drunkard, or monster—these are the roles composers thrust upon us. And I'm sure that our role-playing eventually influences our personalities—or perhaps it's the other way around, and those of us with personalities like elephants simply gravitate toward the big instruments.

Jim Self, who plays tuba in the recording studios in Hollywood, tells me his colleagues have to have a sense of humor not only about music but about themselves. He is in a special group of studio musicians called the Tons of the Pioneers, all of whose members are overweight. He told me:

> There is a lot of pressure when you're playing difficult brass instruments, and when you make a mistake there's no place to hide. You have to have a thick skin. We started out as studio colleagues, five brass players taking a photo of their big bellies. Then we drew up a menu of what we would like to eat at a party. We all wanted the richest, fattiest foods—it was hilarious. And from there, we went on to write and perform production numbers with music, costumes, and dancing.

While I have featured horns and percussionists in previous chapters who have also demonstrated a mastery of courage, they would be equally at home with the bass-clef instruments when it comes to laughter, parties, and jokes!

A smile is infectious, and a laugh can be contagious. When I'm around people with a sense of humor, I feel better. I enjoy what I'm doing, I'm more relaxed, and I play better. It seems to me that when we are having a good time, we work more efficiently—and if I'm right about that, having fun should be a prerequisite for any activity. Humor has the power to defuse tension, to make the workplace more pleasant and productive, and humor on the concert stage helps bridge the gaps between the composer, performer, and audience.

There are many tour stories about the people who play large instruments. Not long after I joined the Cincinnati Symphony, I heard a funny story attributed to our famous tuba player Sam Green (no relation). Sam was a legend among his colleagues, known for his fine musicianship as well as his playful and unflappable personality. In short, he was a nutty and lovable guy. Having Sam Green in the brass section was like an insurance policy: you didn't have to worry about the pressure building or a crisis developing. His verbal comebacks to conductors' musical corrections were legendary. Sam would find a way to bring a smile to the most desperate moments.

In the mid-sixties, Max Rudolf conducted the Cincinnati Symphony in a concert in New Orleans. The story goes that after the last movement in the symphony was finished, the applause began to die down, and Sam left the stage to change his clothes and take off for Bourbon Street! But the audience was more appreciative than Sam had guessed, and their clapping didn't exactly stop. Maestro Rudolf decided he would honor this appreciative audience with an encore—on this occasion, Wagner's Overture to *Die Meistersinger*.

No one knew that Sam was already in the dressing room as the orchestra began to play. Soon, however, the maestro and Sam's brass colleagues noticed that there was no tuba player, even though the piece features a major tuba solo! As the famous tuba entrance approached, a look of panic could be seen on the conductor's face. Sam was nowhere to be seen.

Lo and behold, at precisely the right time, the robust sound of the missing tuba somehow made its entrance. Orchestral colleagues recall watching the brass players and maestro hysterically struggling to retain their composure. As they looked around to see where the miracle had come from, they saw the unforgettable Sam Green in his underwear, with the bell of his tuba extending through the crack of the acoustic shell! It was quite a sound—and quite a sight.

Oh, and I frankly doubt this incident could have happened if a violist had left the concert early. I can imagine that if Sam Green played the viola he might have done the same thing—but that's my point exactly! Sam Green would never have played the viola! Sam is the right man in the right place—playing the right instrument.

Pranks with High Price Tags

Perhaps the most famous double bass story of all time cost the player his position with the Pittsburgh Symphony Orchestra—and sadly, Gerald Greenberg may be remembered more for this stunt than for his very real musical talent.

Tony Bianco, who was the principal bassist of the Pittsburgh Symphony for over fifty years, gave me this firsthand account of the story. The Pittsburgh Symphony was on tour with their celebrated conductor Fritz Reiner in Quebec, Canada, in 1938. Reiner was known for his incredibly small but efficient baton technique—he was a true minimalist! At times he would conduct even the most exciting passages while standing motionless, with his baton held almost still.

A very talented bassist named Gerald Greenberg had just joined the orchestra. Gerald possessed a typically precocious double bass personality and had a penchant for practical jokes. He loved to go shopping for antiques while on tour, and one concert evening he proudly returned from a shopping spree with a new acquisition: he had bought a telescoping spyglass. One of his colleagues asked him, "Gerald, what are you going to do with that?" and he replied, "Just wait and see."

At the evening concert Gerald pulled out his spyglass in the middle of a Shostakovich symphony and extended the telescope as if he were looking for the maestro's tiny but important beat. I'm sure it took quite a lot of nerve to pull a stunt like that—and you can imagine the looks on the faces of his orchestral colleagues! The audience must have wondered if their eyes were deceiving them.

The concert continued, and Fritz Reiner at last noticed Greenberg and the spyglass pointed at his baton. The story goes that Reiner wrote the words "You're fired" on his shirt cuff. That tiny part of the story may be an embellishment—but it was no surprise to anyone that a few weeks later Mr. Greenberg was no longer a member of the orchestra.

A lot of real characters choose to play the bass and tuba, and on the one hand they need outlets for their self-expression, but on the other, you can't go too far and still expect to keep your job. While we all know that a great joke can relax tension and improve the atmosphere in the workplace, musical or otherwise, sometimes pranksters' need for self-expression can make them overlook the little matter of timing. There is a time for jokes, and there is a time to work hard—a time, as Ecclesiastes says, for everything under the sun.

So if there is a lesson to be learned about practical jokes, it is the importance of right timing, of knowing what's appropriate where and when. Because while you can't take the humor out of the musician, if you're not careful you might just take the humorous musician out of the orchestra.

Bear that in mind as you read the following stories, because while the pranks may have been quite funny to those colleagues who were watching, they may not have been as funny to the generals in charge. So here's my disclaimer: do not try the spyglass stunt in an ensemble with your own conductor—even if your maestro's beat pattern is tiny! Remember that we are all in this together, and insubordination for its own sake is not cool.

In the next story I'll tell you, a humorous bassist had the foresight to check with management and her orchestra committee authorities to make sure she would not get into trouble with a prank she had in mind. Inez Wyrick is a bassist and currently teaches young bassists at Indiana University in Bloomington. She has an extraordinary flair for creating humorous diversions. In this particular case, she devised a courageous welcome and surprise for the incoming music director of the Amarillo Symphony. It was important for Inez and for the orchestral musicians to have a working atmosphere where there was room for fun, in big-hearted Texas style. Inez talked her idea over with her management and colleagues ahead of time, and they told her, "It's a great prank, go for it. Everyone will love it." And they did—everyone *except* the new music director.

The new conductor was slated to begin the dress rehearsal for his first concert with Wagner's *Die Walküre*, and Inez had decided to dress the part of Wagner's ancient warrior. As the maestro began to conduct the orchestra, Inez stepped out from behind her bass stool, wearing a Viking headpiece, a long blond wig, pie pans for breast plates, and a huge dress. The orchestra completely lost it—but the conductor was stone-faced, and completely ignored Inez. He finished the piece and stalked offstage.

Sadly, Inez's dress rehearsal gag permanently marred her relationship with the new conductor, and he never said a word to her during his entire tenure as music director of the orchestra. Fortunately for her, he only remained in that job for a few years! I don't know how Inez welcomed the next director of the symphony, but my guess is that she may have chosen more conservative rehearsal attire.

Practical jokes are often more effective with peers and colleagues than with those in positions of higher authority.

Douglas Yeo, bass trombonist with the Boston Symphony, enjoys keeping his trombone section colleagues on their toes. He describes one in his latest round of practical jokes:

Back when I was playing with the Baltimore Symphony, I sat next to one of my old college classmates, trombonist Eric Carlson. The pair of us had a long history of playing practical jokes on each other, both on- and offstage. I thought I had trumped him one time by filling his straight mute with water—which, when he picked it up, spilled out and cascaded all over the stage. But nothing could have prepared me for the night when I picked my own trombone up off the trombone stand for an entrance. When I blew, absolutely nothing came out—for a second—and then whoosh!

While I wasn't looking, Eric had dumped the entire contents of his spray bottle into my slide. I didn't notice the extra weight of water as I lifted my instrument, but when I went to play, the air pressure from my lips ran up against the water, which promptly forced itself out of my mouthpiece. I was showered with water from head to toe!

Doug may have lost this round of practical jokes, but he acknowledges that he played his rehearsals and concerts the next week with a heightened sense of alertness.

Using Humor to Defuse Tensions

Sometimes you just have to laugh.

William Revelli is a celebrated but sometimes impatient band conductor. During a particularly intense rehearsal with an all-state band many years ago, he and his tuba player were not seeing eye to eye. The piece they were rehearsing, by Persichetti, featured a prominent tuba solo, and the young tubist, who had never heard of Mr. Revelli prior to the rehearsal, found himself repeatedly the object of Revelli's wrath; Revelli kept telling him that his entrances on the solo were unacceptably late. After several attempts and several lectures, the young tuba player stood up and told the maestro, "Sir, I don't know when this note is getting up to you—but it's leaving here on time!"

The band members roared with laughter, and Mr. Revelli was able to see that the hostility he had been projecting was not having a positive impact. The tubist's lighthearted comeback forced the conductor to reapproach the problem in a more relaxed manner. He needed to find another way to get the tuba to play earlier, and hit upon the nonjudgmental instruction "Start your entrance one beat after the clarinet finishes his phrase."

Sometimes it's the calm and humor you exhibit under fire that releases tension and allows you to perform at a higher level.

Keeping Our Own House in Order

Jim Self told me about another famous tuba player, the late Clarence Karella, who played at 20th Century Fox studios for many years.

Alfred Newman, the most prolific composer of movie music of his day and winner of many Academy Awards, was conducting. Clarence, as was often the case, was not paying attention. His brass colleagues wanted to teach him a little lesson that might encourage him to stay tuned in to what was happening, so between takes one of the trombone players leaned over and told him: "Alfred just said he wants to add the tuba in this passage on measure thirteen. You must play a fortissimo (very loud) on low G." Clarence marked the new loud note in the place on his score that the trombone player indicated to him. Then they played the take, and he came in with the superloud note "as designated"—but it was completely out of place. This brought down the composer and orchestra—but it also got Clarence to pay more attention, for a while at least.

Rehearsals may at times be boring simply because a conductor cannot pay equal attention to everyone in the group all the time. You may have to be creative about finding ways to rekindle your attention when you need to play, or you too could be embarrassed by your colleagues, the conductor, or yourself. While these lighthearted pranks certainly combat a less-than-productive atmosphere, in some cases they may also increase the musicians' concentration on the music they are rehearsing.

And isn't that what this is all about?

These stories bring home a very important point for musicians and nonmusicians alike: we can't take ourselves too seriously. When our personal and musical goals become so overwhelming that they inhibit our ability to perform or concentrate, it is time to come up for air. The atmosphere in a musical workplace has to be conducive not only to playing your instrument but to the expression of your creativity and musicality, too. We all need to remember at times that we are still human beings and not mindless mechanical robots.

CREATING A LITTLE FUN IN BORING REHEARSALS

Time goes by fast in rehearsals when the players feel challenged and exhilarated by excellent music and the conductor works efficiently. Not all rehearsals are so wonderful, unfortunately. And when you find yourself watching the clock in rehearsal, it is not such a bad idea to have some interesting alternative activities in your repertoire, which you can draw upon to increase your level of interest.

You are more likely to work efficiently—and to enjoy what you do—when your concentration is challenged. When you are having a good time, you will make fewer mistakes and perform at a higher level, and ultimately this positive attitude will be audible in your performance and reach your audience.

Let's explore some activities that use humor and imagination. The main difference between the activities I shall describe here and the practical jokes I described previously is that you are required to pay attention in rehearsal. You may also find that some of these activities lend themselves to the nonmusical workplace—although once again, I absolve myself in advance of all responsibility for the use of anything you read in this chapter!

Should you decide to go ahead and use any of these techniques, you will need to adhere to a few ground rules:

- You must still pay full attention to what is being said or played during the rehearsal.
- You cannot miss a note or entrance—and if you do, you must stop the activity.
- Whichever activity you choose, it must promote musical interest and teamwork.
- It should also keep you alert and on your toes.

I would strongly advise you *not* to engage in these activities at every rehearsal. At times, things may be going just fine. Leave well enough alone; if it ain't broke, don't fix it. This isn't the time for humor. But when things aren't going so well and you can feel real tension or boredom, maybe a little humor wouldn't be out of place. It's a delicate balance you'll be treading here, and sensitivity to the rehearsal atmosphere and your sense of timing will determine what seems appropriate and even delightful and what seems intrusive or offensive.

Your goal, remember, is to stay focused in the rehearsal while also having a little fun.

So if you sometimes explore a humorous musical diversion *which you can only manage while your attention is focused on the music*, the result will be apparent in your increased concentration on music making. With improved concentration and a healthier and happier attitude, you will ultimately enjoy more productive rehearsals and better concerts.

Soloing When No One Can Hear

Sometimes it's just plain fun to play something that isn't supposed to be in the music, or to play spontaneously in a jazz or classical style.

There are fine soloists in any ensemble who may not have many opportunities to express themselves. Some may like to improvise backstage before a rehearsal or concert. Others may play a few licks while the band or orchestra is warming up or tuning. Tubist Martin Erickson writes about how his Washington, D.C., service band colleagues would joke around playing improvised jazz solos during outdoor concerts—when loud jets were flying overhead.

We used to play weekly concerts every summer at the Watergate area. There was a stage set on the Potomac River facing the rear of the Lincoln Memorial. Planes would take off and land at Washington National Airport almost like clockwork during the concerts—literally every twenty or thirty seconds, a plane would pass directly over the spot in the Potomac River where the band played.

The noise from the jet engines was so loud that it wiped out any sound the band made, so certain band members, anticipating the exact moment the plane would pass over us, would just improvise wildly or play something entirely different. Some of my favorite memories are jazz licks on the *Light Cavalry* and *Poet and Peasant* overtures. This went on totally unnoticed by the conductor, as well as by many of the players at the fringes of the bandstand.

Quirky Quotes

Conductors have been known to say some fairly outrageous things during rehearsals. Sir Thomas Beecham's remark to a cellist whose playing irritated him is perhaps the best known: "Madam, you have between your legs an instrument capable of giving pleasure to thousands, and all you can do is scratch it!" But then this was the same Sir Thomas Beecham who described the harpsichord as sounding like two skeletons copulating on a tin roof, and said of the British that they may not like music, but they absolutely love the noise it makes.

There is a well-known list of rehearsal quotes from Eugene Ormandy, famed conductor of the Philadelphia Orchestra, circulating on the Internet. When Ormandy wanted his players to play a passage more romantically, he's quoted as telling them, "Think of your girlfriend or boyfriend!" Another Ormandy quote has him telling his musicians, "During the rests—pray!"

And recently in a rehearsal of a San Francisco Bay Area symphony, I heard our conductor offer a few precise suggestions to the musicians, including "Very sorrowful, but not melancholy," and "Brass, you have got to get those tongues going faster."

Taking a conductor's remarks out of context and seeing whether you can read a hidden meaning into them can sometimes enliven a rehearsal— and waiting for a good pun will also keep your attention focused on what the conductor is saying. You'll find that paying attention is a whole lot less boring than watching the clock.

And what were those prayers Ormandy requested supposed to accomplish? Who or what do you suppose his musicians were supposed to pray for? The mind boggles at the possibilities. . . .

Sometimes conductors' gems should be penciled into the music as a reminder of their wisdom. If your conductor is prone to giving ridiculous instructions, or just describes the musical imagery in overly poetic terms, you might like to write down on the music exactly what was said. Later generations of musicologists may one day wonder why your music contains marginal comments like *elephantine, pray here, like a cockroach, passionate, gay, rambunctious, gross, like a shimmering sunset, like a jet engine,* and so forth.

Like a cockroach? I told you we low-instrument players get some pretty strange instructions from both composers and conductors, didn't I?

Things to Do When You Screw Up

Everyone makes mistakes in rehearsals and concerts. Sometimes you are the only person who knows what happened, other times your mistake might be detected only by your stand partner—and then there are times when *everyone* hears the mistake.

When this happens, it can be very embarrassing. What do you do?

If it happens during a concert, it is probably best to stay professional (stone-faced) and not in any way acknowledge that it happened. If some people in the audience hear something that sounds wrong, but don't see anyone react, they may think it was supposed to be that way.

Returning to Boston Symphony bass trombonist Douglas Yeo, he had an experience which may clarify just what to do when you do make a "big one":

Prokofiev's Concerto for Cello and Orchestra ends with the solo cello playing furiously high up on the fingerboard, all alone—followed by a thunderous unison low E quarter note by the whole orchestra. It's about as dramatic a climax as there is in music.

During a performance of this piece by master cellist Rostropovich with the Boston Symphony conducted by Seiji Ozawa, I was counting through the last bars and played the last note where I knew it was right. Fortississississimo—as loud as I could. But . . . the whole orchestra came in one beat late or, well, I guess it was *me* who was one beat early!

Ozawa looked up with a shocked expression on his face, which changed only when Rostropovich, who was by then standing up and bowing to an appreciative audience, turned around to the orchestra, holding his side and laughing. The soloist's graciousness did nothing to assuage my embarrassment over such a mistake—after all, I had played that note with everything I had!

I went slinking down into the basement of Symphony Hall during intermission, trying to hide from my colleagues. To my incredible surprise a violin player caught my arm and said, with a look of breathless wonder on his face, "Doug, did you hear the mistake the tuba made at the end?"

Too shocked by his question to think to explain my own culpability to him, I simply said, "Yes—but you know, it can happen to anybody!"

Mistakes *do* happen to anyone and everyone. And you can't always get away with it by playing innocent: there are times when you just need to acknowledge that you screwed up.

Using humor or modesty sends a message to your colleagues that you know you are human, and that you take responsibility for what you did. The *worst* thing you can do is to make an excuse to cover up your blunder.

Here are some things to do in rehearsals when you can't hide from your mistake—but be sure to choose one that fits the circumstances:

- Say, "That wrong note sounded pretty good. Maybe I should write it in?"
- If you play a wind instrument, fake a technical problem by blowing air on the keys, as if the mistake were caused by water in your instrument—then smile!
- If you play a string instrument, wipe off your bow as if you were getting rid of the bad note—or you could make a joke at the wind players by blowing on your strings.
- If you play a brass instrument, look in the bell to see where the wrong note came from—then shake your head.
- Look under your chair or around at your colleagues in a confused manner, as if asking where the wrong note came from.
- Raise your hand and proclaim: "I did it!—I'm an idiot!" What can anyone say after you've said that?
- Pick up your pencil and mark something on your music, as if something were wrong there and needs correction.
- Shake your head in disbelief.
- Turn to your colleagues, take a bow, and ask them if they would like you to play an encore.
- If something causes you to stop playing, just continue singing your part as it should have sounded.
- When the passage is repeated, play your mistake in the same place— for consistency.

- If you make a really loud obvious mistake in the wrong place, you might innocently ask your colleagues, "Did anyone hear that?"

Group Ensemble Responses

In large ensemble rehearsals, individuals get few opportunities to talk. It can be frustrating for players to spend so much time playing, listening to the conductor's and section leader's instructions, and never be able to talk back. Sometimes it feels good to remind the conductor that the ensemble is made up of live human beings with feelings, thoughts, and a sense of humor, working very hard together.

The activities I'll describe next allow the entire group to be heard as a community, without too much disruption: some of these are for fun, some are very subtle, some could be considered sarcastic, and in some cases they might even be bad ideas! Use and observe with discretion.

- When someone plays a nice solo in the group, shuffle your feet.
- When someone is late arriving for a rehearsal, shuffle your feet.
- When the conductor uses the word "break" in a musical context—e.g., "We need a break between the flute and clarinet solo"—stand up and turn around as if beginning your intermission break.
- If the conductor himself is late for a rehearsal, have the entire orchestra/band/chorus hide or leave the stage: when the conductor finally arrives, no one will be present! But don't forget to come out after the joke is over!
- Whenever you hear an extraneous sound, mimic it with your instrument—you can mimic birds, sirens, large truck motors, furniture being moved, bells, cell phones, beepers, and so on.

All these games, activities, excuses, and group responses challenge musicians to participate with interest while still playing their parts accurately. Remember that if your humorous diversion causes you to miss an entrance, you are asking for trouble. Use your sense of timing, discretion, creativity, and maturity when bringing some lightness into the workplace.

When you feel "rehearsal-impaired," I hope some of these options will prove helpful.

THE SOLO ARTIST COMEDIAN

Niccolò Paganini (1782–1840), the world's most famous Italian violin virtuoso, drew attention to his virtuosity through his personal magnetism. He mesmerized audiences and critics alike with his bravura, showmanship, and all sorts of antics onstage. One of his most famous works was the "Moses Fantasy," to be played exclusively on the lowest string of the violin. Paganini went to outrageous lengths to entertain the audience with this piece: he often had a stagehand come out onstage with a large pair of scissors and cut all the strings on the violin except for the G string on which Paganini played the "Fantasy." Apparently he was so good at this piece that he sometimes played it while holding his violin behind his head.

While the "Moses Fantasy" was based on the melody of a solemn prayer, the fun that Paganini had while playing a piece with such a serious theme contributed greatly to its success. It seems that after almost two hundred years, most audiences and performers have forgotten some of the more eccentric performance practices of long ago: when most violinists (or contemporary players of the viola, cello, or bass) perform Paganini's "Moses Fantasy" they make it a technical display, completely forgetting the humor that Paganini himself brought to the music.

This piece became a signature piece for my friend and colleague the celebrated bass soloist Gary Karr. Gary was just beginning to establish his career as a solo double bassist in 1961, but he was already both a great virtuoso and a superb entertainer and comedian.

When Gary played lighthearted music such as the "Moses Fantasy" or some of Bottesini's virtuoso operatic pieces, he would accompany his performance with colorful facial expressions and body gestures that precisely heightened what was going on in the music. He would model joy and sorrow, boredom, sarcasm, and silliness, daintiness and abuse, delight and excitement.

Gary's witty expressive interpretations were true to the character of the music he was playing. They helped his audience to see and hear what the composers intended—and he did all this while demonstrating the most impeccable phrasing and beautiful bass tone. Gary's solo recitals touched the hearts and spirits of many audiences, and they came to hear Gary as a great artist and entertainer who happened to play the double bass.

Gary's achievement was truly remarkable and added a new dimension to solo recitals. In the true Paganini tradition, Gary dramatized the humor inherent in the music while dazzling audiences with his musicianship and virtuosity. And his open inclusion of expressive humor as an integral part of his presentation has inspired many other soloists and composers to revive this otherwise forgotten art.

When I asked Gary how he rediscovered this lighter approach to music, he said:

It all started during my first concert tour with the Chicago Little Symphony in '61 playing, among other things, Bottesini's Grand Duo Concertante with violinist Charles Treger. The piece is like a miniature opera, complete with an unrequited love affair and a duel. Being born and raised in Hollywood, I saw this as a perfect opportunity to employ some acting and comedic skills. Although the critics hated it, the audiences ate it up, so after that, anytime I played a corny virtuoso piece, I infused it with humor.

Gary, who grew up in a family of professional musicians, told me he regarded performing as something as natural as life itself. He was bothered by the stiff decorum that classical musicians bring to the stage and determined from the start not to be overly serious when he performed.

I wanted to share the joy I felt in making music, and I found it impossible to fit into the serious mold expected of classical musicians. In fact, during my youth, classical music was called *serious* music—which, when you consider such greats as Mozart and Haydn, couldn't be farther from the mark.

Like other art forms, classical music encompasses the full gamut of human emotions from tragedy to laughter. It seemed to me that classical performers, like jazz and popular musicians, should be more relaxed and communicative. In this way, they could better convey their own personal reaction to the music. This is what I've tried to do in my own career, and so performing has always been fun for me—without up-tightness or unnecessary stress.

As we saw in the chapter on communication, there's a close entrainment that occurs between performer and audience, and if a performer like Gary is enjoying himself, the audience members will likely be enjoying themselves as well. And the contrary is true: if the performer is serious, tense, or very formal, the audience will likely respond in a similar way.

Gary describes an amusing experiment in which he put this very principle to the test:

> One time I gave a lecture-demonstration to a sophisticated classical audience. First I came onto the stage, took a very dignified bow, and performed some humorous pieces in a very stiff and serious manner. The applause was polite. Then I came back onstage and played the same pieces—but with my instinctive theatrics. The crowd went wild!
>
> I have fun playing the bass—why shouldn't I share that joy onstage?

Gary feels it is most important for a performer to be natural. Stiffness is not natural, and fear is not what the audience came to hear. This brings up the question of what the intention of the performer *should* be. I'd suggest that music is not so much about technical perfection as about the transmission of a musical message. If the performer communicates this message, the audience will be moved and entertained, feeling passionate or playful as the case may be.

Animation

While bass, tuba, and low-pitched instrumentalists are most often called on to play humorous or character roles with their orchestras, in their chamber groups, or during solo performances, enhancing the animated character of music can be valuable for musicians of all instruments and voice. Everyone can benefit from emulating the engaging personalities of some great conductors, singers, and instrumentalists.

I have watched the fiery and passionate expressiveness of Leonard Bernstein's face as, hair flying all over the place, he seemingly dances about the podium while conducting Strauss or Tchaikovsky. I have been amazed to watch the expressions which play across James Galway's face as he blows his tin whistle. Itzhak Perlman seems to be having way too much fun while he plays with his characteristic reckless abandon and brilliant virtuosity. André Watts is legendary for expressive facial gestures which reflect the music he plays. Soprano Kathleen Battle is one of the most visually expressive singers in the world; she brings her music to life not only through impeccable musicianship but also through facial expressions and body language. And violinist Nadja Salerno-Sonnenberg has been quoted as saying, "Music is show business." She adds a theatrical quality to her playing with her exaggerated body movements and engaging facial expressions. In a recent interview, Gerhard Mantel spoke of the great cellist Paul Tortelier:

> He was fascinated by the idea that music making has an element of theatrical acting, not as something "imposed on top of the music," but as something elementary that is inherent in effective artistic musical communication.

Regardless of your instrument, voice, or profession, if you enhance the theatrical character of whatever you do, this can not only free you up for a more passionate experience of the music, but also add meaning, interest, and value to your performance. And the audience will reflect the joy that you show in your own performances.

THE VALUE OF HAVING FUN

During my summers with the Cincinnati Symphony, I was given the choice of playing opera concerts in the air-conditioned Music Hall or pops concerts with Erich Kunzel outside in the humid Riverbend Music Pavilion. The first season, I elected to stay cool inside. I thought I would be more challenged artistically playing opera than popular classics.

My first opera rehearsal, however, was with a celebrated but universally despised conductor whom I quickly tagged in my mind as "the Screamer." When he didn't like the way our music sounded, he started to sing and scream the music so loudly that we couldn't hear ourselves play. It was de-moralizing, dehumanizing—and artistically awful. I said to myself, Why do I have to play for this jerk? I thought music was supposed to be enjoy-able. This is no fun—I'm out of here.

I transferred to the pops orchestra—and stayed there for the remaining twenty-eight summers. The music may not have been of the highest artis-tic caliber, but I knew the audiences would love it, the orchestra would play with energy and zest, and everyone would have a good time.

I asked our pops conductor, Erich Kunzel, how he is able to create such a friendly atmosphere in his concerts, and he credited Arthur Fiedler as an early musical influence because he created a new demand for semipop-ular music. Yet I remember that Fiedler was not popular with musicians because of his taskmaster attitudes, and he never spoke to the audience. Erich, by contrast, has a relaxed yet efficient rehearsal atmosphere and loves to talk to the audience.

I wanted to bring the audience into the pops family so the music is more reachable to them. I wanted the people to feel they were coming to get entertainment. My aim was to make them feel part of the experi-ence, as Frank Sinatra did.

Perhaps one of the reasons Erich has such a theatrical side is that he first trained as a classical bass player! That's why he belongs in this chapter.

Having played bass in my school orchestra, I knew how much I hated it when conductors talked so much—all that philosophical stuff. That is just not possible with a hundred musicians.

Interpretation belongs to the conductor, but you don't have to *explain* your interpretation! I want the orchestra to have fun, and we need to feel relaxed to put on a relaxing show. They have to lower their shoulders and dig into the music, but have fun. This is what reaches the audience.

Kunzel likes to tell funny stories, and his conducting gestures were in the tradition of my bass hero Gary Karr, and reflected the character of whichever piece of music we played. By creating a spirit and environment of camaraderie, Kunzel allowed room for our practical jokes and humorous group responses to some of his silly rehearsal images. We had fun working for him and he with us.

For Halloween, Western, or holiday concerts we changed into theme costumes, and we were encouraged to participate in theatrical stunts. Erich could make the audience believe they were hearing Tchaikovsky even when we played Marvin Hamlisch! Fun and humor were high on the list of skills that he encouraged. And friends in the audience have told me that they go to pops concerts not just because of the programs and the style of the music, but because they know they will always have fun.

Learning is fulfilling. Work is productive. Communicating is satisfying. Playing music is thrilling. All these things are wonderful and satisfying on their own—and approaching learning, work, rehearsal, and performance with a lightness of being, a sense of humor, and a spirit of joy can make each of them that much better.

We take up music because it brings satisfaction and joy to our lives, yet it is easy to get caught up in the result-oriented world, desperately preparing for a concert, and lose sight of that original goal. Everyone is under pressure to perform flawlessly. Some musicians will always want to judge your ability to play your instrument and hope to be considered more accomplished than the next person. Others want to impress their colleagues and the public with what they know and how talented they are.

Yet while "being good" is an individual goal, the music is for everyone to enjoy. When we laugh at something, the moment is for everyone to experience. When we are having a good time, we are not usually thinking of ourselves. Most of us choose to play music not for the money, but because we love it. The audience comes to our concerts because they want to have fun. Humor helps us avoid that endless mental chatter and keeps us from getting too self-absorbed. So in the privacy of rehearsal, and when playing our instruments in a solo, band, choral, or orchestral concert for others, let's remember one thing:

It is the *joy and passion of our music making* that will keep us all, performers and audience alike, coming back for more. And let's not forget to have fun.

five

PASSION: THE POWER
OF LOVE

(Cello)

Passion and music have been deeply interwoven since a bird first sang to attract its mate, if not before. Shakespeare's remark about music being the food of love captures the idea nicely, and my own experience at Jewish summer camp when I was still in junior high brought the point home to me: I played my accordion during meals and prayers and at services, and Julie noticed.

Julie thought I was cute, Julie thought I was especially cute when I played the accordion, and I couldn't get Julie out of my mind. Even then, at the passionately romantic and hormonal age of thirteen, I took time to note to myself that music can be a very seductive activity.

I should add that the accordion is not the instrument I associate most strongly with passion, nor is it my own beloved double bass.

I have always envied cellists, not only for their musicianship and the wondrously soulful sound of their instrument, but for the beautiful music that the great composers have created for them. Brahms and Shostakovich consistently exploited the passionate quality of the cello, and Bach's celebrated suites for unaccompanied cello are extraordinary masterworks of passion and beauty.

In writing this chapter about musical passion, I could no doubt have drawn my anecdotes from any instrument or part of the orchestra. I feel, though, that the cello is the most passionate of instruments and the cello repertoire the most passionate of instrumental repertoires—and it is to the cello and to my cellist friends and colleagues that I turn to explore the topic of passion in music.

I would like to talk about three kinds of passion (apart from the kind I felt for Julie) which can touch the lives of those of us who make music: the passion for life, the passion for music, and the passion which music expresses.

The Passion for Life

The passion for life is the hardest of the three to talk about, and it's also the most inclusive and least directly focused on music making of the three. But I have put it at the top of my list, and although I shall only touch on it briefly I would like to signal its importance by quoting the legendary cellist, conductor, and self-exiled Catalonian icon of culture and humanity Pablo Casals, who once said:

> Real understanding does not come from what we learn in books; it comes from what we learn from love—love of nature, of music, of man. For only what is learned in that way is truly understood.

Life itself can be a passion. I cannot improve on those words from the great Maestro Casals, and I shall not attempt to, but I would like to tell you one story about a cellist who brought his passion for life quite uniquely into his playing. It was during the early 1990s while the city of Sarajevo was torn by war that for twenty-two days in a row, Vedran Smailovic dressed for a solo concert in full formal evening attire and walked out into the middle of a street with his cello to sit down and play Albinoni's lyrical Adagio. Smailovic played the Adagio in front of the same bakery each day, played it against a background of sniper and artillery fire and in the lulls which pass for silence between lethal exchanges.

He played it each day for twenty-two days straight, because twenty-two human beings, Sarajevans like himself, had been killed when mortar fire hit a bread line outside that bakery, in that Balkan city already worn down by centuries of war.

When a CNN reporter asked him if it was not crazy of him to play his cello in the street while Sarajevo was being shelled, Smailovic replied: "You ask me am I crazy for playing the cello; why do you not ask if they are not crazy for shelling Sarajevo?"

This cellist is just an ordinary person, but his passion lingers; his courage, his defiance, his imagination, his playfulness, his art, his intention, all of these live on.

Smailovic's story exhibits his passion for life, and the way in which he translated it into the voice of his instrument.

The Passion for Music

This leaves two forms of passion for us to discuss: we can have a passion for music and music making, and we can play music with passion. Music can stir passions in others, I believe, because music can be an expression of our own souls. And I don't mean those words lightly.

A few years after that summer in camp with Julie, I began my own love affair with music. I was playing bass by then, and it lured and seduced me all the way through our fine high school orchestra, the all-state orchestra, and the school jazz ensemble to the All-Southern California Hollywood Bowl Jazz Ensemble! All of a sudden I felt something special in music that kept me going back for more and more. I had to be there. I was in love, and this was a love to last a lifetime.

The love affair can be total. Janet Suzman once wrote of the brilliant cellist Jacqueline du Pré, "Music is life, breath, food and inspiration to her, the element she swims in like a lovely trout." Du Pré debuted at the age of sixteen and was an international star by her early twenties—before multiple sclerosis cut short her career as one of the great musicians of our times.

I have spoken with many cellists about falling in love with music, and each of them spoke of some special memory he or she had of being drawn to music or the voice of the cello. Perhaps their stories will remind you of your own experience when you first felt the seductive power of music in your life.

Joan Jeanrenaud, the cello soloist who recently retired from a twenty-year chamber career with the world-famous Kronos String Quartet, is experiencing a new phase in her love for the cello and music, but when I asked her about the first time she experienced the love for music, she recalled a time when she was studying cello with Fritz Magg at Indiana University:

> I came right out of a cello class where I hadn't played well at all, into a rehearsal conducted by Fiora Contino. We were rehearsing a baroque cantata, and I was playing the continuo cello part. All of a sudden I found myself playing with great emotion, freedom, and passion. I was not thinking about what I was doing, I somehow transcended my personal situation and felt I was caught up in the entire ensemble experience—and I was taken to a higher place with the music. I loved being part of the group, and losing myself in that larger musical whole.

Bonnie Hampton is a distinguished soloist and chamber music performer, and professor at the San Francisco Conservatory of Music. Her story credits her own teacher, Margaret Rowell, as her inspiration. Bonnie remembers herself as a somewhat rebellious teenager, struggling both with herself and with her instrument. She recalls both her mother and her wonderful teacher pressuring her to be a cellist, but it was when she "caught the bug" around the age of fifteen that she first really determined to be a cellist herself.

Bonnie told me that playing the cello helped her understand and communicate with others:

> I was shy and not very verbal, and there was never any question that my best mode of expression and communication was through the music. I found that when you talk with someone, you don't really have to know

them, but when you play music with them, you do—so music is a kind of expression that demands honesty. We all tend to wear masks of one kind or another in social situations—but when we play music, we have to make ourselves more vulnerable, more open to each other as well as to the music.

I consider myself very lucky to have had the cello as my "voice." The instrument's vocal color and expression was always the big draw for me, and it is still what means the most to me.

The wonderfully creative cello soloist David Darling is an ECM recording artist and director of Music for People who began his career with the Paul Winter Ensemble. David and I were classmates at Indiana University, and he has been a passionate musician for as long as I've known him. Dave's original compositions and his playing are reflections of what he sees in the world and how it affects him. I asked him about the cello's natural capacity to express pathos, and he told me:

I'm always on the edge of my emotions. When I visit large cities, I see people all around me in desperate need of help. I do not and cannot understand hunger, and poverty, and crime, let alone crimes against humanity and war—but I can feel them. And the pathos that comes out of the cello is so expressive. It allows me to express my feelings and my attitude to life.

The cello immediately puts one in a place of pathos. And it's not just the instrument, but also the person who plays it. How can we play a sound that makes an audience weep? When we play the opening of Bloch's *Schelomo* or the second movement of the Shostakovich cello concerto, it can be so astonishingly evocative....

Carter Brey, distinguished principal cellist with the New York Philharmonic Orchestra, believes that music offers a more direct language for the emotions than any other art. He recalls first feeling a passion for music at age fifteen, when he first played the Schubert C Major Quintet. He told me:

It hit a button in me—but that barely expresses the strength of what I felt. I needed to dedicate my life to playing this kind of music.

When you are an adolescent, you are able to experience erotic love for the first time, and that is a spiritual and emotional opening which goes in tandem with becoming physically mature. That certainly helped me understand the greatness in this music.

Carter experiences a similar excitement whether he's listening to Schubert's C Major Symphony or the Beatles' *Abbey Road*. Music gives him both euphoria and intellectual engagement.

Euphoria and intellectual engagement, the plight of humanity, pathos, honesty, transcending oneself as part of a larger musical whole—these are not small matters. Once the musical bug bites you, you have experienced something in music that is not as readily available on evening soap operas, in automobile maintenance classes or sales meetings, or at the checkout counter of Macy's department store.

Passion isn't just something we do with feeling or emotion, it is something that compels or defines the artist. At the highest level of artistry, when we experience this passion in our music, our lives too are touched by the love that Casals describes.

The Passion Within Music

This brings us to the passion within the music, the composer's passion which music alone seems able to express, and the player's passion which expresses that passion.

Music touches feelings that words cannot. Music has the power to reach directly into the soul of everyone who participates in this experience. It is inspired by feelings and has the power to communicate the emotions better, perhaps, than any other form of communication. It is truly the international language that needs no translation. Most musical masterworks are inspired by the human condition as it is impacted by the beauties of nature, love, birth and death, and historical occasions.

When Bach wrote the sarabande of the Second Cello Suite, when

Brahms wrote the opening cello solo in his Piano Concerto, when Copland penned the beginning of *Appalachian Spring*, and when Rodgers and Hart conceived "My Funny Valentine," each one was in touch with something immaculate, something perfect. As musicians, we get to put our daily lives down, set our personalities aside, and jump into the middle of that perfection, to join with others in re-creating these great moments in musical history. This is way beyond fun. At its best, it is a spiritual experience, an act of human passion and skill that can be as beautiful as a crystal, a rainbow, or a brilliant sunset.

FINDING YOUR PASSION: SACRED SPACES

One way to bring more passion to your music making is to ask yourself the question "What's the most passionate and memorable musical experience I've ever had?" Once you've figured that out, you'll probably recognize there was a specific trigger or triggers which gave that time its emotional intensity and passion.

I know that my own most memorable breakthrough occurred at a time when several important influences came together—my practicing, my teacher, and a very special place. If I was forced to say which was the most important influence of all, I'd probably say it was that special, sacred space. It all started for me in 1988, at a concert given by my teacher at the time, the world-renowned bass virtuoso François Rabbath.

During a historic concert he gave at the International Society of Bassists Convention in Los Angeles, my hometown, Rabbath premiered an original composition of his own called *Reitba*. In words almost as inspiring as the music itself, he told us how he had been traveling in the African desert and seen heat waves pulsating above the white desert sand: in the distance, he could make out what appeared to be a rose-colored lake surrounded by snow crystals (he later found out the sparkling ice crystals were in fact the lake's salt banks). This unique image, in which a cool jewel of rose-colored water and snow seemed to beckon across an arid expanse of sunbaked sand, inspired a no less mysterious music in the master—aflame with passion and anguish, yet cooled with contemplation and consolation.

Reitba brought Rabbath's audience to tears—and after hearing this performance, I vowed I would study more intensively with the master and someday be able to play this piece of music for myself.

Studying with Rabbath was a painful process; I had to allow myself to learn an entirely different way of playing the bass. And change didn't come easily. It took years for my left and right hands to adjust to using different muscles, while relaxing others that I had used over a lifetime, but over the course of many trips to Paris and one leave of absence from my symphony job, I persevered. Yet while I was anxious to learn to play *Reitba* with all the evocative magic that goes with Rabbath's interpretation and fingerings, François was in no hurry for me to play his music. In fact, after years of technical study, there was not a mention of my playing *Reitba*. Our study was about discipline and not about playing evocative solos. François told me that when I was ready to play his music, I would know.

Eventually, one of my Inner Game seminars took me to a wonderful music course outside of Barcelona called Stage 92. I had been hired to coach chamber music and conduct Inner Game of Music sessions for talented postgraduate students. I borrowed a bass from the local teacher.

Finding myself in a new country where I didn't know the language, I missed my wife, Mary, and felt alone with only my bass and my music to comfort me. That's when I found my own special and sacred space. I took the beautiful old bass I had borrowed into a dark chapel with high wooden pews and stained-glass windows. I wanted to find the notes on this strange and lovely instrument. At first I played the prelude to the Bach D Minor Cello Suite; the tones of that bass resonated through the chapel unlike any other I had ever heard. I felt as though my breath had been taken from me. I was playing with new freedom and passion, and every note seemed to hang in the air in an endless expression of beauty. I thought to myself, If only François could hear me play like this! I was so inspired I had to put my bass down and take a walk outside.

It was a hot summer day as I walked out into a meadow of dead brown grass and sand. There was a mountain in the distance, with what I later learned was a historic monastery perched on its peak. I could feel the heat, the wind, and the guiding spirit within myself. Something told me to sit down on the sand and meditate on my own breath. As I breathed in, I could hear the strains of *Reitba* begin to pulse in my heart. Tears came to my eyes and I began to cry—and as I cried, a sense of calm came over me, and I found myself humming and then singing the melody of *Reitba*.

I knew this music was now inside me, and was ready to come out. I went back inside the chapel and began to play *Reitba* with the passion I had felt that first time I heard François play it several years earlier. Since that day, I have continued to play this wonderful piece, and I have been able to recapture and preserve the special soul quality that I had never experienced in my own playing until I visited this sacred space in Barcelona.

Now when I need inspiration, or feel that my playing lacks passion, I take myself back to that chapel and that meadow, and refresh myself at the source.

Many things may come together to create this kind of magic in your life: your own preparation, your emotional makeup at the time, and endless other factors. It may seem that a particular "sacred space" is the final piece of the puzzle, but more likely it is the interrelationship of many factors that creates these special moments.

In telling this story over the years, I have discovered that this kind of experience is far from unique. When I asked the celebrated English solo cellist Steven Isserlis to tell me about one of his most passionate moments, he told me several things that contributed to his best music making.

Steven Isserlis's Sacred Space

For Steven Isserlis, Wigmore Hall in London is the sacred site, his own equivalent to my chapel in Spain. One of the highlights of his solo concert career was playing his favorite music on his cello in his favorite hall.

Steven's preferred cello is the "De Munck" or Feuermann Stradivarius, dating from 1730. He tells me that all he has to do is dream of a sound and his cello can produce it. He loves the historic ambience of London's Wigmore Hall, which compares in tradition, beauty, acoustic excellence, and spirit with America's Carnegie Hall, and on whose stage so many distinguished cellists have made music, Casals, Rostropovich, du Pré, Starker, and others, for decades of the most appreciative audiences and critics. *The audience at Wigmore is there to listen and be involved, and they make up a big part of the musical experience,* Steven says. And his favorite music is Bach, the Bach of the six great unaccompanied cello suites.

It was here in Wigmore Hall that Steven pulled off a great feat of concentration and artistic achievement, performing all six of the Bach cello suites on his Feuermann Strad in one day; it was a memorable musical event, one that he still carries with him.

We cannot visit our favorite chapel or concert hall, or the desert fields and monasteries of Spain, each time we want to make music, but we *can* create a sacred space in our own imaginations.

Visit and practice in a chapel in your own neighborhood, and use your imagination to transform it into the Cathedral of Notre Dame in Paris. Or play outside on a high school football or soccer field—and transform the greenery into an imaginary place among the clouds, on water, or in the mountains or desert. You can imbue your instrument or voice with a sense of history and your responsibility to the great musical traditions of the past, honoring others who have come before us in your own imaginary concert setting. With imagination, you can create a sacred environment so filled with feeling and meaning that it can overcome and transform any feelings of doubt, anxiety, or loss of self-confidence.

And here is a secret that artists, musicians, and poets perhaps know better than most: imagination is not some gossamer web of illusion, *it has the power to transform reality.*

The Spirit or Loss of a Loved One

Natalie Clein, the talented young award-winning British cellist, learned about egoless cello playing while playing Bach at a memorial service for a dear friend who had passed away.

> I realized I was playing both for my deceased friend and for his wife, sitting in front of me—and what struck me about the experience is

that it was a sort of communion with them. I know that sometimes in a concert I'm thinking about how I'm playing, and it can all be quite ego-centered—but in this very powerful and moving situation the ego disappeared completely, and I felt the music had an extra poignancy and beauty.

For people who are grieving, music can be a really beautiful thing. It can be a chance for beauty and optimism to blend in with the tragedy of loss. And I believe I learned a lot from this particular experience. I always try now to forget my own security and ego, and turn my music making into a human situation.

Grief at the loss of a friend or family member is among the sincerest expressions of love. It is a pure gesture from the heart, and reaches into the emotional depths of the soul. Playing in memory of a loved one can inspire a calm expression of passion from deep within your soul, and playing from the place of love or honor can be the purest and most honest kind of musical communication.

Lynn Harrell, the great concert cellist, lost both of his parents when he was very young. He was raised by friends of his family and lived out of a suitcase until he was eighteen, at which point he joined the Cleveland Orchestra. Lynn said it took a long time for him to come to terms with the death of both his parents, and that it was an experience that he wouldn't wish on anyone. But in his loss, he learned about the resilience of the human spirit.

In an interview for the Internet Cello Society, he told Tim Janof:

I think now, due to much introspection, and with the help of self-help and psychology books, that I have learned to recognize the pain that we all experience and that none can escape. Some people have more than others, but we all have it. Part of the artistic process is to channel these feelings of pain and sadness through music to the listener. In my teen years, when I awoke to music, I didn't really share it with my parents because I was very inhibited, since they were professionals. When they died and I couldn't share it with them, there was this need to really give to others, a need I now try to fulfill by giving to the audience.

One of my own beloved teachers, the celebrated concert cellist and professor Janos Starker, told me about losing his two brothers in the prime of their lives. He said that you become aware there must be a reason why you are still alive.

I was further reminded of this by my mother's passing, because the concert I played on the next day was one of my most emotionally charged concerts ever, and this concert in turn reminded me of playing one particular concert with the Chicago Symphony on tour in Dallas, Texas, with Antal Dorati.

We had already played more than ninety concerts with the Chicago Symphony that season, and I couldn't understand why Dorati was suddenly doing some things with the Brahms symphony that he had never done before. He was a very private and distant person, but a great genius. After he finished the performance, he passed me in the hall, and said to me in Hungarian, "My father died yesterday."

These things make one aware of one's own mortality—and other considerations like career and money become less important.

Playing in honor of a loved one or friend has the emotional and physical power to take our music making to a higher level. In a sense, grief gives us a more urgent appreciation for life, and channeling this energy and emotion into our music will intensify and even purify our reasons for playing. The ego takes a backseat, and we can tap into a very deep place in the soul where the music resides in all its glory.

Anytime you are playing music, it can be an opportunity to dedicate your performance to a friend, whether living or dead, and to connect with that place of honor and spirit.

THE ROOTS OF PASSION

I have often wondered how environment, family, genes, instinct, or even cultural background can contribute to someone's ability to make music. It certainly seems reasonable to suppose that both family and cultural environments may exert a strong influence on love or talent for music at an early age, and who knows what other influences may or may not play a role? Even a particular instrument may be a vehicle for musical passion.

My friend and colleague bassist Glen Moore, who plays with the eclectic New Age ensemble Oregon, makes music on a three-hundred-year-old bass. He feels his bass is a "living spirit" and has a voice of its own. And my own great teacher François Rabbath has only allowed a few people to play his treasured Quenoil bass. Rabbath feels that when someone else plays his bass, the instrument takes on a different energy from his own. He claims he can even tell if someone else has touched his bass by accident!

Cultural Heritage

Given the bewildering variety of possibilities for transmitting sound, spirit, and musical passion through inheritance, family expectations, environment, tradition, and even concrete objects, I trust you will bear with me if I express my pride in the distinctive musical heritage of my own Jewish upbringing.

On the one hand, the large number of outstanding Jewish string players and composers might suggest that perhaps there is something in Jewish culture which supports the passing down of a style of playing, as demonstrated by such celebrated musicians as Itzhak Perlman, Pinchas Zuckerman, Robert Cohen, Leonard Bernstein, Gustav Mahler, George Gershwin, and Daniel Barenboim. That's a thought that I take pride in.

On the other hand, I have heard numerous non-Jewish musicians play with the same spirit. Yo-Yo Ma and Rostropovich play with a soul that would be the envy of any Jewish musician. Bach certainly wasn't Jewish. This passionate style is then in no way exclusive to the Jewish people. Do I take less pride in that? No, because I am human. And perhaps that's the point.

Each one of us may have a "local" culture or tradition in which we take pride, and from which we derive strength. But we are all also heirs to the great human tradition of music making, and Carlos Nakai's Navajo flute can be as rich an inspiration to me as Perlman's violin.

Having said that, it is also very likely true that music which expresses grief, persecution, and pathos may attract and reflect the imagination of people from a familiar cultural background. The brilliant English cellist Natalie Clein believes Jewish musical tradition closely parallels that of the Eastern European Gypsies. She explains that the Gypsies—a people without a land to call their own—have also found a special sense of community in music, using it as a way of holding themselves together and expressing their sorrows.

It's a sentiment that Robert Cohen might well agree with. Robert certainly acknowledges his Jewish culture, and also identifies with the spirit of the roaming Eastern European Gypsies and their music. He talks about the feeling of rootlessness, and the poignant way music can address suffering:

> I'm Jewish, and there is no question for me that what I have to say in music reflects my understanding of humanity, suffering, and communication. In a very subtle way, I think I identify more with music in a minor key. In the Bach suites, when I hit the minor keys, I feel it's more poignant. The pain that's expressed in the minor keys is somehow acute for me. I am sure that every musician's makeup includes cultural and historical dimensions, and feelings deepen as we develop as individuals. The better we can understand our feelings, the better we can express ourselves, which is why it is often more interesting to hear people play as they get older.

Jacqueline du Pré converted to Judaism when she married Daniel Barenboim—and in her case, Judaism and music seem inextricably intertwined:

> Life is incredibly important, and one must try to cherish every minute. Since I changed my religion, I don't think I've made any leaps in character. When asked if my Jewish faith helped me cope with my MS I always reply, to be quite honest, not as much as music, because for me

the Judaism is almost bound up in the music. I just cannot separate them or indicate their boundaries. I know through all my troubles, I could never say that I am not a lucky person, because I am blessed.

And perhaps it's in religion that the passions and emotions—and thus the music—run deepest. Daniel Rothmuller, associate principal cellist with the Los Angeles Philharmonic, comes from a Middle Eastern Jewish background, and he spoke to me about the Jewish liturgy:

> On your knees you are either praying, or giving thanks. The history of the Jewish people is a history of suffering and prejudice, and that's reflected in our prayers, and also in our lives.

There is enormous emotion in Jewish liturgical music, he explained, the prayers that are sung are prayers of pleading, mourning, or praise and thanksgiving—but always full of emotion and yearning.

Gypsies and Jews have long experience of struggles and horrors and dispossession which enrich their music making, but what of others? How can one bring passion, suffering, and other deep feelings into music when one has less experience of these qualities in one's life?

These things are not culturally exclusive, but they may be culturally influenced, so the answers have to be found in your capacity to empathize. Spend time looking into the history of any culture and you will find war, prejudice, and persecution. The history of every population has its times of struggles. *Feel globally, dig locally* is my recommendation. Value your own cultural history, dig into it, learn its sorrows and its triumphs, and, at the same time, foster a global awareness within yourself of humanity's social interactions with humanity worldwide.

And, of course, listen passionately to passionate music. If passionate and expressive music is not a part of your culture or family background, you can expose yourself to the anguish and joy of the blues and jazz, or the spirit of flamenco guitar. The quickest way to learn the style and nuances of any kind of music is simply to listen to it—whether it be jazz, popular, sacred, folk, rap, or classical music.

Indeed, Daniel Rothmuller believes that *listening* is an absolute prerequisite for musical artistry.

Without immersing yourself in a style of music, you can only play the notes. Whatever repertoire you are working with, you must understand its language to the point where you are able to speak it fluently. You must understand music if you hope to interpret it, and that's when you need immersion.

Teachers Open Horizons of Culture, Art, and Spirituality

Some wonderful teachers have integrated cultural sensitivity and an awareness of humanity and the beauty of nature into their teaching of musical expression. In this section we will meet several inspiring teachers who on occasion ask their students to put down their instruments—to find inspiration in life and nature which they can then bring back to their music.

Margaret Rowell (1900–1995) was a remarkable teacher who lived in Berkeley, California, and taught at the San Francisco Conservatory of Music. She was an extraordinary human being who touched the lives of many cellists, both celebrated and unknown. Studying the cello with Margaret was not just a matter of the mechanics of playing, fingerings, bowing, and dynamics; it was more about life, it was about the human spirit, it was about inspiration, and falling in love with the world around us.

Bonnie Hampton studied with Margaret Rowell and recalls how Margaret would open doors to broader horizons of culture and spirituality:

Margaret opened up the world of books and literature to me as a person. She really wanted to develop musical characters as richly as possible and was always working away at her students' artistic and cultural sensitivities. She took us to art shows, nature was very important to her, she liked to take walks after a lesson, and she would talk about Einstein and Gandhi. Her physical energy came across both in her per-

sonality and in her teaching: there were no barriers. When I was studying Bloch's *Schelomo*, she so much wanted the human expression to come
through—and wouldn't stop until I got into the spirit of it.

Margaret was never trying to create the perfect instrumentalist—it
was the whole person she was after. She wanted me to grow as a human
being. She felt that whatever maturity I might achieve would ultimately
be reflected in my music making. In later life when her health was on
the wane, I would want to visit her to lift her spirits, but I was always
the one who left with the gift. Her company was always such an inspiration.

Margaret Rowell knew that expressing love and passion with music
means loving life and living passionately too.

Musical Partnerships

Inspiration often comes through others: partners, teachers, coaches, ensemble colleagues, and producers—even perhaps from a higher power.
David Darling, a cellist and man of great passion, told me the highlights
of his musical career came via the production, coaching, and encouragement of his ECM record producer, the brilliant Manfred Eicher. He said
Manfred somehow had the ability to take him deeper inside himself so
that he could come up with music that was passionately fresh. Simply
finding himself in Manfred's presence is enough to take David to a different place to find his musical voice. David himself also produces recordings for other musicians and draws on Manfred's spirit as he coaches
others to access their own inner resources.

When David was invited to record his first solo record with Manfred
in Stuttgart, Germany, he was very nervous. He brought all his music and
laid it out on the floor. Manfred first asked him to play anything he liked,
and since David had been experimenting using the cello as a guitar, he
started with a cute, funky piece. *I didn't hire you to do that shit,* Manfred commented, *I hired you to go as deep as you can go; just play your cello!* At which point
David put his bow to the cello and dug in.

This made me go into my inner drive. Rhythmic strumming has something to do with cute dollar signs, perhaps, but it's not the same as diving into the soul—what a lesson! Manfred demanded a direct line to the heart or where your real emotions lie.

For me the cello is the clearest instrument to sing through. On my first record, he made me recompose on the spot. The music had to come straight from my feelings—and the result was something that made everyone cry.

Robert Cohen loves to experience the extraordinary chemistry that can arise between two musicians—even for a few bars. He says that when two people play together, they can be so closely bound together it can be a spiritual experience. You can actually sense yourself being elevated by the power of two as opposed to the power of one.

It seems that whenever I play with Italian violinist Massimo Quarta, we are each always reaching to play with the qualities of the other person—but then realize that we are doing the same thing. It's an uncanny experience to strive for unity and find that every vibration matches, that each of us is doing exactly the same thing as the other. It is like playing with a soul mate, with a brother, perhaps.

Carter Brey recalls that the most passionate highlight of his musical career was inspired by a perfect combination of colleagues: the New York Philharmonic Orchestra, Zubin Mehta conducting, and Carter himself playing the solo cello part in Strauss's *Don Quixote*.

Carter said he felt very much at home with Mehta directing such a great piece of music and an orchestra of such high caliber behind him.

I felt so much at ease that I was able to play at my very best during three straight performances. I felt as though I was actually creating the music as it went along, able to do anything that I wanted to do. I could play around with my basic mind-set each night, and was able to subtly alter the quality of each performance—but I knew it would still be together. Maybe the moon was in the right phase—it was like riding a wave or being in a groove. I felt a profound happiness, and it came from my sense of being with all the right people, in the right place at the right time.

Janos Starker told me of the immediate bond he felt with colleagues who had studied with his chamber music teacher, Leo Weiner. He said that when he was with the Roth String Quartet in 1950, they performed six Mozart string quartets after only one day of rehearsal.

Because we had all studied with Weiner, his way of music was embedded in all of our minds. Leo Weiner taught us how to hear and listen; he taught us the difference between a rhythm line, melody line, bass line, and middle harmonies. He taught us how to evaluate a dot, and how to play an agogic accent that created freedom within the phrase.

Finding great chemistry with special partners was no accident in this case, but working with companion players who share cultural background and family history can generate electricity between performers. And while studying with the same teacher may promote a very close-knit sense of unity, when two people fall in "musical" love, it could just as well be diversity and contrast that draws them together. Contrasting and complementary styles can bring drama to musical partnerships when one player contributes a quality to the whole which the other partner lacks.

Special moments inspired by people, partners, or ensembles may still be few and far between, but it is important to keep oneself open to receive the unique spiritual gifts of collaboration which other musicians can offer. *Seek and ye shall find.* Everyone is unique, and has an individual chemistry which can add its own effect to any relationship. Being open and available to receive the guidance, imagination, inspiration, and direction of others, you may find you come in touch with qualities in yourself that you did not know you possessed.

The Art of Passionate Expression

The real art of passionate expression—the trick that allows you to let passion pour through you in a way that can reach and move others—is the art of balancing emotion with discipline. Passion without technique can sound terrible, unless you're the loving parent of the one who is playing. And technique without passion doesn't sound much better; it's a dry, formal, pedantic way to play music. So the art lies in finding a balance, and allowing your passion to speak through the discipline of your technique.

All musicians have to strive for a balance between their own love of the instrument, the voice they have chosen, and their responsibility to communicate the message of the music. And this may be particularly true of the cello, which is a very romantic instrument not only because of the sumptuous sounds created by its resonance but also because the cellist must literally cradle it with his or her body. I'm teasing a little here, of course, but the cello is a very lovely and beautifully voiced instrument, and I'm serious in saying that all musicians need to avoid falling so deeply in love with their instruments that they lose sight of the music.

Once you understand the music and how to communicate it, don't get so emotionally involved with your own playing that you absorb it into yourself and can't transmit it to the audience. If you step back just a little, all of a sudden the music will take on its own power and personality and have the potential to project even better to the audience. This balance is one of the hardest things to master, even with years of experience. Both teachers and performers are constantly challenged to sustain a relationship between music and emotion without going overboard on one side or the other.

Different players naturally have different ways of talking about this kind of balance. Pamela Frame, soloist and teacher from Rochester, New York, believes that the performer needs to be in the driver's seat with a piece. Technique should be taken care of first, she feels, and students should not need to focus on technique while they are playing the music. When a musician looks at a page of music, the process should start with imagination and finish with a technical solution. Rather than playing through a passage for bowing or dynamics, she recommends students start in the imagination, deciding what would be the best possible sound for the piece. That way, the entire process is aimed at the musical goal of the imagination.

> The music must be dominant, not the technique. The two things are not of equal importance. You have to have both craft and emotion to make art, but when you focus on your goal, you had best see it as a musical goal. When I'm playing, I don't want to think about technique.
>
> A true artist is someone who can express emotions in such a way that it creates those emotions in others. When my seven-year-old throws a tantrum, that's not art. You can't just throw paint at a canvas and say that's art. You can dump a paint bucket on the floor in a fit of anger and say it expresses anger—but it isn't art. It takes organization and discipline to create art.

It's a paradox: discipline needs passion to bring it to life, and passion requires discipline to give it expression.

I asked Carter Brey how he helps a student find passion in his playing, and his response was quite the opposite of what I expected, though very much in line with this paradox. Carter told me he would work like Socrates, questioning his students to ensure they would understand that music making was an art, not just an emotional display onstage.

> My ideal conception of an artist is one who has balance. Mozart was able to balance technical perfection with expressive power. So I would discuss the decisions my students have to make and how each one affects the music. It is a mysterious process to explain, and difficult to teach, but it can definitely be fostered.

Janos Starker has yet another approach to the same issue. He tells his students he doesn't believe in expressing his own emotions in a piece of music; he believes the appropriate emotions are already in the piece. During his interview with Tim Janof, he said:

Whether it's Beethoven, Brahms, or Tchaikovsky, I allow the composer and the piece itself to set the emotional tone of the experience. My obligation is to do the most I can with a given work. To put it crudely, I don't want to be one of those musicians who seems to be making love to himself on stage. And my approach must work for audiences, or I would not have been invited to give so many thousands of concerts throughout my life!

Starker is another who points out that discipline gives the musician freedom—that it is mastery of your instrument and technique that leaves you free to serve the composer and the piece.

I'm an ideal realist, he said with conviction.

You may have the greatest musical thoughts in the world, but if you haven't got the muscles to press the strings down in the proper places, all your idealism is for zilch.

PASSION, CELLO, AND VOICE

Cellist Carter Brey of the New York Philharmonic says his favorite instrument, and the one he feels is the closest to the human voice, is the saxophone; he loves it for its flexibility and natural lyric tendencies, and as a cellist he envies what sax players can do. The great operatic tenor Plácido Domingo once told Jacqueline du Pré that the cello is his favorite musical instrument, and that he loves to imitate it with his voice, especially during *legato* passages. When he told her this, Jacqueline at once began to teach Domingo to play the cello.

Cellist Danny Rothmuller's father was the celebrated Metropolitan singer Marko Rothmuller. At Indiana University, Marko's studio was located next to that of Danny's cello teacher, Fritz Magg. One evening Janos Starker, who also teaches at Indiana, was talking to Fritz Magg and commented that the most important thing was to put the cello down and sing it, dance it, but not be bound by instrumental constraints. To this the voice teacher Marko responded that he would tell his voice students to sing like a cellist!

Cellists that love saxophones, tenors that love the cello, cellists that sing...maybe the lesson here is that you shouldn't think of music in terms of your own instrument, because your technical knowledge is all bound up with your own instrument, and the expression of music is a purely imaginative idea.

As a bass player, I have heard it said that the cello is an instrument that falls nicely in the register of the human voice, but obviously it is not the only instrument that can claim this register, which is proudly shared by bassoons, basses, horns, English horns, clarinets, and saxophones. The cello does, however, have a range that spans baritone, tenor, and soprano vocal ranges, an almost complete sampling of vocal arts. And there is no doubt that the music written for cello in the orchestra as well as in the solo and chamber music literatures values and emphasizes the expressive vocal nature of the instrument.

It seems to me that the common thread here is that all musicians, instrumentalists as well as singers, strive for the vocal quality of singing, regardless of what instrument or voice they want to imitate. Furthermore, most of the great conductors usually express themselves in some kind of vocal style. The musical art, I'd suggest, is in some sense basically vocal in nature.

Janos Starker taught me that the string instruments should always sing. He said it's a daily chore for him to persuade students to *breathe according to the phrase*—and this is one of the major principles in his teaching. Starker believes that all musical functions are controlled by the breath.

David Darling is very much at home integrating voice with his cello playing, and in teaching people to find passion and expression in their music. He tells me that the most powerful technique he teaches at his Music for People workshops is based on the principle: *Sing what you play, play what you sing*. David finds this creates the perfect timbre and allows his students to tap in to their most expressive feelings.

Cellist Lynn Harrell is one of the most animated and colorful performers on the concert stage today. He freely shows his feelings in his facial expressions, in his body movements, and in the great dynamic intensity of his performances. At times he seems more like an opera singer than a cellist, almost as though he were *getting into character* for each piece. You might find him smiling at a theme, or even laughing with the audience throughout a performance. When Lynn played the Shostakovich cello concerto with the Cincinnati Symphony, I saw his bow fly off the strings as if he were waving a sword in triumph at the audience!

Lynn responded to a question about these extroverted displays of character in his interview with Tim Janof by saying:

> Every piece moves me in such a way that I act it out. It's a bit like method acting: once I get into this state, I don't have to act, I'm there—and if I don't get into this state, then my performance is just a bunch of empty gestures. I have enough maturity and confidence in my career and in my musicianship at this point to let myself go and let my inner self speak—even if it upsets my control and playing technique at times! I know that I sometimes hit the cello a little harder than maybe I should, but that's how the music moves me.
>
> And if the music doesn't move me . . . where's the music?

PASSION IS LOVE

When all's said and done, it is love that brought most of us into the wonderful world of music in the first place. One of the greatest challenges, whether in life, work, or relationships, is to keep the love alive.

I asked the distinguished San Francisco cellist and teacher Irene Sharp what she would like to be remembered for when she is no longer around to play or teach, and she replied:

> My love and passion for music—that's what I want to be remembered for.
>
> And I also want to be remembered for a lifetime of learning. I'm so excited by human beings and what they can do. I couldn't live without music, it is such an amazing thing. It can enhance the human soul.
>
> Music brings beauty to the world.

A famous Israeli critic known for destroying artists in his reviews once described one of Robert Cohen's performances of the Dvořák cello concerto with the words *Cohen is a musician of love*. Robert felt this was an important comment, and he showed the review to his agent, saying he had the feeling that for the first time in his life someone had written something about him that he really believed in. Interestingly enough, his agent didn't want to use this quote; he felt it was too soft, that people wouldn't take it seriously, that it might make them uncomfortable! And yet for Robert, it was probably the most important thing anybody could have said.

He told me:

That's one of the things that matters to me most about making music—and about life—the uninhibited feeling of love. I see love as the central point which everything stems from. . . . I'll communicate love through the music itself, or my love of the music, or the love and passion of the composer. And when the note comes out in a way that is truly thrilling, even for me perhaps—it's like I have found the core communication of love.

I feel this is what music is really about—in the most serious terms. When music goes straight into your heart and gives you a feeling that is beyond what you could feel at any other point.

Why not call this passionate love?

six

TOLERANCE: THE VIEW
FROM THE MIDDLE

(Violas and Management/Musicians)

To your right sits the first violinist, brainwashed from the beginning (as are all violinists) in the belief that he will be the next Heifitz or Perlman. The violinist says to the cellist, *Do it my way*—with just a hint of mafia in the phrasing. The cellist, on your left, is less than convinced: he knows violinists crave the limelight and are just a tad superficial as a result—whereas his own deeply felt sense of the music translates directly into the rich timbres and resonances which give the cello heart and soul. "Your way? I think not," says the cellist. "You're missing the feel of the thing. It goes like this. . . ."

"Relax, both of you," says the violist, "and try listening to each other. How many years have we been playing together? Let's try to figure out where the problem is."

Sitting between violins and cellos, and listening with great care to more than one musical line at a time, the violist enjoys a unique perspective on the music—and on the dissonance that can arise between players. As a result, violists often find themselves hearing both sides of an argument, then helping to bring it to a harmonious resolution.

If you play the viola, crossfire confrontations between violinists and cellists are nothing new to you—you are used to them, you have come to terms with them, you know how to deal with them. You are, in effect, a practiced mediator. Cool under fire? I'd say so! Not only have you learned to resolve other people's problems, you've also managed to tolerate their constant jokes about your competence, character, and supportive musical role.

You're the people person, the glue that holds things together.

I suspect it is because violists often play this mediating role in the string quartet that so many of them go into music management at some point. In orchestral management, you have to harmonize trustees' wishes, conductors' egos, audience preferences, composers' musical intentions, musicians' schedules, agents' demands, employees' complaints—and the budget! For other musicians, it might sound like a nightmare: for violists, this is just life in the string quartet.

Violists and musical management will be our models for tolerance. And you shouldn't be surprised to learn that the four people representing the administrators in this chapter are all current or former musicians. While tolerance may be the quietest and least self-assertive of the ten pathways to true artistry, it is a critical component for achieving interpersonal and musical harmony in any ensemble.

THE VIOLIST MANAGER

Violists and managers haven't always had the best reputations in the musical world, but this has been changing over the past decades. For more and more players, the viola is the instrument of choice, not a poor cousin to the violin, and the level of viola playing has improved dramatically as a result. At the same time, advances in management practices that have brought a less confrontational and more human resource-oriented style of leadership to business have seeped into the musical world.

Craig Mumm, associate principal violist with the Metropolitan Opera, recalls that when he "came out of the closet" as a teenager, telling his father, the concertmaster of the Milwaukee Symphony, that he intended to switch from violin to viola, his dad's old violin buddies shook their heads in despair and muttered, "So young, and already a violist," as though they were mourners at a wake.

These days, the stigma that was once attached to being a violist is no longer there. Alan DeVeritch, former principal violist of the Los Angeles Philharmonic and Professor at Indiana University, says the situation has changed markedly over the last ten years, and that it is now more common than not to find violists who have only played viola, and not switched from violin.

If you ask viola players, most will tell you they just like the sound and feel of the instrument better than the violin. There's this sense that when you want to go high, you can still sound like a soloist, and when you want to go lower, you can reach for a richer, deeper sound to rival the cello. Violists have a lot of versatility since they are very much in the middle range—and in the middle of things.

Besides, it is only natural to feel pride in playing the instrument played by great conductors such as Carlo Giulini, not to mention composers as great as Hindemith, Beethoven, and Mozart.

The Pathway from the Middle

Craig Mumm takes great pride in being in the middle and serving as the glue that holds the whole orchestra together. *The violists are the ones who pull the different solo lines together and make a piece work as a whole*, he says. He told me that he cannot find it in himself to feel jealous of the oboes or violins, and doesn't crave their roles: he enjoys the violist's role as an essential part of the orchestra and has no need to play the star.

Craig was recently invited to introduce the viola to his audience, and told them, *The viola is like an onion—it's rarely the main ingredient in a dish, but it makes every dish it's in come alive!* By filling out essential harmonies, the viola gives body and depth (and flavor) to music—and that modest and unassuming role is an important one.

Providing Support

Both chamber and orchestral music are team activities, and as with any team activity up to and including putting a man on the moon, the stars couldn't put in their stellar performances without the help and support of a great many others who also take pride in their mission's ultimate success. In music, it takes many supporting artists in the cast to allow the limelight to shine on the one soloist or conductor. Frequently it is the violists who create a harmonious work environment—and then go on to provide harmony and rhythm so that the distinguished soloists can be heard with the right color and character.

James Dunham, the former violist with the Cleveland Quartet and now professor at Rice Shepherd School of Music, explains that the viola and the second violin play similar roles, and the personalities of their players feed into this function.

> In the Cleveland Quartet, when we had two competing ideas about a passage, we always went with whoever had the leading line. It is important for the leader to feel and sound good, so the group as a whole needs to yield. We all sound better if we can help the person with the leading role, and the music must come first.

Getting People to Work Together

Jeremy Geffen was a viola student of Donald McInnes's, but had to quit playing because of a physical problem with his hand. Jeremy then brought his personal skills to orchestral management, first as associate artistic administrator of the Aspen Music Festival and currently as artistic administrator of the New York Philharmonic. Jeremy played viola because he really enjoyed making music with other people, and he still loves working with others to create something larger than himself.

Those colleagues who have chosen to contribute to the musical product through their roles in management share a role similar to the violist's. While their individual part is not necessarily seen or heard in the same capacity as the first violinist or a piano soloist, their supportive actions make it possible for a great concert to take place. They have the personal satisfaction of knowing that without their help in contracting musicians and soloists, arranging sufficient rehearsals for the preparation of the music, ensuring that the pacing of these rehearsals and the pieces being rehearsed are not overtaxing to some of the players, managing personal conflicts with musicians, directing stagehands, and, most important of all, promoting the concerts and securing an audience, there would be no program and no music. When the audience is thrilled at hearing a wonderful program, the management stands proud knowing they made the event possible.

Jeremy Geffen compares his management role to playing the viola:

> In many ways what I do as an artistic administrator is similar to the role I had while I was playing chamber music. I work with a music director, an executive director, an orchestra and guest conductors, and an audience, and it's my job to keep the integrity and interest of the institution in mind, and bring the greatest strengths of each of these individuals together to build something interesting.

PAYBACKS FOR TOLERANCE

Bored stiff? No chance to solo? Stuck in an office doing administrative work while others get to make the music? You might think violists—and managers, for that matter—have a hard time of it, that you wouldn't be able to tolerate their situations for a moment! But violists and managers themselves don't tend to see things that way. And if there are times when the work is boring, or when colleagues snipe at violists or managers, remember that these are the folks with the gift for tolerance.

Getting to Hear Everything

Paul Silverthorn does better than tolerate his situation as principal violist with the London Symphony; he loves the fact that playing the viola puts him right in the middle of the orchestra. He says he chooses to be in the middle of things, understanding the workings of the whole musical ensemble rather than dominating it with his own voice—and by the same token, he also enjoys playing the role of mediator, helping to bring harmony out of discord in nonmusical as well as musical ways.

Cecil Cole, the artistic director of the Jacksonville (Florida) Symphony and former double bass player, has to endure a lot of stress on his job. He has to plan programs that sell enough tickets to fill a concert hall not once but many times a season. He has to meet tight budgets not just for his family but for a large arts organization. He has to keep the board members, the press, and the public happy with his program offerings— and hey, he also has to deal with some very demanding musicians! Did I mention that musicians can be demanding?

Cecil tells me he can tolerate almost *anything* as long as he gets to hear the concert at the end of the week.

Shaping and designing a program is creative work, to be sure—and when I get to see an audience that's thrilled by what they have heard, it's very satisfying and moving. People call or write in to share their enthusiasm, and I get the smiles, the compliments—I get to see their faces! I'll admit I get great satisfaction when we are able to do the planning and put an entire season down on paper—but finally hearing the program is the ultimate payback. Wonderful. It is like birthing a baby.

Musical Satisfaction from the Inside

Nardo Poy, violist with the Orpheus Chamber Orchestra, tells me he even gets excited about playing the repetitive offbeat accompaniments in Strauss waltzes. He says that playing *pa-pa* with panache, even without the *oom*, is really fun and stimulating. Hard to believe? When you hear great Viennese musicians playing their waltzes, you *know* there is something different about their sound. And when you apply this sensitive approach to playing what might seem a boring part at first glance—a sort of concentrated zen glee in the task at hand—it can be incredible. When Nardo plays these offbeats with style at the Metropolitan Opera, he brings the innards of the music alive.

I don't care if it's not the melody . . . it is still great stuff! When you look beyond the part, you go to the music as a whole. . . .

Craig Mumm, violist with the Metropolitan Opera Orchestra, says that his personal payback comes when he senses the feeling bordering on adoration from audiences during curtain calls:

> I don't have a great craving for individual recognition. When we give a good concert and the audience is really enthusiastic, it is very satisfying to have been a part of the team.

Playing Multiple Roles

Nokuthula Ngwenyama is an outstanding young viola soloist who also enjoys playing chamber music, because it allows her to see the larger scope of things. Nokuthula gets to be a star and assert her musical personality when she plays as a soloist, but as a chamber musician she gets to take a break from her star role—and she loves doing it. ·

> It is so nice to be there for someone else, and then at times to hear that unique viola voice coming out from its supporting role to take the lead role, and then move back to the supporting role. I love the way the viola's role changes from harmonic support to rhythmic assertion, then to a flash of melodic solo! I don't always need to be at the center of the music. . . .

I have heard violinists actually complain that they are always playing the melody. After a while, this can become less interesting. As for bass players, while one would think we are always playing a dull rhythm part, on the contrary, we share all the musical functions with all the other instruments in the orchestra. Like the violists, sometimes we have a robust melody, other times we are paired with winds and percussion to provide a rhythmic part, sometimes we sustain and reveal the most important harmony changes that give the color to the sound of the orchestra. Many times we play with the cellos and the violas. Just being aware of the many musical roles our instruments play in the ensemble helps us to understand and play our parts with more insight and sensitivity. Violists, being right in the middle of all these voices, have the ideal perspective. They can link up with the higher instruments or the lower instruments or even have their own moment in the spotlight.

Managers' Paybacks on Several Levels

There's one personal reason in particular that I decided to include managers as well as violists in this chapter: I wanted an appropriate way to acknowledge the generous and tolerant personality of my wonderful boss at the San Francisco Symphony Education Department, Ron Gallman.

Ron, who also sings with the San Francisco Symphony Chorus, told me there are three things that make the long hours that music managers spend attending meetings, preparing tedious budgets, and keeping on top of a large department all worthwhile:

> First, we want to promote the art of music to as many people as possible, and ensure that it maintains itself as a positive force in our society. Second, our job is to make life as close to problem-free as possible so the artists can create their art, so our decisions and preparations contribute directly to the artistic product and help it reach that widest audience. And finally, the relationships are extraordinary; we have very high regard for our colleagues, both musical and managerial, and enjoy the interactions with them.

Artists, stagehands, light and sound technicians, management, promoters, and agents—all have a unique contribution to make, and all share in the great success of a wonderful production.

Tolerating Jokes and Tension from the Job

Violists may be the recipients of the most abusive and insensitive jokes of any instrumentalists. To be sure, some of these jokes originated at a time when the playing level was not as good as it has been in recent decades—and furthermore, the uniqueness and richness of the viola sound are less familiar than those of the violin or cello. But even so, all those jokes must have some impact, right?

Danny Seidenberg, violist of the Turtle Island String Quartet, told me he is not the least bit bothered by viola jokes—the fact that there are viola jokes is just a gentle commentary on the nature of the beast. In a way, he says, these jokes are supportive, because they recognize the unique difficulty of the instrument and acknowledge the courage of violists who transcend it. While he admits it is possible to lose perspective and take the jokes personally, he thinks they are basically a nonissue.

Donald McInnes is not bothered by viola jokes either. He says he doesn't let them get to him. He feels that the violists who are offended by viola jokes may be the ones who have not gone as far in the profession as they might like. *If you know you have played well, it is not so difficult to accept the ribbing.*

In fact, Nokuthula Ngwenyama loves viola jokes, because she thinks they are funny. She loves to root for the underdog:

> I think all the joking is sort of cool—but then again, I really don't think any of it applies to me personally. You need to have a bit of a thick skin; you have to be confident about yourself and be able to laugh at yourself, and then just go on from there....

Tolerating the Hot Seat

In any case, dealing with a few jokes is not as challenging as handling irate musicians, difficult stand partners, stress on the job, and even outright abuse. But Nokuthula Ngwenyama's perspective still works: engage your self-confidence, know that the tension is really not about you, and don't take it personally.

Orchestral management has to deal with many different groups, each one pressing its own agenda or concern, from a hostile press or impatient audience to nonsupportive board members or irate musicians. Deborah Borda, the former violist who is currently executive director of the Los Angeles Philharmonic, says the key to harmony is to bring the different parties together in alignment with the overall vision and purpose of the organization.

> When difficult questions arise, we can do some soul searching to recover the core purpose of our being there in the first place. My immediate task is to get them to dream about our common goal and then to put their unique insight into their own words. Then I can share them with the rest of the organization.

Many confrontations can be handled effectively if you understand where the conflict is coming from. For example, I heard about an emotional explosion that took place at the prestigious Salzburg Festival, when a very important conductor was making his debut there with his own American orchestra. Something minor happened—a door creaked—and the conductor screamed at the first person he saw, who happened to be the artistic administrator, but also a close friend of his. The chewing out that administrator took had nothing to do with him at all—it was about the conductor's anxieties.

Jeremy Geffen is very sensitive to tensions of this kind, a trait which makes him particularly keen to know the best way to handle them:

> When someone is upset with me, the first thing I ask is "Can you tell me more about why you are mad? Is there something you think I should have done better, or differently?" I find it may help if I explain myself. And the best thing in a conflict is to *keep talking*. The *worst* thing you can do is to walk away.

Cecil Cole said he can tolerate someone yelling and screaming at him, and it just doesn't get to him personally. He learned how to handle this sort of thing by working behind a hotel desk.

> I was in hotel management before I went into the symphony business. I was a desk clerk at a huge convention hotel in Richmond, Virginia, and what I learned was that everyone that walks up to that front desk is *dif-*

ferent. I had about thirty-five seconds while I was registering that person to assess where they were at, what kind of mood they were in, and how receptive they were. This really helped me learn how to "read people" well. I would do my best to figure out what was going on with them. What's eating this person? Is there any way I can bring this one back down to earth?

Musicians can have many things on their minds, too. Perhaps they've had an injury, or the conductor has been a real jerk. So when someone screams at me, it's a little like being behind that hotel desk again, and I try to figure out what the problem is. I don't take it personally, I just see if I can help resolve the problem. Each and every personal relationship I have is important to me. And I like to finish things with a positive statement, to end on a good note!

Tolerance is a wonderful tool for defusing hostility. It takes two to argue—and if someone is yelling and screaming at you and thinks he is getting to you, he will probably keep right on doing it. Show him your violist's tolerance, and let him pop his steam valve! When he sees all his sound and fury isn't making much of a dent, he will likely back off.

Cynthia Phelps, principal violist with the New York Philharmonic, believes that one person's obvious truth is another one's patent falsehood. She notes that people simply don't all see things the same way, and it follows that there are many more ways than one to look at any problem. All successful negotiators know that there has to be a place where differences of opinion can coexist:

Orchestral musicians are told constantly that we are behind the conductor, but it never felt that way to me, and it wasn't clear to me how true this was, until I played a concerto in front of the orchestra—and heard the lag myself for the first time. The others were right on this occasion: we *were* dragging!

Knowing something of how tolerance defuses situations can help us understand why certain people are able to stay calm and focused in the face of conflict and chaos. But where does one learn tolerance? Is it something some people are just born with? Is it something that can be taught and learned, or "caught" from role models, perhaps? Or is tolerance something we all just have to pick up from difficult life experiences, as best we can?

All kinds of influences may help shape who we are as musicians and as human beings. By exploring where we can learn tolerance, we are likely to develop some tools that will help us to be more sensitive in our own communications with others, both musically and in life.

LEARNING TOLERANCE

Donald McInnes feels that violists don't learn tolerance as such, but that musicians with a tolerant temperament often seek out a musical role that suits their personality, and wind up in the viola section! People learn tolerance from many different kinds of life experiences, and my personal view is that with willingness, openness, and desire, you can learn tolerance regardless of your family background or musical role. Many will agree that we learn most easily when we are young, and lessons in tolerance often begin at a young age in the home.

Learning Tolerance from Parents and Family

James Dunham's father worked for the State Department as a U.S. diplomat, so James grew up with a heightened awareness of body language as well as verbal language, and his sensitivity to the nuances of communication taught him volumes about how to say something—and how *not* to say something. When James was asked to substitute as principal violist with the Boston Symphony and again with the Dallas Symphony, he applied lessons he had learned both from his diplomat father and from his pianist/violist mother, and led by listening.

Coming in as a guest leader, I wasn't privy to the way things were usually done and I didn't yet know the people, so I would ask the players for help. If an issue came up, I would say something along the lines of "Have you noticed this problem? Can you help me out here?"

This attentive and collaborative leadership style draws out the best in a team by making its members feel included, and it quickly gains respect.

Cynthia Phelps was the fourth of five siblings, and learned her own lessons in tolerance from being a sister, mother, spouse, leader, professional, and teacher. In each of these roles, she had to constantly adjust to the needs of others.

Constantly changing these hats is really a challenge, perhaps the biggest challenge of my life. You really give up so much of yourself. I have to have the energy for my spouse, I have to be there for my children, and I have to have energy for my conductor and my section. The challenge is to deal with every problem that comes up in the day as if it was the first problem and not the twentieth! Just keeping a balance between these different roles has taught me patience and tolerance.

It's easy to talk about diplomatic remarks and tolerant behavior, of course, and to forget just how deep the lines of intolerance can run. Cecil Cole grew up as an African-American in the segregated South of the United States, and also learned the lesson of tolerance in his own home. For Cecil, the form the lesson took was an uncompromising emphasis on excellence.

You have to be really good at what you do, Cecil's father would tell him, *really, really good.*

Back in the days when Jackie Robinson was the first black man playing baseball, if someone came up before him and got a home run, the announcer would call a home run and the crowd would roar. But when Jackie came up and he too hit a home run, the announcer would ask, "How far did Robinson's home run go over the fence?" He'd always want to qualify his praise.

My father would ask me, "If it went over the fence and it's a home run for the white guy, why are they measuring how far it went over the fence for the black guy?"

Cecil's father taught him that just being good isn't enough—but if you know you are giving 150 percent, you have the self-confidence and tolerance to handle anyone's criticism.

There's a common thread running through each of these ways of learning and practicing tolerance. In each case, the focus is not on an attempt to change the attitudes of others, but on the individual's own attitude and performance. It is notoriously difficult to change other people, but we can choose our own beliefs and behaviors. We can rise above criticism and hostility by focusing on what we can do better to serve our ultimate goal, and we can help others to handle their issues and problems by practicing inclusion and acceptance.

Learning Tolerance from Teachers or Mentors

Jeremy Geffen credits three colleagues from his first administrative position at the Aspen Music Festival with helping him learn how to maintain good relationships with a diverse group of musicians. Robert Harth, Ara Guzelimian, and NancyBell Coe taught Jeremy the model he uses in management, which resembles the "brainstorming" technique for creativity that's increasingly used in business. It involves encouraging free discussion, but with a taboo on negative or dismissive responses.

I try to be very informal and not put up any barriers. I don't like treating people differently just because of their position or what they do. NancyBell taught me that you don't always have to be right, and that, on occasion, if it will soothe tensions you might decide to take responsibility for something you didn't do. It is also good to say "I don't know" and also to ask for help.

A big part of Jeremy's work involves maintaining and nurturing these relationships. Jeremy is able to do this by ensuring that everyone feels that her or his contribution is important.

The musicians have to feel appreciated, conductors have to feel special, staff and administrative personnel need to feel valued—we all do! And when everyone feels included and appreciated, something happens—everyone finds new reserves of energy and ability.

Alan DeVeritch credits his teacher, celebrated English viola soloist and chamber artist William Primrose, as the biggest influence in his life. When Alan began to study with Primrose at the age of twelve, Primrose had just suffered a major heart attack, while his young wife, the love of his life, had just died of cancer. Then Primrose lost everything he valued, his manuscripts and personal possessions, in the wartime bombing of London. His second wife was alcoholic, and Primrose too became dependent on alcohol. At the height of his playing career, he lost some of his hearing—and this was followed by his own cancer.

Primrose was a brilliant man who had a beautifully eloquent way with the English language, and he maintained a positive outlook on life right to the end. I spent a great deal of time at his bedside learning about his philosophy of life and his theories of humanity. His life brought him fame and glory, but also great tragedy, and I was in awe of him. What he told me helped me form my own approach to life. His way was to find the good in things; his message was always one of optimism, understanding, and tolerance for others.

What is the lesson that each of these master mentors and teachers gives to his students? It is about being positive. It's about accepting who you are and the position you find yourself in, and inspiring others to feel good about themselves. In the space that's opened up by a positive and accepting attitude of this kind, everyone feels welcome, everyone feels accepted. There is room under the sun for us all to work together in a positive spirit—and this is one of the great gifts of tolerance.

Tolerance from Faith

Like William Primrose, Donald McInnes has had major upheavals in his personal life, and he told me that if he didn't have a strong faith, he would not have been able to get through them.

I don't feel any one of us should dictate another person's religion or faith, but I do feel it is extremely important that one has some kind of belief system. There are times in your life when you realize you cannot be in total control of who you are and what you do. If we don't have a certain amount of order in our lives and they get too chaotic, we gradually lose our self-respect. I firmly believe each one of us needs to have a relationship of some kind with a higher being, something that makes me a better person and more humble.

When you are making music, you are placing yourself in a vulnerable position in public, and it's only natural to get defensive if your vulnerability comes under attack. It is important to *listen* very carefully to what the other person has to say when someone is criticizing you. If you can put yourself in the other person's shoes, without judging him to be right or wrong, you may find you see yourself in a different light. Values that include a willingness to learn from the suggestions of others can be learned from the home, from a conscious regard for fellow colleagues, or from your own faith or spiritual practice.

Moving Beyond Tolerance

Conflicts that get us all stirred up can also seem frankly trivial in comparison to more important issues of life and death.

Nokuthula Ngwenyama tells me she used to be very highly opinionated. She describes herself as having been a nonconformist anti-authoritarian. She left Los Angeles before she finished high school to attend Curtis Institute in Philadelphia. At the end of her second year at Curtis, both her father and the brother who inspired her to play music died within a few months of each other.

For me, that was really the crossover point between adolescence and adulthood. That changed me, and changed the way I saw and related to other people. Things I used to think were very important were no longer as important. People waste a lot of time in rehearsals with conflicts about things that can just seem so superficial, like arguing over a bowing, or nitpicking the dynamics of a piece. I'm just not there with that kind of conversation, it's just not worth it for me.

Life is just too short!
Remember Tim Gallwey's "Stop" tool from the chapter on discipline? The same principles apply to being sucked into confrontation.

Step back and put some distance between yourself and whatever you are involved with.
Find your balance and find your center.
Think about what is really important.
Are you being ruled by your emotions or by good sense?
Is this supporting the ultimate musical product?
Does it really make a difference?
Organize your thoughts.
Prioritize what should happen first.
Could you possibly postpone this discussion?
Proceed only when you see and feel the clarity that comes from the practical experience of stepping back.

If after all this the situation still remains tense, and you honestly don't feel you can back down, ask yourself, *Is this something I need to pursue—regardless of my personal health, or maintaining friendships?* If the answer is yes, then stick by your position—and you will either find tolerance and acceptance from those around you, or you will find the inner peace to move on.

TECHNIQUES FOR TOLERANCE

When problematic situations arise in the workplace, it is often inappropriate to ignore them and hope they will go away. Sometimes situations of this kind will require you to exercise your tolerance, even when you might otherwise prefer to disengage. Coming prepared with *strategies for hanging in there* will increase both your patience and your ability to deal with a variety of challenges.

Start with Flexibility

Randall Kelley, principal violist with the Pittsburgh Symphony, says that *flexibility* is the hallmark of great leadership in any organization, that the best leaders are the ones who are always watching and listening, who know what is going on because they are constantly reevaluating situations and devising new strategies. Randall believes it is tolerance which gives them flexibility, and flexibility which brings them success.

> If I'm working with someone, then I try to be flexible—and conversely, if I find someone is not flexible in their dealings with me, I tend to rebel. I think this is the real reason orchestral musicians like or dislike particular conductors. If a conductor doesn't listen to the orchestra, I put up a wall. That was the problem with Mazel. If I made a mistake, he wouldn't tolerate it, but he never admitted it when he was the one who had made a mistake. The man was a supergenius on the podium, but he made his players feel very uptight. He would make people lose their confidence, and then they would sound tense or harsh! To me, that's where the flexibility comes in. We all make mistakes, and if you are going to jump on someone for making a mistake, you should take a look at yourself first.

When you as a musician can open yourself to others' ideas, it quite naturally generates a strong sense of collaboration, and this can feel (and sound!) even better than "having things all your own way." You really aren't giving anything up, you are creating a greater whole out of the musicianship of the group.

Ron Gallman believes there is always room for latitude and tolerance, as long as dialogue doesn't turn into a lack of personal respect. If someone has a different point of view, he is interested in hearing it, and believes the best way to handle a conflict of opinions may be to find some kind of middle ground between them. He points out that lives are seldom in the balance when musicians disagree!

Nokuthula says that when she plays chamber music with a new group of colleagues, she likes to hear what the other players have to say and discover their approach to making chamber music, and rarely goes into a group with guns blazing.

> I usually keep my mouth shut at the beginning. I like to listen. And where there's more than one point of view, it's important to avoid negativity at all costs. If we all feel good about each other, our performance will be far better. My advice is to just have a good time—and if disagreements come up, remember why you wanted to play music in the first place!
>
> If I don't like the way things sound, I like to ask, "Can we take this over again? It didn't feel right"—and let the problem fix itself. This usually results in some kind of a compromise, which I don't take personally. This is simply what you do when you play with others. You need to be okay with compromise, and realize that one performance with an approach that isn't entirely your own is not going to ruin your life forever.

Nokuthula recalls rehearsing the third movement of the Brahms B-flat Major String Quartet, op. 67, where the other strings are supposed to be muted and the viola isn't. On this occasion, the cellist she was playing with felt strongly that she should be playing with a mute. She explained that Brahms's score didn't call for a mute for the viola. The cellist replied heatedly, "That's bullshit!"—so Nokuthula said, "Look, if you care that much about me using a mute, I'll use a mute."

It isn't worth it to defend my ground and get nasty with him at re-hearsal. And in the concert, if the issue is important enough to me, I can do what I want anyway. I like to be totally unthreatening on the outside, but I also know that on the inside I can take care of myself if I need to.

Self-Tolerance and Self-Responsibility

Danny Seidenberg believes it's important to be tolerant and understanding of yourself and your situation:

> You just cannot do passage work on the viola as easily as you can on the violin. The viola is an unyielding instrument, and it is physically very taxing to play. It's a large instrument, and your arm is extended, so you're playing in a difficult position, whereas the violin is much easier to play. You can play a note on the violin with no inflection, and it sounds good. If you play a note on the viola without inflection, it sounds as though you're sneezing! But if you just add this single viola note to a chord . . . beautiful. It's beautiful.
>
> The viola is a wonderful instrument, but it's harder to play than the violin. That's just a simple fact. And that simple fact requires you to be more tolerant of your own playing.

Being tolerant of yourself is also important when you're improvising. You have to be able to take chances, to risk falling on your face. You have to accept that you will have good and bad moments; otherwise you just cannot do it.

Being intolerant of yourself and others produces stress, anxiety, and tension, and will result in a poor performance. Accepting the world around you for what it is, while also maintaining tolerance for your own limits, leaves you "in the present" with your music. You will discover that when you are in the moment in this way, new opportunities open up with every note and every phrase. This open state of mind allows you to tap into your full potential.

Nardo Poy applies this principle while playing in a large orchestra.

When you see things in the widest perspective, it's really never about the other person, but about yourself and the music. Of course, conductors can really get in your way at times, of course your stand partners can sometimes be problematic, but the music is still great, you can still love the music! The way I see it, you can be miserable—or you can find a way to shield yourself, and just do your job as well as you can. Tolerance is really important here; the best thing to do is to go within yourself and exercise tolerance.

Show Tolerance! Support Your Competition!

Auditions can be highly competitive and very stressful. Sometimes you will only have five to eight minutes to play for a committee—often behind a screen—and you know that if you make just one small mistake, you may be excused on the spot. And to add stress to an already stressful situation, before your audition you may have to warm up in a large room with other competitors, and the environment may be tense or even hostile, since others may view you as the competition.

I don't disagree with them; in a way, you are the competition! But here is the real question, the one that allows you to see things in a different light: *Are you competing against your colleagues—or are you competing with yourself?*

Craig Mumm says the atmosphere at a viola audition is quite different from that at a typical violin audition. He sees the competitors socializing, interested in each other, carrying on pleasant conversations, and wishing each other good luck. That attitude is much less stressful than feeling hostility for everyone in the warm-up room!

And as Alan DeVeritch reminds his pupils, you will likely be competing with the same other players for future jobs throughout your career! Alan won't accept students who can see things only in terms of a competitive dog-eat-dog attitude: *You need a keen competitive sense,* he told me, *but you also need to understand the concept of team support.*

The real competition is with yourself, and your aim is to do your personal best. That attitude allows you to support your colleagues, and to be happy for them when they succeed. It's essential. Think about it. You have no control over what others do, and there will always be someone who can play faster or louder than you. But you are your own unique personality, and there will always be room under the sun for excellence, integrity, and artistry!

Being in Control

Feeling in control is a very important concept for most musical managements. I'll never forget how I felt when the great violinist Yehudi Menuhin talked to me about the concept of control. Visiting backstage after a Cincinnati Symphony rehearsal twenty years ago, he told me, *You are most in control when you are least aware of it.* When I thought about this, I recalled it was indeed true. When everything is going just fine, we say, "It's under control." If you are constantly "controlling" things by telling yourself everything you have to do, on the other hand, it isn't very much fun. When we are clear on our musical and administrative missions, we can let go of authority and even trust others to do their part as well.

Our misconceptions about control start with conductors, who need to feel they are in charge of the musical interpretation, the players, and even the organization. Then management feels the need to control the business side of things, which from management's point of view includes the conductors' desires, the musicians' demands, and the audiences' satisfaction. But this leaves the musicians wide open to discontent, as they have little control over their musical leadership, the music they play, where they sit, their schedule, their salary, or their vacations! Often musicians cannot even choose the city they wish to live and work in.

However, the industry is rapidly changing, conductors are becoming more flexible and open to their musicians' ideas, management is increasingly allowing musicians a share of authority in artistic and business matters, and in general everyone is beginning to collaborate, be inclusive, and work together, so that no one is left out of the process. When people work together with open-mindedness and tolerance of each other's needs, ideas, and feelings, not only are they happier, but everyone's performance improves too. So by letting go of your need to control, you actually increase your chances of achieving the desired outcome. It's just one of those zen paradoxes, which Yehudi Menuhin reminds us of when he says: *You are most in control when you are least aware of it.*

Cecil Cole sees no harm in letting other people get credit for his ideas, if they can express his views for him. *I love it when I can get someone else to say what I want to say in a committee meeting,* he told me. *I have the satisfaction of seeing my thought conveyed, and they are happy to get the glory.*

I used to work with Joseph Silverstein, the former music director of the Utah Symphony. Joe likes to be in charge of choosing his own programs. After eight or nine months, I learned that as long as he felt it was his idea, I could negotiate my own agendas with him. By the time I'd been there a couple years, I even learned I could plant an idea with his wife and she would bring things up with him.

I remember the time I wanted the orchestra to play Carl Orff's *Carmina Burana.* Joe, who is Jewish, didn't want to play it because of Orff's connection with the Nazis, but I believe every audience should hear the *Carmina* at some point. I went to Adrian and told her how good it would be for the audience, the chorus, and the public, and she decided to discuss it with Joe. Then Joe came to me one day and said, "I think we ought to play *Carmina Burana.*" I almost fell out of my chair!

But that's not the whole story. Joe was giving me what I wanted and felt we needed, to be sure, but he was still faithful to his own feelings—so he added, "But somebody else can conduct it!"

TOLERANCE IS AN OPEN DOOR

Tolerance is like opening a door and entering a world without walls or ceilings.

Tolerance gives us patience and space for others. It can turn adversaries into collaborators, and it can allow collaborators to create together something far finer than they could have managed if one person's view had triumphed over all the rest. Tolerance means inclusion, cooperation, sharing, delegating, and banding together. It's about not taking things so seriously, and being able to laugh at yourself. It's about knowing who you are and accepting yourself. It's about accepting your roles and responsibilities and being a part of a team. It's about appreciating what we do have, and not being jealous of what we don't. It's about letting go of your need to be in charge.

One Step at a Time

The pathway to tolerance is traveled one step at a time, but the journey does not have to be a painful one, as Deborah Borda learned when she was a young viola student.

> I remember when I first started to study the Bartók viola concerto, it was too difficult. I told my teacher, the late Jacob Glick, that I just couldn't play this piece. He said to me, "What do you mean it is too difficult? Is there one note that you can play?" I said, "Of course I can play most all the individual notes," and he said, "Well, let's just play one note in the middle of a passage that you absolutely cannot manage!" So I went to the end of the introduction to the first movement, and picked out this one note, and he asked me, "What's the next note?"—and then asked me to connect the first note to the second note. So I did that, and we went on to the note after that—and within thirty minutes, I could play the entire "impossible" passage.
>
> What I learned is that there is no problem you cannot handle if you start with a very simple step and work methodically onward from there. Nothing is impossible.

Deborah learned to look at a problem from the middle and work outward. Learn tolerance, and you have learned a pathway that resolves discords into harmonies. The willingness to see all sides and bring them together is the path from the middle. Those who have mastered this art of tolerance, with any instrument or voice, are able to enjoy music from a special point of view.

seven

CONCENTRATION:
THE SPIRIT OF THE ZONE

(Solo Instruments: Violin, Piano, Classical Guitar, and Harp)

There is a state in which musicians, artists, writers, doctors, philosophers, scientists, inventors, and athletes sometimes find themselves in which they move through their tasks with an assurance and presence, a sensitivity and precision, beyond normalcy. Something changes dramatically when a young musician or a great artist moves into this highly creative space; the focus shifts from questions of identity and performance into a fluid awareness which seems able to tap effortlessly into the highest levels of artistry. The brain is the key to this state of peak performance, in music and in life.

THE ZONE

Mihaly Csikszentmihalyi calls this state of optimal functioning "flow," and notes that we enter it when we feel neither challenged beyond our means (overloaded, paralyzed) nor lacking all sense of challenge (uninterested, bored); essentially it is the state that occurs when risk and skill are in appropriate balance. Others such as Abraham Maslow speak of this state as "peak performance," and yet others know it simply as "the zone." Timothy Gallwey in his many Inner Game books has helped the public understand the delicate balance of skills that have to be in place to reach this flowing state of peak performance, which he terms "relaxed concentration." This seemingly paradoxical name is Gallwey's way of accounting for the fact that being in the zone includes an intensity of focus on what you are doing with a relaxed and seemingly effortless ability to do it.

For the past twenty-two years, I have enjoyed helping musicians balance the three Inner Game master skills of *awareness* (attention), *will* (commitment), and *trust*. I believe that mastering these mental concentration skills is as essential as mastering the physical technical skills of playing any instrument. Over the past two decades, I have observed that the musicians who spend the most time immersed in this pursuit of mental skills are those who play the primary solo instruments. While I could easily have gleaned the materials for our exploration of the zone in this chapter from psychologists, scientists, athletes, creative writers, or other groups of musicians, I have chosen to explore the zone through one representative of each of the classic solo instruments: violin, piano, classical guitar, and harp.

Our journey into the zone will be in three parts. First we will *define* the state of concentration that many refer to as "the zone." Second, we will consider some of the many ways to *get* there. Human nature being human nature, however, even those who enter the zone can fall back out of it, so our final challenge will be to explore ways to *stay* in the zone as long as possible.

Discovering and Defining the Zone

My first guest is one of the world's most recognized violin virtuosos. Anyone who has ever seen and heard Joshua Bell play the violin has some understanding of the zone: the handsome and youthful figure playing the violin with eyes closed, the soaring purity of sound, the body so rapt it almost seems ready to lift off the stage, the face an image of transcendence, perfection, passion, and beauty . . .

I recently watched Joshua Bell perform as a soloist; he was playing the violin fantasy based on Leonard Bernstein's *West Side Story* with the Sun Valley Summer Symphony, and from my seat leading the bass section I could see that Joshua's performances *defined* what we are talking about when we describe the zone.

Joshua told me that the first time he ever experienced the zone was when he was only eleven. He had entered the Julius Stulberg competition in Kalamazoo, Michigan, where he played the first movement of Lalo's *Symphonie Espagnole*:

It begins with this difficult opening way up on the E string. I slipped off the fingerboard and botched the entire thing. I was angry with my-self for ruining it so soon. I said, "I want to start over so I can get through it," and something clicked after the first line. I remember feeling as though I could do no wrong. It was the first time I had been in the zone, and whatever I thought I could do, I did. I felt technically confident. I wasn't looking to get into the zone, you understand, and I remember it being such an incredible feeling. From that point on I just let the music take me there. It was a visualization thing: I could "see" the zone happening, and then I could make it happen for me.

Scientists have proved that accessing this state of peak performance is associated with changes in brain function. Brian Hatfield of the University of Maryland has published research confirming that during peak performance, the mind relaxes its more analytical left side and lets the right side direct the body. Anxious thought has to allow relaxed muscular memory to take control.

When in the zone, one pays complete attention to the task at hand. The performer is almost entirely focused on relevant cues, and disruptive internal thoughts are essentially blanked out. It is interesting to note that achieving this sort of undistracted focus is a major part of the teachings of zen masters.

Exploring the zone is a lonely pursuit. The golf sensation Tiger Woods said in an interview, *I play better when I can prepare in solitude and peace*, and that's surely true for many of us. Violinists and pianists seem to be most comfortable spending great amounts of time studying and practicing alone. They practice in isolated and sometimes barren environments; they must be able to focus on the music, tune out distractions, and connect both with their own souls and with the spirit of their music.

The violin has an endless body of literature that includes unaccompanied solos, technical études, duos, chamber music, and many great concertos. A pianist could spend a lifetime learning nothing but a fraction of the technical studies written for piano and never find the time to play a live recital! With so much literature to learn and practice, solo artists who play piano and violin are accustomed to being alone in their pursuit of excellence; they get a lot of practice feeling at ease and productive in this "solo" environment.

Our guest celebrities for exploring the zone include one champion each of the violin, piano, classical guitar, and harp. We have already met virtuoso violinist Joshua Bell, and we'll turn now to Jeffrey Kahane, another virtuoso musician. Not only is Jeffrey a great concert pianist, he is a fabulous chamber music artist who has performed and recorded with Joshua Bell, Yo-Yo Ma, and the great improvisational pianist Fred Hersch.

Jeffrey Kahane is also a popular conductor of major orchestras throughout the world and artistic director of the Santa Rosa Symphony and the Los Angeles Chamber Orchestra. Jeffrey is a gift to the music world. Here he describes one of his most profound experiences performing one of his signature repertoire masterpieces—Bach's celebrated *Goldberg Variations*.

Jeffrey acknowledges that there are times when we are performing when the music is coming out quite well and yet we are still worrying about the right fingerings, or mortgage payments, or dinner plans. We can keep going, to be sure, but the quality is just not on the same level as in those blissful moments when such thoughts are totally forgotten and we are simply lost in the music.

On this occasion, it was different for him:

I played at the Oregon Bach Festival, in a beautiful small hall with perfect acoustics. Everything sounds good in there. The hall was full, with people behind me and in front of me, and I knew that some of my good friends were in the audience. I just remember feeling at a certain point in the piece as though everything disappeared—myself included. There was no audience, there was no me—everything was gone except the music.

Jeffrey believes that music making is at its best when the performer is completely absorbed in the act of making music. This has always been the premise of the Inner Game; when the internal voice and obstacles are removed, what remains is pure music.

When our attention is held by technical or other nonmusical concerns, less awareness is available for the music. This has been recently demonstrated in scientific terms with the publication of a survey about driving and talking on the cell phone. The crux of this study, led by Dr. Marcel Just of Carnegie Mellon, is that the brain appears to have only a finite amount of space for tasks requiring attention. When people try to do two tasks at the same time (like concentrating on the music and attending to other concerns simultaneously), brain activity does not double, it decreases. The result is that the two tasks are performed simultaneously less well than one task alone. The brain becomes less efficient when it performs more than one complex task at a time.

The clear implication is that any artist, athlete, or professional is less likely to experience the zone when attempting to micromanage technique at the same time he or she is hoping to be inspired by great ideas. Joshua Bell believes in having the mind and body totally available to the guidance that the music can bring. In this state, you are not presenting your own ideas, your ideas are arising naturally from the greatness of the music.

Joshua described for me the way he experiences the spirit of a renowned composer's music. When he plays the Beethoven violin concerto, he sometimes finds himself feeling nervous about coming in during the big orchestral introduction, but then he experiences a sense of calm just as he is about to play.

It is as though I must succumb to this world that Beethoven has created, and I suppose I almost treat it in a religious sort of way. In the world of his music, Beethoven is God. I'd never thought of it that way before, but it is as though I begin to warm up to what religious people refer to as a loving God within that musical world. I feel as though I surrender to this. I feel that there is somebody who knows this world so much better than I do—and it is Beethoven himself, who created it— and there is something very comforting about that. Somehow that gets me feeling very relaxed.

I think what a privilege it is to be a part of this great, beautiful piece of music. And this helps me get rid of my nerves and stops my extra-neous thoughts about technical issues and what I did or didn't do in the practice room.

This concept of "being captured by the music" or "surrendering to the composer's spirit" explains why many accomplished artists experience a sense of calm just before an important performance. When they studied two groups of parachute jumpers, scientists found that inexperienced jumpers had greatly elevated heart rates just before they left the plane, but the heart rates of experienced jumpers actually *decreased* before they jumped. This suggests to me that the prepared performer has the ability to "surrender" into the state of relaxed concentration.

The Zone Is a Fearless State

When you are in the zone, it seems you are in a world of your own, a world in which you have an inseparable connection to your music. It ap-pears to simultaneously exclude your audience and include them. They are drawn into your experience by the intensity of your absorption in your art. And the intensity of this absorption is nothing less than fearless. It's as though one has been possessed by another character—the character of the music, or that spirit of the composer.

Yolanda Kondonassis is a concert harpist, professor at the Cleveland Institute of Music and the Oberlin Conservatory, and Telarc recording sensation. She explains that playing the harp involves a lot of hopping around with your arms, hands, legs, and feet, combined with precise land-ings on strings, which in turn require accurate estimations of distances. What this all means is that harpists necessarily have a very physical and tactile approach to their instrument.

> For me, that fearless state is defined by a sense that there is not even the slightest possibility of failure, as if slipping or missing isn't part of my reality. When I don't get into the zone, it's usually because I haven't prepared my body properly. In my experience, the whole process of achieving that perfect flow starts with the basics: rest, the right food, and exercise. My mind needs to feel sharp and flexible since playing the harp requires keeping track of many elements at once.

> The optimal state for me is one in which I can switch comfortably between an automatic, or muscle memory, mode and a very focused, conscious mode. I need to be at this master panel and flip the switch back and forth as need dictates. When technicalities don't require my direct awareness, I prefer to lose myself in the music; that's when it's good to get into the automatic mode. Muscle memory can be a powerful tool as long as it's backed up by a strong conscious awareness in preparation. That's why a controlled blend of the conscious and automatic is so important.

I find it interesting that Yolanda talks about switching back and forth as a means of finding an appropriate blend of skills. The sense of balance or blending comes about when these two elements work together to create a single musical statement rather than two separate physical and intellectual entities: we are striving for a proper mix to make a unified musical product. When you tune a radio, you hear both treble and bass sounds, and can often adjust the volume of either one; but when these two separate adjustments are fine-tuned, you are no longer conscious of either level individually, and you can respond to the music as a whole.

That's our ultimate goal.

The Audience Connection

When performers are in the zone, it may seem that they are in a world of their own which excludes the audience. Musicians who seemingly escape in their own worlds to capture the beauty of Brahms may forget that it is possible for them to include their audience in their inner voyage to this zone. And I think we can all vividly recall times when performers have left concert audiences pretty much to their own devices.

When performers only reach out to the first few rows of the audience and leave the others out in the cold, they are missing out on another form of musical connection and transcendence.

Joshua Bell says that one danger to avoid when performing is going so far into yourself that you don't include the audience in the music you're making. There is a balancing act here that we all have to achieve, staying inside the world of the music while projecting our voice to the audience. Josh says that when he is playing he is not *thinking* of the audience as such, but his *sense* of the audience affects him enormously.

> I can feel the audience, I can sense their commitment and their spirit. Definitely, the audience's participation is crucial to the music I make. I have a much harder time playing without an audience. And I've had some experiences in Japan where the people in the audience were so quiet, I felt that what I was doing might not be getting through to them. It was almost eerie.
>
> There is a definite sense you get when an audience is hanging on to what you are doing.

What this suggests to me is that performers can consciously include the audience as an active participant in their own musical process. I'm not just thinking here of a cabaret audience or comedy club, where the performer actually gestures to and winks at the audience. Even in a classical, operatic, or theatrical setting, there is an energy that exists when the audience is really there with you; there is a palpable, visceral atmosphere in the room which is created when everyone is part of the experience. Audience members clearly don't want to disturb performers by their own presence, but they do and should want to be drawn into the performer's world, and this inclusion of the audience within the artist's zone has a great impact on any artist.

The Imaginary Fishnet

Jeffrey Kahane speaks of casting an imaginary fishnet over the audience when he walks onstage. He told me he wants to reel in as many fish as he can:

> I will cast this spell: I know I can open this door and show you something unforgettable and transforming, and I'm determined to take myself there and to take you with me. I invite you to step out of the world with me and come beyond everyday reality—not to escape the world, but to transcend it.

Sometimes the spell is pretty palpable. Jeffrey recalls playing the Beethoven A Major Sonata with Yo-Yo Ma at the Paola de la Musica in Barcelona. The audience was very attentive and quiet, not to say spellbound. Then at the end of the first movement someone coughed—and about thirty people emphatically went SHHHHHHH!!! They were protective of the special atmosphere or spirit that had come over performers and audience alike, and very much resented one person's destroying it.

Joshua Bell said that communicating with the audience is perhaps the closest thing there is to ESP, because he can totally sense whether the audience is with him or not:

> I don't know how, but I can feel it. I can feel an entire audience, or even one person in an audience, that is really with me. And this inspires me to want to take that person or that audience along with me.

Yolanda Kondonassis stresses the importance of consciously including the audience in the music. While she plays by memory with her eyes closed, she knows that the music she makes is really for the audience.

When I perform, I have a strong belief that it's not just "all about me." You always try to go to that intimate place in the music that you think the composer had in his or her mind. And while most of the positive energy has to come from deep within you, it's still possible to make a space in the hall where everyone is included. There's nothing I love more than creating a special finish to a piece, like the beautiful slow movement of Ginastera's harp concerto. To take that last sound and carry it farther than anyone thinks possible with the vibration of the string and the motion of my hand, folding music into sacred silence, is like wrapping everyone in the entire hall together in this one spiritual atmosphere. It's an incredible feeling.

Kondonassis knows how to play in the zone. Daniel Buckley interviewed her recently for the *Tucson Citizen* after her performance of this Ginastera concerto with the Tucson Symphony, and he wrote:

Kondonassis is much more than a technician. In tandem with her virtuosity, her musicality borders on the metaphysical, lending the sense of a shaman in the throes of a transcendental ritual.

Most artists welcome a transforming feeling of this kind, but it may not be something we can attain every time we take the stage. It seems to me more like a delicate gift that comes to us on the breeze. I believe in the *let it happen* school rather than the *make it happen* school, but recognizing that this zone exists and making yourself available to its power may be the first step in getting there. And the difference between good and great artists just might be that the great artists are those who live and breathe the atmosphere of the zone like natives.

The Zone Can Be Out of Control

The zone is a place of flow, not of control, and the attempt to control things so that you stay in the zone can be a fast way *out* of it! Many great artists take pleasure in accepting and welcoming a sort of craziness or recklessness in their greatest performances. The legendary guitarist Christopher Parkening described his mentor the master musician Andrés Segovia's performances as having a sense of excitement because the maestro *wasn't being careful*. He told me that Segovia never played at the "safe" tempo, he was always right there on the edge:

> This gave a certain electricity in performance which wouldn't have been there otherwise. There are times when you have to take things to the edge—and even falling is okay. There is a certain presence, an excitement that spontaneity creates, which being careful can never reach. When an interviewer asked the Olympic ski champion Jean Claude Killy how he had won four gold medals, Jean Claude responded, "I skied out of control." He went for it. There is a time for risk taking in musical performance, too. You can really hear the difference.

Yolanda says that when she's in that totally fearless state, she strives to take it as far as she possibly can. She is willing to risk everything—and then be able to reel it all back just in time, at the point where the intensity of the music making crosses an invisible line and becomes just too much.

Jeffrey Kahane sees a connection between improvisation and this kind of musical excitement. His teacher, Howard Weisel in Los Angeles, encouraged him to improvise:

> I have always loved improvising, it comes easily to me, and I feel there's a freedom that it brings. Quite often when I'm playing with an orchestra, I'll approach something in one rehearsal very differently from the way I'll tackle it in the next, and someone will ask me, "Well, are you going to do that in the concert?" And I say, "I'm sorry, you will just have to wait and see!"
>
> We have lost sight of this in recent decades—the aspect of spontaneity.
>
> It is just so important to keep that element of creating in the moment.

GETTING INTO THE ZONE

Entering the zone requires 110 percent of your energy and concentration. It isn't really an accident; a musician can prepare for this much the same as an athlete prepares for a big championship game. This involves being rested, and taking time to prepare for entering an entirely new and different world. You need your physical rest, and you also need to clear your mind of the clutter that remains. This requires some extra effort, perhaps even the adoption of a routine for separating yourself from the concerns of others. Entering into a state of concentration can be physically demanding and exhausting. Quiet and solitude are critical.

Yolanda Kondonassis mentioned the need to be rested before a performance. Joshua likes to pace himself before a concert, then use up all his fuel on the program. He said, *If you are going to have a great meal, you don't want to eat too much beforehand, you want to be really hungry.* Joshua prefers to feel supercharged when he goes onstage.

> For me, this involves resting for a couple hours in the afternoon so I feel fresh for the concert at eight p.m. I'm just pacing myself, so I'm ready to pop with all my energy when the time comes. Having little or no stimulus before a concert helps me, too. I don't like to talk too much before a concert, I don't like making small talk while I'm being taken to the concert in a car, or having music on the radio. I've found I have to gather myself beforehand and get into the right state of mind. It's very important.

When I asked Joshua Bell how he is able to enter the zone, he pondered the question, and then speculated that people who meditate may have an easier time getting there.

Meditation is a discipline of concentration, so those who have practiced a meditative discipline should be able to shift these techniques to the music as well. Meditation is the simple act of focusing all your concentration onto one specific point. Some people focus on the act of breathing—inhaling and exhaling. Others focus on a single sound or image, a candle flame perhaps, or a feeling, or even "nothingness." When you practice concentrating on a specific focus in this way, your mind will begin to wander; but as you continually refocus your attention on the object of your choice, extraneous thought begins to lose its grip on your attention.

Joshua told me that he hasn't quite yet figured out how to meditate, but when it comes to music, he is able to move almost instantaneously into this other world. He believes that great music has that effect.

Sound can be your focus of meditation in this way if you wish to concentrate on one sound, one pitch, one volume, or one tone; but since music is constantly changing and requires attention to a variety of landscapes, feelings, and energies, meditating on *music* as such is a slightly different exercise, closer to the "wide-angle awareness" style of meditation popular among Buddhists. And remember that even meditation is a pathway to heightened consciousness, not the end of the journey!

If you are working on *entering* this state, the act of focusing on a specific element in the music can serve to quiet the mind, so the music can release its spirit on both listener and performer. Once in the zone itself, you are not working at anything: you have left the process of conscious listening and are in a state of silently experiencing and re-creating the music.

The Inner Game is based on utilizing three master skills of concentration. Its value, in terms of getting into the zone, lies in a simple method of being able to filter out those distractions that are not essential to actually making music. This liberates the artist to escape into this "sacred space" without being concerned with outer game issues of success or failure, following instructions, doing the right things, pleasing the crowd. Instead, the artist can devote 100 percent of his or her attention to merging with the energy of the music.

The First Inner Game Skill: Awareness

The first of these three skills is *awareness*. Awareness encourages you to pay attention to (or just notice) what is actually happening while playing. There are four things to focus on while we play. One of these is *sight* (looking at the notes, seeing your body in the act of playing, or the images implied in the music or the text of a song). Instead of worrying about your hand trembling, for example, you can put your attention on the visual contour of the notes as the melody rises and falls. The three other awareness foci include *sound* (volume, rhythm, timbre, pitch), *feeling* (quality, feelings in oneself and in the music), and finally *understanding* (of form, harmony, text, function, meaning).

Here's an example of using an awareness technique to bring your own feelings in line with the music. Jeffrey Kahane was feeling scared at the final round of the Rubinstein competition in Tel Aviv. He told me he didn't want to be scared, he wanted to make music. When he wants to switch his focus from anxiety to the beauty in the music, he often plays his favorite British folk song, "The Water Is Wide," which takes him to a place of heart and feelings of love.

> I would play that piece until I found the place inside that I wanted to be in, and that I wanted the listener to be in. When I finally reached that place, I knew I could go out there and play. It's usually the music itself that takes me to the place where I feel I have the confidence, will, strength, and power to lift the audience and take it with me. At other times I'll sit down and improvise. I might use some aspects of the music I will be performing. If I were scheduled to play the Prokofiev Third Piano Concerto, for instance—it's wild and pumped, like running a race—I wouldn't choose to go to the peaceful heart place. "How I get there" depends on where I want to go.

What Jeffrey does involves a process of assessment. He first notices how he feels: he *becomes aware* of his feelings, his emotions and even his state of mind *as they are*. Then he asks himself, *What feelings are implied or expressed in this score?* Next, he compares his feelings with those expressed in the music, and this gives him a sense of where he wants to go and what he has to do to get there. This is a classic example of being aware of the feelings in your body, and allowing them to align themselves with the feelings of the music. The demands that music makes on awareness are many and varied, and are in constant flux, and it can take all your physical and mental resources to be able to respond instantly to every shift. While keeping yourself emotionally available and tuned to the music you are about to play, you also need to maintain a sense of simple, focused concentration.

It is important to stay focused on one element at a time. If your attention wanders, you will need to direct it back to the music. There may be a lot of things vying for your attention, and it may be helpful to go from several foci to just one musical focus.

Many artists connect to the music in this way by limiting their senses and closing their eyes. Just as a blind person can develop hypersensitive touch and feeling, limiting your sensory input with conscious focusing can heighten other critical connections to the music. Yolanda frequently performs with her eyes closed; she feels that if you have to be staring at the keyboard or strings all the time, you are at some level not ready to trust yourself with the music. She told me that playing with her eyes closed allows her to utilize her other senses a lot more and helps her to "go where she wants to be with the music."

The Second Inner Game Skill: Will/Commitment

It is really difficult to be in the zone when you are not completely clear on what you are doing and precisely how you are doing it. This involves knowing exactly how the music should sound. You have to be clear on the style, the melody, and the rhythm, and know your music so well that anything that doesn't exactly fit your internal vision can be immediately recognized and changed.

You also need to be clear on how you are performing on the flute, bass, keyboard, or voice. This involves remembering the technical fingerings and bowings and when to breathe, and being aware how you are articulating. You have to be clear about these things, or you will be a host to distractions, doubts, and memory slips—a true recipe for disaster.

This principle was reinforced for me when I asked Jeffrey Kahane, Yolanda, and Joshua how they help their students identify how they truly feel about the music they are playing. Jeffrey Kahane told me that when he would ask his Eastman piano students to explain their musical intentions, he often got a blank stare. A student would ask him, "How should I play this passage?" and Jeffrey would sidestep the question:

> I'm not going to tell you what to do. I'll help you to develop your ideas once you have a purpose and intention. It has to come from desire, imagination, passion, and soul.

Yolanda believes that listening to other performances is a great way to absorb the musical experience and build your personal archives of musical gestures and ideas. But the result of all this listening and study should be a tapestry of your own, not an imitation of someone else's vision. There's no right or wrong when it comes to interpretation, there's only "Did it work or didn't it?" And Yolanda believes this question is answered by the sincerity with which the interpretation is delivered.

Joshua asks students the same kinds of questions.

> I try to strip away the recordings you have heard, and what your teacher has told you to do, to get to the basic issue of what this music does for you. Sometimes it is a matter of asking the question "Is this sad, is it happy, is it both?" I have my students describe it in their own words. And if what they tell me isn't happening in their playing, then I must tell them that it's not coming out: "I'm not feeling that from you." Students will often take one idea from a teacher and another from a recording, and these ideas may be completely contradictory in terms of what the musician has to say. So this all comes down to having integrity in what you are thinking and expressing.

Having a clear sense of your musical objective is really crucial if you hope to achieve a magical state of concentration, and yet I often find that less mature players don't have their primary musical goal clearly identified or conceptualized. Where is the music that we so desperately aspire to play located? What is a composer expressing through all those notes, rhythms, dynamics, fingerings, and articulations? What is the composer's actual intent? When you can answer these questions with the conviction Evelyn Glennie described in the chapter on courage, you are ready to take the stage.

The Final Inner Game Skill: Trust

The Inner Game skill of trust has a lot to do with letting go to the music. The score may show an accent mark, a crescendo, or the metronome marking that a quarter note equals 126 beats per minute, but these are signs composers wrote to express their musical intentions, and once we have understood them, we should move from the marks to the music itself, and trust its dynamics. Why not play the accent mark as an explosion, or the crescendo as the energy of a giant geyser erupting, why not play the excitement that the composer was thinking of when he made that notation that the quarter note equals 1/126? Why not trust your sense of the music and play the piece as if it were a song?

In these cases, you are putting your trust in the qualities of the music itself. This will get you much closer to the music. And once your concentration is refocused, you can begin to slip back into the state of relaxed concentration we call the zone.

The great classical guitar soloist Christopher Parkening stressed the importance of focusing on musical expression as a way of sustaining his concentration on the music:

> For the most part, I like to focus on the expression of the music. It can be the calmness or its sheer beauty. I basically know what I'm going for, and I'm trying to express that to the audience.

The key to staying in the zone is to stay with the music, to stay with your role as the messenger who brings the audience this gift. This is your obligation, and your pleasure.

Jeffrey Kahane strives to think, feel, and exist in a place that is beyond the printed notes, and enters a special space where he is both composer and performer at the same time.

When things are really working, I feel as though I'm making the music up: it's as though the spirit of the music has become so much a part of me that I can trick myself into feeling like I'm composing it.

Becoming the composer in this way is a form of letting go. It is a trust technique. Instead of playing like a performer, a student, or someone who is reading, play as though you are the composer and it is your piece!

All these Inner Game techniques will help you narrow your focus to include only the music, so that when you enter the spirit of the zone, you are not carrying any excess baggage. When you have completely merged and become one with the music and its qualities, you are there. Now the challenge is to stay there for as long as possible.

STAYING IN THE ZONE

When you have done your part in preparing for that heightened state of consciousness, good things can happen. But as those precious moments begin to manifest, you will find yourself facing a new challenge: the challenge of sustaining yourself in that zone for as long as possible. Human nature is quirky at best, and may at times choose to sabotage a great performance. It is up to you to focus your will to remain in this zonelike state as long as possible. And while it is likely that you will lose your focus momentarily, your goal is to return to it as soon as you can.

This is one of the great gifts Timothy Gallwey has given us all in his Inner Game books. He offers us tools to refocus on the good stuff when mental interferences keep us from playing at our best. Approaching music with a toolchest of strategies for keeping it at its best will be our final strategy for staying in the zone. The techniques remain simple, and each one has to do with staying connected to the music. In the final analysis, the best choice will be to do what is most natural in the moment—and that moment is ultimately determined by what is happening in the music.

Duration

Don Greene, Ph.D., sports psychologist and stress coach to top executives, has written a wonderful book, *Fight Your Fear and Win*, which is completely consistent with Inner Game techniques and is full of resourceful strategies for sustaining optimum concentration.

Dr. Greene stresses the importance of being able to control the *duration* of your concentration, and he outlines specific ways of doing this. He strongly believes in using pre-event routines, rituals, or repetitive actions that have a lulling effect on the left brain. The process Jeffrey Kahane described in which he plays specific music in advance of a performance would be an example of this approach. Greene believes in engaging in a ritual that is strongly visual, kinesthetic, or auditory for the purpose of disengaging the left brain, and explains that this causes the brain waves to shift from high frequency to flatter beta and into mellow alpha waves.

I would also like to refer you to the final chapter of my own book *The Inner Game of Music*, which suggests a three-part pre-event routine. This consists of a progressive muscle relaxation (or any other physical activity designed to release excess physical tension) followed by a form of meditation to quiet the mind and clear out extraneous thoughts. The final component is a visualization of your actual performance, phrase by phrase. If you get into the habit of running through this three-part ritual before you perform, it will put both mind and body in a more focused place, making it easier for you to enter the zone of concentration.

The sports psychologist Harvey Dorfman stresses that distractions can be eased and minimized by staying focused on what you are doing rather than on outer game issues like winning, being right, and being successful:

> Dwell on external results, and pressure will build. Focus on execution, and pressure will lighten.

What Dorfman calls "execution" involves bringing the three Inner Game skills of *awareness, commitment,* and *trust* to bear on the music.

Pacing

Another thing Don Greene stresses is the tremendous stamina required to sustain awareness and the need to pace your energy over the duration of your performance. You can't just put your all into the first phrase and expect your concentration to last for a thirty-minute concerto appearance or a two-hour recital! This is why Joshua Bell takes such care to rest before a performance, conserving his energy.

Greene also advocates *adversity training*—practicing with noise around you, or engaging other musicians to distract you. Practicing performing in front of any kind of audience, parents, friends, and colleagues, will strengthen your resolve for those times when you find yourself playing under pressure.

Bill VerMeulen, the horn professor at Rice University, keeps his horn students on their toes by spontaneously calling them to perform their excerpts on demand at any time of the day or night. He also encourages them to challenge one another to play a particular musical excerpt perfectly. This kind of adversity training strengthens their ability to concentrate under the pressure of performance.

Noises and Distractions Beyond Your Control

Your audiences can be quite a distraction at times. The legendary classical guitarist Andrés Segovia had a way of taking his cause directly to the source of the problem. Segovia was so critical about extraneous noises that if there was coughing at a concert he would glare and stare at the audience. Christopher Parkening once saw him smash his foot to the ground, pull a handkerchief from his pocket, and tell his audience, "It disturbs me and it disturbs the listener. When you have a cough, you do *this!*"—at which point he covered a cough with his handkerchief. The audience responded with cheers of approval. After that you could have heard a pin drop. The zone was restored.

There can be other distractions besides audience noises. Perhaps you have to play with bad light, so that it is difficult to see the movements of your hands, the conductor, your partner, or your music. You may run into mechanical problems that affect your instrument, such as a string going out of tune. Do you stop? Do you adjust? Do you get another instrument? And what happens to your concentration when you have to play in a state of physical exhaustion, or with a physical injury?

Letting the Zone Work for You

Christopher Parkening told me an inspiring story of how he was able to access some of his best music making under adverse conditions. In 1991, Parkening was engaged to play at the Hollywood Bowl with the Los Angeles Philharmonic. Just six days before that particular concert, he was up at a ranch fly-fishing with his sister, her husband, and her two boys, who had slept in a couch bed. Christopher was folding up the couch bed when somehow the ring finger of his left hand got caught between two folding metal struts. His finger was severely lacerated. With the impending concert only days away, the obvious question was whether he would be able to play, or whether he should cancel. Christopher wasn't ready to cancel. For the next three days, he was unable to play at all: his hand was so stiff that it was impossible for him to press his finger on the string.

The third day before the concert I started to play a bit, and it wasn't good. Even the day before I wasn't up to par by any means. The night before the concert, I read a particular passage of scripture, Second Corinthians 12:9, which says, "My grace is sufficient for you, for my power is made perfect in weakness." So the suffering that humbles us is the very source of power in our lives. When we are weak and without resources and left totally to trust in God's power and grace to sustain us, we become channels through which God's love can flow.

I remember going to sleep at peace that night, just trusting in God's grace. The morning of the concert I avoided showing my finger to the orchestra manager, Ernest Fleishman. I felt such a sense of peace beyond myself, and it was one of those magical concerts when you play so much better than you really felt you were able to. It was really almost humanly impossible for me to play that well, yet this was one of the highlights of my playing career.

Some readers may be reluctant to attribute Parkening's brilliant performance that day to the New Testament, although he is perfectly clear on that point himself—but his experience is in any case a testimony to the potential that lies within each individual, and Christopher's letting go of his physical struggle while connecting with his musical goals has much in common with the kind of *surrendering into the spirit of the zone* that we have been discussing in this chapter. In terms of the Inner Game, there was an element of trust in his letting go. Rather than playing in pain and with physical limitations, he entrusted his playing to a power way beyond himself.

You may recall that Joshua Bell talked about succumbing to a world that Beethoven had created—what J.R.R. Tolkien would call a "secondary world." Joshua calls this sense of letting go to the author of the music "surrendering." Yolanda Kondonassis recalls using sound and motion to guide her audience into a sacred silence and spiritual atmosphere at the end of the slow movement of Ginastera's harp concerto. And Jeffrey Kahane managed to locate a state in which there was *no audience, no me— everything was gone except the music.*

For a musician, the zone is music.

When we recognize that the zone exists and allow ourselves to be touched by it, we can enter a world of balance, perfection, and beauty. In this space, we are able to perform from a place of potential that we often don't realize exists within each and every one of us. This is the place we strive for, and when we are there, we want to stay there as long as possible.

Enjoy the search. Enjoy the experience. Enjoy the journey. And remember, this place of musical magic is always there, as close as your own concentration, just waiting for you to return.

eight

CONFIDENCE: FROM BRAVURA
TO INTEGRITY

(Trumpet)

Susan Slaughter has been principal trumpet with the St. Louis Symphony since 1972. Each year she plays the national anthem in front of more than twenty thousand St. Louis Cardinals fans; it's a ritual she takes seriously. In 1991, a Cardinals official came up to Susan while she was preparing to play, told her that Baseball Commissioner Fay Vincent was attending the game, and asked her, "Don't you want to meet him?"

Polite but firmly fixed on the musical task ahead of her, Susan replied, "Well, uh, if you would like me to meet him, fine, Marty." Her tone was accommodating, but not thrilled. The official gathered that Susan was more interested in warming up than in meeting a baseball VIP, but he also knew that social contacts are important, so he gently pressed the point: "Well, Fay Vincent is the commissioner of baseball." Still polite and obliging, and still focused on her musical preparation, Susan said, "Okay."

She shook hands with the commissioner and then played the national anthem.

Two weeks later, Susan received a call from Fay Vincent's office, and he invited her to play the national anthem for the upcoming World Series.

On October 21, 1991, Susan was flown to Atlanta for the game between the Braves and the Minnesota Twins. Just before she was to play, someone on the staff of the Atlanta Braves came up to her and said, "Do you realize you are going to be playing for twenty-plus million people tonight?"

Polite but still firmly fixed on the musical task ahead of her, Susan replied, "Well, if you say so, that's fine. It doesn't really matter to me." Once again, the tone of her voice was agreeable, but not thrilled.

Preparation is important because it's what gives Susan her confidence. Susan told me she tries not to let herself be distracted on these occasions, and just concentrates on remaining in her own comfort zone, where she knows what she is doing and where she can focus on playing.

> I was focused on what I wanted to do—to just do what I have to do, just play the anthem and not worry about how many people are going to hear it. When I practice, I set myself the goal of playing something through perfectly three times, and then stop. I know that in performance, I'll only have to do it once, so this practice goal tells me I *can* do this—and I follow that up with an act of determination that I *will* do this.

Confidence has a face that is easily recognizable. You often hear a sports commentator or television analyst say something like "You can see his confidence" as some athlete performs without doubt or hesitation. Confidence is no accident. It is based on preparation, momentum, and, most important, experience. It is something that you acquire. And like a snowball as it rolls down the hill, it gets bigger and bigger.

But confidence can also be based on a fragile foundation. We all know how devastating to one's self-confidence a bad experience can be. There are many ways to acquire confidence, and to sustain it once we have it. We will explore different kinds of confidence in this chapter and learn which kind is the most enduring. With this understanding, we can access confidence more frequently, and also know what will allow us to perform with lasting confidence. Preparation and Will.

Armando Ghitalla, the late former principal trumpet with the Boston Symphony and Professor at Rice University, defines confidence as:

An accepted and unheralded evidence within a person that gives a person the unconscious knowledge that he/she is able to produce outstanding results in his/her chosen career under almost any circumstances.

Full technical control is a must: this "evidence to oneself" provided by preparation and determination is what fosters confidence and it becomes stronger with experience.

TWO KINDS OF CONFIDENCE

Doc Severinsen told me that there are really two kinds of confidence: an "innocent" kind that's powerful but fleeting, and an "enduring" kind that's based on hard work, experience, knowledge, and preparation.

When Doc was only seven, he started playing solos:

I was just a little kid, and all of a sudden everyone is telling me how great I am, and I believed it. I won the state competition when I was nine. That's the first kind of confidence I had—confidence born of instant success.

But then I began to lose my confidence: every time I went out to play, I was terrified. I think this was because my dad had taught me to play by rote—I didn't study any technical stuff out of the instruction book. And at one point I developed a confidence and a lip problem, and I just broke down.

That's when I went to New York and studied with Benny Baker, who had been Toscanini's trumpet player at one time, and we just started from scratch. I did all the things I should have done from the very beginning. This time I was able to know and accept what I was doing intellectually: I put together a series of positive reference points to build on. And as I got better and better, I went back and played with high school bands and college groups as a soloist and clinician—and all this experience helped me to accumulate the second kind of confidence, the kind that stays with you.

Doc can look back and compare the difference between what he calls the "innocent" kind of confidence and the confidence that is acquired over time through preparation and knowledge.

Michael Sachs, principal trumpet with the Cleveland Orchestra, would agree. He believes that real confidence is not something that happens overnight, but builds very slowly over a long period of time. He points out that someone can tell you that you sound great, but until you can really hear it yourself and believe it, outside praise will not bring you the lasting kind of confidence.

> Real confidence comes from a combination of getting encouragement from teachers and colleagues and *then* having breakthrough experiences that you can validate for yourself, where all your effort and preparation culminates in a successful event. You *feel* the success, and realize that you haven't done this for anyone other than yourself.

I find it exciting to see how someone's confidence can build momentum and speed like a great freight train. Confidence can be a self-fulfilling prophecy. Success breeds success, and the same principle applies to confidence. When you know you're getting a little better from practicing, you want to practice more. Then you get a little better still from this renewed effort, and it makes you want to practice even more. You get still better, and you want to practice forever. It's like a freight train that you just can't stop!

The legendary jazz trumpet player Clark Terry believes that confidence is about knowing how to survive. It's a matter of being prepared so that you know that you can perform under any circumstance. Real confidence, for instance, often means being able to make something good out of a mistake. Clark told me he learned this from mice and rats while living in the ghetto.

> We used to take tin cans and put them over a rat hole, and then use cheese as bait; but the rat always finds a way to get the cheese without getting caught and get back home safely.

You have to know many ways to get back home. When you are improvising on a jazz tune, there are times when you can get so far removed from the melody and harmony that you are lost. You have to stay so focused on the tune in your head that you know multiple ways to reflect its sound and feel, without losing the spirit of the piece—like the rat escaping and knowing many routes to safety and refuge.   ·

Don't lose track of your home base.

Clark also told me that the confident musician keeps his rhythm section in his hip pocket, very close to him; this way he never strays very far from the beat. So much depends on pulse and rhythm, and when you are tapped into them, you can go forward and improvise with confidence.

PATHWAYS TO CONFIDENCE

There are many ways to build and gain confidence. Once you begin this journey, you will find that you are moving through a landscape with its own fair share of straight and narrow paths, tough uphill sledding, detours, and dead ends, but also steep and exhilarating drops into mysterious valleys, beautiful vistas and views. You have to be prepared to change course at every given moment, though. It takes constant alertness and multiple strategies to keep moving ahead on this never-ending journey.

What I'm offering here is a map. Some of these suggested pathways will help you get started, others will be important when you lose confidence and need to rebuild it. One strategy will lead to the next, and so on to others that may spring from your imagination, your teachers, and your own experience.

Enjoy the journey, and remember there is no end to the pursuit of artistry.

Preparation by Overpreparing

Michael Sachs describes a level of preparation that goes way beyond what most people might consider necessary, and there's a lesson for us here. His preparation for winning his seat as principal trumpet with the Cleveland Orchestra epitomizes being prepared for everything—and then for everything else.

Mike was twenty-six years old and playing fourth trumpet in the Houston Symphony. As is normal for most auditions, the Cleveland Orchestra published a list telling candidates what music they would likely have to play, and added in smaller type, "plus sight reading from the standard repertoire." This means you may have to play anything they put in front of you.

In preparation for his audition for the Cleveland Orchestra principal trumpet position, Michael wanted to be prepared to play any possible piece in the standard repertoire. He acquired all the orchestra scores, recordings, and complete trumpet parts to the most frequently asked audition pieces not on the list. His stack of music for the audition was over two feet high.

> I just couldn't be too well prepared for this audition: I needed as much knowledge at my disposal as possible. When the time came, I wasn't nervous at all. My extra work had given me a backlog of information to feed off of, and I knew that I'd left no stone unturned. It didn't matter what they put in front of me, because I was prepared. I wanted to take as many potential variables out of the equation as I could.

Barbara Butler, former professor at Eastman School of Music who currently teaches at Northwestern University, describes this kind of "above-and-beyond" approach as "preparation by overpreparing," and recommends it highly. She says that if a piece goes to a high C, you prepare for a high D. If the piece ends with a high short note, then you practice so you could end it with a long note. If you have a long passage, then you should be able to play it with two or three repeats. If you have a one-hour recital, then you should be able to play a two-hour recital.

That is the essence of *preparation by overpreparation*. You do more than enough in preparation ahead of time, so that doing enough on the occasion itself will be a breeze, and in the event you have the confidence that comes from preparation.

Know the Product

When I asked my former Cincinnati Symphony colleague principal trumpeter Philip Collins about confidence, he said the most important requirement is being convinced about what you want to convey. (Remember Evelyn Glennie talking about courage in this way?) He explained that a great performance is the result of musical concepts being clearly communicated to the audience. Therefore a musician must be more than a right-note machine. Music is not about just playing all the right notes and rhythms. It is more like a drama class, where we have to convey the message or play a role. If our only task is accuracy, then the pressure is on. But if the goal is to accurately deliver a message, then the fun begins! Philip said:

> Confidence becomes instinctive when the performer takes on the challenge of communication. Inspiring performances consist of excellence not only in the technique but also in the character, style, and the spirit intended by the composer. Know exactly what you want to do. It's like carrying a cup of coffee filled to the brim across the room trying not to spill a drop. Looking only at the coffee, you will probably spill some of it. But if you look to the place you want to take it, you won't.

State Your Case with Passion and Meaning

Powerful expression springs from confidence, and musical expression is no exception. There is no point in playing bland music without any message, meaning, or color. One of Phil's teachers once told him never to lose the élan (dash, verve, character, spirit, or, as conductor James Levine calls it, pizzazz). Playing with élan is not only confidence-building, it's an expression of confidence too. Phil describes vividly:

> My heroes always capture this style in their playing. They put their stamp on the music without spoiling the overall balance or blend with the rest of the orchestra. Not only does the product need the appropriate character but it must usually travel a great distance through the orchestra to the back of the hall. I have a picture on my wall showing just

the bell of a trumpet with many multicolored streamers shooting out like it was the Fourth of July. If great sounds were also visible I believe they would look stunning. I can still remember the Zarathustra trumpet call belted out over the orchestra in the shed at Tanglewood years ago. You could almost see that high C spiraling out over the audience! Such brilliant playing kept me inspired for months.

When one hears music played in this manner, there is no doubt as to what we experience. It is almost as if we can "see or feel" the confidence, it is so convincing. When you believe in and know the character of what you are expressing, you can deliver the goods as Collins described.

Maintain Courage in the Face of Criticism

Charles Schlueter, principal trumpet with the Boston Symphony, learned to believe in himself by studying with an extremely demanding teacher, the legendary former principal trumpet of the New York Philharmonic, Bill Vacchiano.

Charles told me that when he would go for his lessons at the Juilliard School, his hands would start sweating before he walked in the door. He remembers that in his first lesson with Vacchiano, Bill didn't like his trumpet, his mouthpiece, his sound, or his phrasing!

Then he said to me (mispronouncing my name): "Hey Schloiter, where you're from in the Midwest, they have cows there, don't they?" I said, "Yes," and he said, "Did you ever see a cow do his business?" I didn't know quite what to make of that, but I guessed, and he went right on and said: "That's what your attacks sound like!"

Talk about vivid visualizations! But I don't think I ever made another one of those attacks again! This certainly raised my sense of what was expected of me. Bill always seemed to know just what to say that would challenge me to "work harder and do it better."

In retrospect, Charles realizes that the reason no conductor has been able to rattle him is that Bill made him so scared in those forty-five-minute trumpet lessons back at Juilliard that everything that followed has been pale in comparison. Charles now has confidence in himself and he knows that it's his own evaluation that matters. He went on to say:

> To play for the conductor, the audience, my colleagues, my parents, friends, or God would be a hell of a burden. I think that's what screws people up when they're playing for auditions: they may be thinking, "I wonder what they are listening for." When I'm on the jury, I couldn't even tell you what I'm listening for. But when I hear something special, I know it.

Auditioning for any ensemble is probably the most musically unrealistic kind of performance there is. It is also very hazardous for anyone's confidence, because it is an unfair process of evaluating how one will actually perform on the job. When Charles auditioned for his job as the principal trumpet with the Boston Symphony, he was quite content as the principal trumpet with the Minnesota Orchestra. So rather than enduring the standard "behind the screen" or "committee" audition process, he could afford to ask the orchestra to evaluate his playing based on actually performing a concert with the Boston Symphony. Charles felt more confident in this kind of audition, and didn't care if they rejected his proposal. Actually playing with the orchestra would be a more natural way to show how he could blend with the section and perform his part.

When you play an audition behind a screen or in front of a jury, there is a quite natural tendency to want to play perfectly. This desire creates an environment in which Self 1 demons can sabotage your performance. *Don't make any mistakes! Use the right dynamics! Impress the conductor and score points with the jury!* Charles reminded me that what works best is believing in one's training and experience acquired over many years (tone, style, intonation, dynamic range, ensemble, musicianship)—in other words, in one's proficiency or command of one's instrument, rather than on specific repertoire. That is what confidence is all about.

> Each individual player is responsible for the music, but there is no "product." As soon as something is played, it's gone, good or bad.

Playing is a "process." There is no anxiety in the present. Anxiety is either in the past, worrying about what was just played, or in the future, worrying about what you are about to play. Nothing can be done about either! Don't judge or evaluate while you're performing.

Confidence begins from within. When you get to a point where you can acknowledge and feel comfortable with what you can do, you are ready to build on it and take the next step. Each successive step involves choosing the high road (courage): will you take the safe path, or will you take the higher road? You have to leave your doubts behind. The courage to step up to the plate despite all the risks of failure is critical if you are to continue accumulating good experiences. So courage actually helps us to gain the positive experiences that will result in building confidence. As I said earlier, confidence is like momentum, it builds on its own successes.

George Graham tells me that the Hollywood studio guys he plays with are some of the best in the world—but I know George is one of those guys himself. I asked him what their secret is, and he said they *don't leave any room for doubt.*

We develop "ice water in the veins." Stuff that would be scary to other people just isn't scary here. Most of us have learned how to take the fear and turn it into a positive energy.

Before he moved to Los Angeles, George played shows in Reno, and he recalls playing "America the Beautiful" in one show where the last eight bars were an unaccompanied trumpet solo. He played, and he listened, and he heard himself sounding better than ever before. Risk had turned into reward.

I remember seeing a poster that said, "Ships are safe in harbor—but that's not why ships are built." I took this cue as an invitation to return to L.A. and do some even more high-pressure studio work.

That's how confidence builds momentum.

Confidence Is a Journey of Learning

You can be the cause of your confidence or lack of it. Andrew McCandless, principal trumpet with the Dallas Symphony, believes that when he doesn't play a passage too well in rehearsal, if he is conscious of how he got there, he can retrace his steps and find and fix the problem. To maintain this consciousness of his own process, he keeps a journal of everything he does in practice. He said:

> This way, when I get to the point where something is going to shake me up, I can go back to see what I was doing that led up to it. I keep a log of what works and what is not working, and it helps me to teach myself.

That's another point. Somewhere along the line, anyone who aims to be a professional musician will have to stop taking full-time lessons. This doesn't mean you should close yourself off to other ideas, or stop improving. But eventually you have to be on your own. If you can learn *how* you learn, you will continue to improve beyond that point because you'll be your own teacher. And that in turn will keep on building your self-confidence.

Michael Sachs believes it is possible to trace and fix virtually all mistakes. The problem could have to do with fundamentals, airflow, embouchure, or body position, or perhaps it is purely a mental distraction: not thinking about the musical character, or not being thoroughly prepared.

Michael told me about a student who had a horrible experience playing the offstage solo from Respighi's *Pines of Rome*. He missed just about every note. It couldn't have gone worse.

> What I got him to do was describe *exactly* what happened and how it felt. We re-created the event phrase by phrase and figured out what went wrong each step of the way. Then we mapped out solutions to every problem. I told him, "This was only one moment in time and it's already gone. But, because we've now traced the problems to their cause and fixed them, it won't happen that way the next time."

You never have to lose your confidence long-term. There are always so-lutions to get you back on track. Mistakes are opportunities for you to learn. Learning from your mistakes and finding out how to solve your problems helps to build your self-confidence, step by step. In fact, it is the actual solving of problems that is the accomplishment! This in turn builds momentum, which fuels more confidence—and so your progress on this endless journey continues.

Stay Within Your Limits

Vincent Cichowicz, formerly with the Chicago Symphony and North-western University, believes it is important to stay within your limits. When considering a new job, you must ask yourself whether you would be doing something that is totally out of your league.

> Taking a job you know you will struggle with can shake your confi-dence and hurt your career. If you need to play above the level you can manage on a regular basis, that's a sure way to become anxious—and there's a great chance the attempt will defeat you!

There is a famous story about a San Francisco trumpet player who is also a composer. So the story goes, he's invited to write the music for a film, takes time off from the trumpet, works hard on the project, and wins an Academy Award for his music. Not too shabby, you might think. But in the meantime he hasn't had a chance to practice. When he gets back to the Bay Area, he meets a friend and tells him he has been away in L.A. doing this film work that has turned out quite well, in fact he's won the Oscar for his soundtrack. And his friend says, "Gee, I hadn't heard about that—that's fantastic!" and then asks him, "What have you been doing since you've been back from L.A.?" So the trumpeter/composer says, "Well, I just played Pier 32 the other night, and my chops were so bad I was embarrassed."

And his friend says: "Oh, yes, I heard about that!"

It is important to protect your confidence and avoid situations where you know you aren't going to be able to do your best. It might be a good idea to make sure you are in shape before you get there and play!

SUSTAINING CONFIDENCE

Confidence is a fragile commodity. You can acquire it through good preparation and meaningful experience, but it remains a challenge to sustain it when faced with irritable critics, negative suggestions, bad experiences, the muttered opinions of your colleagues and teachers, and your own negative demons. In order to sustain your confidence in a potentially hostile world, here are a few strategies you can follow.

I have always believed that the best teacher lies within you.

To put it another way, it's not so much *teaching* as *learning* that's the real key to success. A music teacher can give you all the right answers, but nothing much happens until a lesson sinks in, and at that point *you* are the one doing the learning. Furthermore, no one knows how you best learn better than you do. It follows that the best music teacher you can find will be the one who can help you to teach yourself, and that the most wonderful tool for learning from yourself is your own awareness of what is happening.

And so we come back to one of the three primary skills of the Inner Game and revisit *awareness*. Awareness is the skilled use of attention. It is like a wonderful searchlight: it illuminates everything it shines upon. It works like this: when we can see and know what is there, *What Is*, as Tim Gallwey might say, our Self 2 knows just what to do; but without awareness, it is crippled. Use your self-awareness as a guardian of your own confidence. You don't have to forget your own instinct for what is good or bad, right or wrong, just because someone gives you a suggestion or makes an observation. Your own awareness can be your best friend when it comes to feeling confident about what you believe is right.

John Copola played first trumpet with Woody Herman. He recently had some major dental work done, and when he tried to go back to playing, he found that he couldn't play at all. He told me he needed to discover a way to focus his breath more comfortably.

When you get into a spin over something like this, you begin to ana-lyze—and analysis is paralysis!

I used to study with this famous but dogmatic teacher in Phila-delphia. I believed every word he said was true—but after my third day of lessons, I could not play any high notes at all. My teacher went through this detailed description about how my airstream should go to the left, and I'm a downstream guy, and that when I pass C on the staff I should move my head to the right, and so on. So I went to my friend Bill Harris, who was playing trombone with Woody Herman. I showed him all these papers that this teacher had written. And Bill—who's a pipe smoker—took out his lighter and set the lot of them on fire.

In later years, John learned to teach himself through awareness. He told me that he started with one note in the middle of the staff. He no-ticed where he felt most comfortable and when the sound was good. Then he added a second note, and finally a third note. He continued very slowly from there, applying his awareness to each new note; before long, he had solved his own problem.

John's awareness did so much more to build his confidence than this fa-mous teacher who only filled his mind with criticisms. He turned out to be his own best teacher.

Don't Think, Just Play

Doc Severinsen says that when you miss a note on the trumpet, you know it—and it can really upset you and your confidence a great deal. Harry Glanz and Benny Baker both told him that the notes he misses are the ones that he *thinks* he is going to miss: *if you think you are going to miss it, you might as well go ahead and miss it, because it is going to happen.*

So what does Doc do?

You just never think about missing a note. You have to have a positive visualization that it is all going to be right. If you have done everything you can do, then you shouldn't let one wrong note bother you much. Just keep those thoughts about wrong notes out of your head.

Benny Baker has this expression about making music: if you never miss any notes and you never make any music, what have you gained? If you concentrate on getting the music out, you will be less likely to think of missing the notes.

While good and bad thoughts come and go, we still have the ability to focus our attention on what we decide is most important. In this case your ability to choose the sound of the music will put you in a better position to make fewer mistakes, which will ultimately help build your confidence.

Focus on the Music, Not on What People Think of You

Some people use relatively destructive ways to maintain confidence while playing. John Miller, formerly a trumpeter with the Philharmonia Orchestra, London, as well as the world-acclaimed Philip Jones Brass Ensemble, told me a powerful story of how he got support from his colleagues while learning a very important lesson in performance.

John used to be very concerned about playing utterly correctly. He wanted to play all the right notes and avoid making even the smallest mistakes. His reputation was very important to him, as was being popular with the guys. In his late teens, he discovered a wonderful thing: if he drank a couple of beers before a concert, he felt more confident about what he was about to do. It was as if all his worries and fears had been medicated away! He told me:

I began to rely on drinking as a crutch that would bolster me up in difficult playing situations. In the seventies this caused both myself and many of my colleagues a lot of grief: I quickly developed quite a problem.

This reached a crucial point where I had to reassess myself and my methods, and I decided I had to start performing without any artificial aids. I also took a look at the basis of my fears. Some of these were not well founded. Fundamentally, I was basically frightened of what other people thought of me and my playing.

But then I started putting the music first and getting away from my self-image. This did not change entirely overnight, but I confided in certain colleagues, who were highly supportive. Thus began the best part of my career. Through the course of my recovery, it gradually dawned on me that people were not concentrating on me, but on the interpretation of the piece. You might say that my confidence was not earned the easiest way, but, above all, I discovered that in a concert hall it's the music that's on display—not the performer.

Once again the same principle rings true. When the focus is on the music, you can get lost in your natural ability to express yourself and the message of the composer. When your focus is on people's opinions or playing accurately, the music is lost and so will be your confidence.

Focus on What You Have Accomplished and What You Can Do

Bud Herseth is the former principal trumpet with the Chicago Symphony. Barbara Butler told me about a time the orchestra was playing a concert at Carnegie Hall. They were performing the Bach *Brandenburg* Concerto No. 2, which contains a famous virtuoso piccolo trumpet part. To add to the pressure he felt, Bud had not played that piece in New York before under their music director, George Solti. The performance was truly fantastic. Trumpet colleague Charlie Geyer, who was not playing in the Bach, heard Bud play from the balcony. But when he congratulated Bud backstage afterward, Bud muttered something like "Ugh—the worst day of my life!"

Later, a colleague asked Bud what he had meant by that comment. It appeared that when he was warming up before the rehearsal and tried to play his piccolo trumpet, nothing happened—nothing came out!

What Bud did was to go onstage twenty minutes before the piece was to be played and just sit in his chair. All his colleagues were warming up feverishly around him—but he just sat there, and didn't play a single note. Instead he thought about all the performances he had done in his life, and all the successes he had enjoyed. He thought about the good times in his historic career, and only the good times. Then, when it came time for his entrance, he put his horn up to his mouth and played brilliantly.

Taking a moment to remind yourself of who you are, what you have done to get to this place in your career and the many accomplishments that reflect your mastery of your instrument, puts your mind in a positive state. It also helps to silence the Self 1 voice of doubt and replace it with a sense of self-confidence that helps your playing. Barbara Butler, who teaches trumpet at Northwestern University and also specializes in playing piccolo trumpet, said that she had a similar experience of self-doubt before a concert and recalled the Herseth story. The same principles of focusing on her abilities and experience worked for Barbara as she reminded herself of what Bud had done onstage in Carnegie Hall.

Enjoy Your Anxieties—You Are Not Alone

I very much hope that those who read this book and *The Inner Game of Music* come to accept the idea that experiencing the symptoms of anxiety and stage fright is not unique, nor is it a problem—it is human nature.

Stage fright means your body is getting ready for the challenge—and that can be way better than overconfidence. If you are overconfident before you perform and don't feel that excitement and that jolt of adrenaline, you may not have the same mental and physical capacity for dealing with the split-second decisions you need to make in the heat of battle!

Overconfidence can result in complacency; it's like that first type of confidence I described at the beginning of this chapter. It might last for a while, and you may begin by thinking, Gee, I sound great, that went so well! But then comes the flip side, and you think, Oops—where did that mistake come from? And so the downward spiral begins. I call it "crash and burn."

John Wallace, the world-famous trumpet soloist formerly with the Philharmonia and London Symphony Orchestras, has learned to welcome feelings of anxiety before a performance:

> Right before a performance I become very nervous, but then I usually get calm just before I go on to stage. I get this feeling that the audience

hasn't come here to hear me screw the music up. You really have to be out of your regular state of consciousness to play well, so when you get nervous before a concert, it helps to give you the heightened awareness you need. No kidding, those nerves we have are part of the process of playing well!

From my own experience of playing solo bass recitals, I know the most dangerous situation I can find myself in is to play a great dress rehearsal right before the concert. If ever there was such a thing, this is an omen for upcoming disaster. If I have a bad rehearsal or a so-so rehearsal, it reminds me of what I really need to do to play better in concert. I get more focused and more determined to make sure this concert truly reflects what I want to communicate.

When I approach a program with this same heightened sense of anxiety, I'm actually more determined to play what I have prepared. These qualities of preparation and will are once again what focuses our efforts to produce the confidence we see in a good performance.

Not all performances and dress rehearsals have to be this way. Some are effortless, some are a struggle. What is always within our power is to have prepared properly, to stay focused on the music, and to be able to filter out our own mental bombardments. Just let the music speak—you will find many ways to allow it to come through.

MIND-BODY CONFIDENCE

Recent research has developed an extensive body of physical and psychological knowledge which can help us to improve our concentration, performance, and confidence, whether we are athletes, salespeople, or artists. It has become commonplace for professionals under pressure or in competition to seek both physical body training and mind control to improve overall performance. Our confidence, since it is so closely linked to preparation, will no doubt benefit from bolstering both our physical and mental strength and resilience as artists. In fact, demonstrating confidence is also demonstrating strength, both physical and mental. Musicians are small-muscle athletes, so the same principles of physical conditioning which apply to athletes also apply to musicians.

The Body

When I called Doc Severinsen for an interview, he was working out in his own gym lifting weights. He tells me that since he is getting older, it is even more important for him to do everything he can to stay in the best physical shape.

Preparation and physical conditioning have by now become an accepted part of preparation for musicians, especially those like brass and wind players or singers, who have to perform with stamina and depend on good cardiovascular breath control. All musicians can benefit from muscular strength so they can relax under pressure! Doc reminded me of a recording session he'd had with the Cincinnati Symphony when he was under huge pressure to play virtuoso classical favorites when he normally plays popular music and jazz. Watching Doc from my seat in the orchestra, I'd been amazed at his stamina and his ability to stay relaxed during this session. He told me how he was able to do this:

> We were working so hard, and it was absolutely unbelievably physically exhausting. Erich Kunzel, the conductor, was standing there at the podium, laughing at me. He thought it was hilarious that he was putting me through all of this. And my answer to all this tension was that during the short recording breaks we took, I was backstage down on the floor doing push-ups! Somehow this exercise not only gives me strength, it also takes tensions and worries out of the body, so that I return to the stage relaxed and confident.

Lifting weights and doing push-ups are just two examples of the many ways to strengthen and condition the body to play with relaxation and confidence. Strengthening and warming up the small muscles inside the throat and lips is closely related to confidence. Many of the artists I have interviewed have offered their prescriptions for keeping the body strong and relaxed, including such things as walking around the block, running, Nordic track, Alexander technique, Pilates, yoga, deep breathing, meditation visualizations and biofeedback for relaxation, and swimming. Several artists also mentioned commonsense preparations with respect to smoking, diet, nutrition, avoiding drinking and avoiding beta blockers, and taking care of your teeth and ears.

It is good commonsense advice to discharge excessive physical energy and anxiety before any performance with some form of physical activity. A brisk walk or simple stretching exercises can help you rid the body of unnecessary physical tension. Maintaining a commonsense diet and getting adequate rest will put the body in a better position to perform with confidence.

The Mind

According to Armando Guitalla it is also important to approach playing with an *uncluttered mind*.

> It helps to have a mental exercise to shut out intruding thoughts that have little or nothing to do with music making. Concentration is easier and confidence will be better.

Doc Severinsen took the Silva Mind Control course not to help him play the trumpet but for business reasons, but he found the techniques were also very helpful in preparing to play with more confidence. He explained:

> It's all about desire, belief, and expectancy. When you desire to have a good performance, then you visualize it and then you believe it will be. Then you go out and play—and you have a positive point of reference. This is not based on wishes or hopes, it is based on your desire to do it and picturing yourself doing it. And each time you build your belief system this way, it gets stronger and stronger. It all contributes to your confidence.

Many of the distinguished trumpet teachers and players I have talked to consistently mention the power of visualization. All you need to do is take time to close your eyes and think about the great experience that you are about to have with the other musicians.

Hear what you want to sound like before you play. See yourself playing. Feel the connection to your muscles, sense what it feels like to play. Let yourself experience the emotions inherent in the music as you scan passages you are about to play. Listen for the accompanying voices you will be playing with. I have found that while musicians may find many ways to quiet the mind and relax the body, there is simply no substitute for the final, powerful act of mental visualization.

While it is obvious that any performance can benefit from the artist's being in good physical condition and being mentally quiet and relaxed, one cannot forget to prepare the actual muscles that will be used in performance. When I arrived early for a concert with the Cincinnati Symphony, I would always hear my friend trumpeter Marie Speziale doing her warm-ups. In fact, those long tones and scale-type exercises really drove me crazy. But when I asked Marie about this she said:

> I think that a solid, focused warm-up routine contributes greatly to building performance confidence. I value the physical and mental preparation that a good musical warm-up affords me. It sets the stage, if you will, for the high level of concentration that must be engaged in while performing.

These principles of preparation that help build confidence are the same principles that assist in promoting courage, discipline, and concentration. And when you think about the chapters on fun and creativity, I hope you will find new ways to include these essential mental and physical exercises.

TYPES OF CONFIDENCE

While Doc Severinsen described how youthful innocence led him to self-doubt and a major loss of confidence, he also learned over time that true confidence is built from experience and good preparation. This kind of confidence has integrity. The trumpet is one of the loudest and most visible instruments in the orchestra, and trumpet players lead their ensembles. When they assume this musical role without the foundation of preparation, experience, and integrity, their bravura attitude can be short-lived.

Bravura!

Trumpet players seem to have a swagger to their attitude. They have bravura.

When I began to explore the ideas in this book, that was one of the first things that caught my imagination. Granted, composers often give the trumpet a heroic role to play in their music: think of Richard Strauss's tone poems *Don Juan* and *Ein Heldenleben*. Perhaps the exposed nature of the trumpet part and the heroism it often portrays work together to evoke a certain cockiness among trumpet players . . . but let's just say I have often admired their characteristic bravura and panache. Sometimes this look is a natural reflection of a player's preparation and intention, but at other times it may be a facade.

Andrew McCandless believes in what he is doing, and he always assumes that things will work for the best.

When I was a student at Eastman, David Effron was my conductor. He once stopped me in the hallway after we'd played Mahler's Fifth and said to me, "Every time I look back and you are getting ready to play, you look like you're thinking, 'You're not going to believe how good this is going to be!'" I wasn't trying to look that way, I was just excited that I was going to play. I really did feel, "You are not going to believe this!" This confidence comes from strength and preparation.

Vincent Cichowicz says that for some people the swagger effect can work just fine, even if they are not as prepared as Andrew McCandless.

There is the moment in playing where bravura can be in character, but the real challenge is in the moments before you play.

Perhaps this is where the stereotypical swagger comes in. If you are about to play, it may be better to put on a positive facade of confidence than to pace up and down predicting disaster.

Some trumpet players, like any other musicians and singers, may build a wall of bravura to protect themselves. Inside that wall, they may feel some insecurity, because they know that they will miss notes sooner or later. Tom Erdmann tells me he recognizes this bravura onstage, but that offstage the true greats know how to turn it off, and can be among the most humble and honest people in the business.

Michael Sachs, principal trumpet of the Cleveland Orchestra, cautioned me against overuse of the bravura image or sound, which at times can produce fleeting results and shallow playing.

True confidence is more about having an inner sense that you are completely prepared. It's about knowing what's coming: what you want to do and what you have to do. The brass players I respect are complete musicians and can play with bravura in the appropriate context, but can also play with the tenderness of a lyrical soprano. While bravura can be an outward mask of insecurities and self-doubt, it will not help you to be consistent.

Positive thinking is not the same as bravura. Look at your motives for playing. If you feel you are in competition with others, or trying to prove something to someone, this will swing back around and undermine you. And all that bluster will sound mechanical when it manifests as higher, faster, and louder playing, rather than playing with more color, character, and emotion.

What is important here is that bravura can often be traced back to that first type of confidence—the kind that doesn't last very long.

If you need to put on a certain bravado to mask an insecurity, or as a short-term aid to help you repress negative thoughts just before you play, then may the force be with you! Furthermore, if bravura is a natural reflection of your preparation and intention, and if these same qualities are reflected in the character of the music, you can proudly own your bravura. Finally, if you have the bravura habit but bravura doesn't fit the music, then you need to rethink your obligation to the composer, your colleagues, and your conscience.

Inspiration

The pathway to confidence can be a bumpy road. There will be times when we lose our focus. There will be times when we get shaken up and have to rebuild our confidence. The alternative of "quitting" is not an option for many musicians. For most artists, music is a way of life, not a job that we can leave to take a higher-paid position in another field. Perhaps this is because the rewards this work so richly offers include the joys of playing and hearing music, the joys of learning and growing and mastering, the joy of the journey. But as rich and rewarding as a life in music may seem, there are still times when we need further inspiration to continue our journey to artistry. The sources of inspiration are infinite: the few examples that follow may serve as a sampling of what inspires confidence in the people who play the music.

National Pride

British soloist John Wallace said that whenever he gets into trouble with self-doubt or self-esteem and needs to bolster his confidence, he draws on the memory of one specific occasion of pride in his place of origin and the people he feels privileged to play for.

John hails from bonnie Scotland, and he recalls one of the greatest performances of his career when he performed James MacMillan's *Epiclesis* Concerto at the 1993 Edinburgh Festival in Usher Hall, with the Philharmonia Orchestra conducted by Leonard Slatkin. John was truly inspired that night by his national pride in being Scottish and playing for his friends and family. He tells me that he draws strength from that experience even now: regardless of where he is performing, in his mind he is playing for the mother country.

Whenever an occasion or inspiration dominates or transports a performer in this way, the musical expression is tuned to something of far greater importance than any one individual. It is a higher purpose and a higher calling.

Playing for Your Higher Power

When I asked my former colleague Marie Speziale, who now teaches at Rice University, what inspired her confidence, she told me she was a believer.

> I had little to do with the talent that was given me—it was between Mom and Dad and God. I do the work I need to do to prepare the music. Then before each performance, I say a prayer. I put it in God's hands and hope that everything goes well. I started doing this when I was a kid. It has been a source of inner strength. My career has been blessed beyond anything I could have ever dreamed of.

Many artists, athletes, and professionals from all walks of life feel their work is really a vocation, something they are *called* to do. They may also believe that they are a channel for the grace of a higher power, and that if they do not interfere with their source of inspiration, it will pass through them. This is a humble and honest way to keep our interference at bay while surrendering to the power of the music.

Gaining Confidence from Your Colleagues

There is an expression in sports that says, *You rise to the level of your competition,* and in music we often hear people say that a great artist can *elevate the performances of those around them.* When I asked jazz trumpet legend Clark Terry what inspires his confidence, he told me it was playing with a great rhythm section. He said that when you perform with drummer Max Roach, bassist Ray Brown, and pianist Oscar Peterson there is no such thing as not feeling confident.

It isn't just what these great artists do by playing, but also the generosity and space they give to others, to allow them to express themselves.

John Miller has often experienced a similar kind of self-confidence when he plays alongside Maurice Murphy, the legendary principal trumpet in the London Symphony Orchestra. Murphy's own confidence exudes from his personality, and it seems to infect everyone in the section and sometimes the entire orchestra. John described playing with Murphy:

Maurice Murphy was everyone's inspiration. When I sat next to him, his confidence would rub off on me, and would just make me feel good. The amazing thing about this was his ease of playing: nothing ever seemed difficult. Nobody would ever dare ask him how he did it, we just let it rub off on us. Confidence spread from him by osmosis.

Having heard so many wonderful things about Maurice Murphy from many of his colleagues, I called Maurice and asked him if he would like to talk more about the topic of confidence. His response was simple and direct: "I don't have anything to say about that."

His colleagues tell me that is typical of the man and point out that in his own characteristic way, he's answered my question! You remember that saying *Analysis is paralysis?* Maurice Murphy doesn't need to analyze his confidence: he's got it!

Confidence from Mentors

Andrew McCandless learned to believe in himself because others believed in him.

His own story of generosity, humility, devotion, and faith comes from a time when he began to study the trumpet in middle school. He lived in Louisville, Kentucky, back when school busing brought suburban children to inner-city schools in an effort to achieve racial integration. Andrew attended a school with a large African-American student population.

His band teacher was an African-American named Robert Jarrett. Mr. Jarrett was a man of style in the seventies, when bell-bottoms, white shoes, and the Afro haircut were still in. He was also the sweetest man anyone had ever met. For some reason Mr. Jarrett had decided that Andrew could play the trumpet, so he started staying after school to give him trumpet lessons. When Andrew showed signs of improvement, Mr. Jarrett bought Andrew a Bach trumpet with his own money. Andrew showed even more improvement, and Mr. Jarrett didn't think he had anything more to teach him, so he started paying for Andrew to have lessons with members of the Louisville Orchestra.

Andrew said:

Whenever I begin to think, This isn't worth it, or I'm frustrated with a student or a rehearsal, I think about Mr. Jarrett. This man had such a wonderful spirit, and went so far out of his way to help me out. He believed in me, and I believe I owe it to him to keep going.

Can you recall a Mr. Jarrett in your life? Teachers, mentors, friends, or colleagues who have inspired you at a critical time in your development can remain a source of strength and encouragement throughout your life.

Integrity

All these examples of inspiration suggest that confidence has nothing to do with having a sense of one's own self-importance. In fact, it seems that when a performer can get rid of his or her own agenda, and can stop wanting to make an impression on colleagues, stop trying to play right, stop fearing that a note will crack and so forth, the sense of musicianship that remains somehow becomes more transparent to the spirit of the music.

Bravura is short-lived. It might get you through the first phrase, but if it isn't backed by preparation, knowledge, passion, focus, experience, sincerity, and technique, it lacks integrity. Integrity is the pathway to mastering lasting confidence.

nine

EGO AND HUMILITY:
FROM FAME TO ARTISTRY

(Opera, Jazz, and Theater Singers)

At first glance, ego and humility don't seem to have much in common, but finding the appropriate balance between them is a key to the behavior of divas and prima donnas. It is to singers that we shall turn for inspiration in this chapter.

DIVA! PRIMA DONNA!

I remember Kathleen Battle as a fellow graduate student at the College-Conservatory of Music in Cincinnati. She had an irresistible, utterly friendly smile. Her performances with the Cincinnati Symphony and May Choral Festivals were breathtaking. She was a star. When Kathleen came to the Metropolitan Opera in 1977, she was a happy and unaffected woman, attending rehearsals in casual Midwestern dress. And then around 1989, as Johanna Fiedler observes in her recent book, *Molto Agitato*, something seemed to change. Kathleen became less outgoing, arrived at rehearsals at the last minute, and began to isolate herself from her fellow singers in other ways. When she toured with the Metropolitan Opera, she made her own travel and hotel accommodations. She became increasingly unpopular with her fellow singers, conductors, management, and staff. She became a diva, a prima donna.

Interesting, isn't it, that those two words, "prima donna" and "diva," both started out as factual labels for leading singers on the operatic stage?

One of Kathleen's most famous confrontations came about when she and Carol Vaness were both singing in Mozart's *Marriage of Figaro* at the Met: Vaness was singing the part of the Countess, and Kathleen's role was that of Susanna, her maid. As it turned out, the management of the Met had assigned the principal soprano's dressing room, which Kathleen herself usually occupied, to Carol Vaness. Battle became incensed at this; she physically removed Vaness's belongings from the dressing room, leaving them in the hall, and took the room for herself.

Vaness avoided an immediate confrontation with Battle, but after many other incidents, she approached Kathy at the conclusion of a long Japanese tour and said that she would never sing with her again. Johanna Fiedler reports that Vaness told Kathleen, "You are the most horrible colleague I've ever encountered in my whole career!" Kathleen turned in shock and astonishment to her fellow Ohio native James Levine, under whose baton she had performed her Metropolitan debut more than a decade before, crying over and over, "What did I do? I've never done anything to her!" By this time, Kathleen had alienated almost everyone who worked with her—in orchestras, opera companies, and recitals—except for James Levine.

Kathleen was ultimately fired from the Metropolitan Opera Company in a power struggle between general manager Joseph Volpe, artistic director James Levine, and manager Ronald Wilford. Ms. Battle claims that she was never warned that she was acting unprofessionally, and that she was always striving for perfection.

Diva behavior is by no means unique to singers: there have been prima donna oboe soloists, violinists, conductors, surgeons, business executives, and athletes. I myself have worked with self-centered, perfectionist, inconsiderate, insensitive, narcissistic, self-pitying, insecure, attention-grabbing double bassists! All of the above have exhibited behavior that dominates and alienates colleagues and frustrates everyone who comes in contact with them. Marilyn Monroe was like that—but when she walked on camera, she was magical. We tolerate some people who behave this way because they consistently produce world-class work. Others we isolate. In the case of Kathleen Battle, we took away her stage.

What causes this kind of behavior? Are there reasons for it that we just do not understand? Does this behavior help such people perform, or contribute to their success in some way?

Perfectionism

Beverly Sills, legendary soprano, former artistic director of the New York City Opera, and recently retired director of the Lincoln Center for the Performing Arts, compared Kathleen's situation when singing to someone threading a tiny needle over and over again in front of thousands of people. She said, *You have to get it right every time—and if you don't you are a failure.*

The great jazz singer Kevin Mahogany believes that artists are always striving for some vision of the perfect performance, but that they will never be able to attain it—not because perfection is never there, but because they themselves will never *accept* it as being perfect.

> Even when there is no problem whatsoever, the mind of the artist will imagine something. Even when I sing every note perfectly, everything goes smoothly, and I get to sing many encores, I will still find something I don't quite like about my performance.

Kevin also believes that when you have reached the highest artistic levels, there may come a point in your career when you are less tolerant of irritants and distractions. He mentioned to me that the great jazz guitarist Pat Metheny makes the stage into his private castle before a performance. He has incense burning. He allows no one to go onstage—or backstage. Metheny has achieved a level of success that allows him to shut out the rest of the world and do exactly as he likes to create the perfect atmosphere in which to work.

Catherine Keen, the gifted mezzo-soprano with the San Francisco Opera and other great houses, believes that singers are held to the highest standards set by the current and past legends of opera history. If you are a Rossini mezzo, you will inevitably be compared to Marilyn Horne. If you are a Verdi mezzo, the comparison will be to Fiorenza Cossotto or Dolora Zajick. If you are a Wagnerian mezzo, people will wonder whether you are the next Christa Ludwig. When the young tenor Roberto Alagna was scheduled to make his Metropolitan debut, the hype was enormous: he was called "the next Pavarotti." Now the poor guy has to live up to that! What happens if he comes down with a cold and gets a horrible review in the *New York Times?*

That's the kind of pressure that opera singers are under every time they take the stage—and sometimes it can make them a little crazy.

Frederica von Stade, one of the great mezzos of our time, is simply not bothered by the eccentric behavior of great singers. She defends Maria Callas, known for her diva behavior, on the grounds that everything she did was for her art. What seemed egotistical and self-centered was her way of protecting what she believed in.

> Many of the great singers of our time are like that. Barbra Streisand and Frank Sinatra are innate perfectionists. They cannot bear the lack of perfectionism around them. It hurts them down to their soul. Kathy Battle has a terrible reputation, but if you have ever worked with her, you know she has this intense devotion to what she is doing, this real conviction—and it costs her so much psychic energy! But once you have been around someone like Kathy who really expects so much of herself, you can understand these things, and they no longer seem so offensive.

Flicka (it's the name Frederica prefers) loved working with Kathleen Battle, and compared it to playing tennis against a better player.

> The great players pull you up to their level.
> When you are around Kathy, you really zero in on everything be-

cause she is very zeroed in. She wants to look good—and if you are around her, you are going to be sure you look good too. Musicians with that kind of perfectionism pull everybody into their own energy: it is wonderful. I'm enormously grateful to people like that, who demand a certain amount of concentration that brings everybody up to their own level.

Perhaps there's method in the diva's madness!

The Voice: Most Difficult of Instruments?

The voice is a peculiarly troublesome instrument. It's stressful enough working for that perfect performance with any instrument, but the more I have learned about the singer's world, the clearer it has become to me that singers experience a whole *world* of vulnerability that pianists, percussionists, and other instrumentalists simply never have to face.

The problems arise because the singer's instrument is within the singer's own body.

Think about that for a minute. Singers cannot see their instruments. Indeed, since the sound of their voice is transmitted to them through their facial bones, they cannot hear their own voice "from the outside" in the way their audience does. And because every individual body structure is so different, different people have different vocal-cord lengths and facial structures: some have bigger noses, or receding jaws. The voice can get too dry, or too tired, or just plain sick.

Anyone who wants to take up the violin plays basically the same size of instrument, and that instrument will likely respond consistently to the same stimulus or manner of playing. When you play the violin, you can cry and play at the same time without too much problem. But if you are singing, you can't be crying at the same time, because every emotion you feel affects your vocal instrument: it is in a constant state of change. If you get a cold before a concert, your career could be in jeopardy. Do violinists ever worry about their *violins* catching a cold?

Flicka emphasized this vulnerability:

When an athlete pulls a muscle, it's nothing to be ashamed of, but singers can feel a lot of shame if they have a cold or may not be able to perform. Singers have to fly all over the world, which tends to dry out the voice. I may have to cross the country six times in a month, and perform the next day, and sometimes I don't have my instrument at my disposal. There is a lot to worry about.

And besides the voice as a physical instrument, there is also the fragile psyche of the singer to consider. Flicka points out that you cannot *separate* your voice from your body or soul, because it is directly subject to everything you are thinking and feeling.

It's a tremendously exposed position. Going out there in front of three or four thousand people every night, hoping and praying for their approval, knowing there are many factors from the tempo or style of the music to the balance with the orchestra which you simply cannot control—it's not surprising if singers feel fragile and vulnerable. And despite that vulnerability, we singers are the only musicians who turn and face directly towards the public, with no instruments in front of us.

It is a challenge to master *any* instrument, but the challenge involved in mastering the voice is even greater, because the voice itself is so dependent on the changing body. Tenors cannot guarantee that those notes will be there all the time. You can find and play the perfect flute, but you can't just pick the perfect voice up out of your voice case! This is what is so thrilling about the singer's life—but it is also what makes the singer's task so difficult.

Perhaps there's a relationship between the eccentric and sometimes intolerant behavior of the divas and their need to achieve perfection on a fundamentally unreliable instrument. They feel under constant pressure to perform a high-wire act in full view of a critical audience with no safety net. Their instrument may not be in working order. They only get one chance, and nobody cares in the least about their excuses should they fail. Catherine Keen told me:

When I'm doing a big part, I have to cocoon myself and take care of myself. I have to save my voice. I even leave my husband at home during the rehearsals until the show opens. I have to be able to put up the goods: everything rides on how healthy I am. It's a difficult lifestyle. And I am only as good as my last performance.

Perhaps this is part of the reason that Kathleen Battle chose not to be with other singers during the Metropolitan Opera tours. Anyone feel like socializing? How about going out with the gang for a meal and a movie? I believe that the daunting array of problems the great singers face each and every night would stretch the personal boundaries of *any* fragile human being. It is only natural that they might want to focus in on their art and be alone.

Good Reasons for Diva Behaviors?

I spoke with Nnenna Freelon, the celebrated soul/pop singer and Grammy nominee, the day after her Kennedy Center solo concert with the vocal jazz ensemble Take 6. Nnenna was trained as a social worker, and it was only after marriage and a family that she decided to pursue a singing career. Our talk turned to pop stars and the sometimes outrageous-seeming demands they make on concert management. What, I asked, is the reasoning behind requests for (and, indeed, contract riders demanding) special foods, humidifiers, flowers, bottled water, smoking restrictions, and even black towels? Nnenna didn't persuade me that the demands stars make are always on the level, but she did help me to see that many relate in straightforward ways to the ongoing attempt to protect the human voice.

A lot of this is common sense, really. If you want a smooth performance with no problems, you'll need to make sure your musicians have enough time when they arrive in a new city before they have to perform. They, after all, are the ones who will please or displease your audience. In practice, this may mean you need to bring them in a day earlier: I know this is more expensive, but it is very important for a singer to be rested in soul and spirit.

Then you must feed us: full musicians make a happy band. But I have to warn you, food can be a problem. I personally cannot eat before I sing. That's not just some whim of mine, it has to do with the way I prepare myself for a concert. I like to eat after I sing—but when on tour, a lot of people don't quite understand this, but there are often no eating options after the show.

It's also important for me to have access to bottled water that is at room temperature. Does that make me sound like a prima donna? Cool water hurts my teeth and chills my throat, so I can't sing with that. Pure water that's at room temperature is a necessity, not a luxury.

You might think the food and drink issues were okay, but wonder about the flowers. Flowers make me happy. I don't need roses, they could just as well be dandelions. But the colors, the scents, the wild shapes of flowers are all beautiful. A single flower can remind me that when I walk out onstage, I aim to open up like a flower and release my gift into the air. . . .

And lastly, no cigarette smoking please. This is not some strange request that only a diva would make: my throat is my instrument.

The more I spoke with singers, the more I came to understand that some of their quirkier requests and stranger behaviors do have their own rhymes and reasons. I don't think it's so unreasonable, for instance, for performers to come onstage feeling comfortable about where they are and the way they've been treated. Going onstage demands a peculiar personal transformation for the artist, a transformation that in some cases involves assuming a role that's quite different in personality or character from their usual "offstage" personality. Some people can make this transformation with ease, for others it's a source of great difficulty. But it is a *necessary* transition. And while the support systems that facilitate this transformation may seem eccentric or over the top to some of us, they may in fact be essential to the success of the performer's presentation.

Reviews

When Johanna Fiedler explored Kathleen Battle's transformation from a down-to-earth, blue-jeans-clad brilliant young singer with a bubbly personality to the quintessential unapproachable diva, she found it coincided with the time when Battle's reviews went from enthusiastic to worshipful:

> Even the pictures on her record album covers were perfect enough to run in *Vogue*, and one critic called her Sophie in *Der Rosenkavalier* the finest portrayal of the role in the opera's history.

What happens when a singer (or anyone else) reads a worshipful review? Kevin Mahogany addressed this point. He told me:

> As soon as you start believing in your own press, you have a problem. If people tell you how good you are and how great you sound and look, then what incentive do you have to continue? Part of any artist's incentive is to develop, to improve, and to learn. Joe Williams told me just before he passed on, "Yeah, I'm still learning now." But it is our goal to learn something, to improve every time. Don't let the Grammys and other awards go to your head: they are only an affirmation of something you did well.

Take encouragement from your past successes, and keep on learning. When a critic says, "You've arrived, you're the best," it's high time to begin asking, "How can I build on my present success and make it better?"

Leaving the world of your normal personality and entering into a stage persona may require some unusual accommodations, as we've seen, but leaving a stage persona behind and returning to normal can also be a problem. Handling the adulation of fans, the ego boost that comes with wonderful reviews, and the fame of stardom can make it hard for the artist to know who he or she really is in "real life." What does all this acknowledgment represent? Who is the real you?

There are artists who are impossible to work with because of the unreasonable demands they make on conductors and colleagues, but when they step offstage, they are the nicest people in the world. Unfortunately, we see all the other combinations as well, great onstage, terrible offstage; bad onstage and bad offstage—and there are even singers who are great onstage and off!

HUMILITY OR EGO?

Humility can be both a curse and a blessing, and the same can be said for ego, too. Flexibility or firmness, gentle concern or ruthless determination, collaboration or competition: which is more important, which will contribute most to our music making? Do we even have a choice?

There is a time for every purpose under heaven, the Bible says, a time to be born, and a time to die; a time to plant, and a time to harvest: perhaps, too, there is a time for aggressive attack and a time for gracious withdrawal. There are certainly times when it is important to acknowledge others and work together with others to build that elusive quality called community. The entire musical enterprise would fall apart if the singers in a quartet tried to outpace each other like racecar drivers in the final laps of the Indy 500. And yet there are also moments when it's important to stand up for who you are and what you have to say.

Egotistical behavior can alienate, antagonize, and polarize those around you, isolate you, and even help you to lose your job; and yet every artist I have interviewed feels that a healthy ego is essential to artistry. The question remains: how do we strike a healthy balance between humility and ego?

The Roots of Humility

Most artists I have interviewed learned the value of humility at home or from their participation in a spiritual community.

Cleo Laine, the great English singer, told me that humility is something best instilled in you by your parents. At the opposite end of the spectrum, we have all heard stories of aggressive and intolerant parents pushing those values on students of music, ballet, sports, or academics. It works both ways; it just depends on how you are raised:

You shouldn't go onstage and say, "Here I am, you have to embrace me as a great goddess." I don't agree with that. My father, who was black, was the one who made me aware that all people are equal, that they should be revered by other people and not downtrodden. The music you make is something that you have worked hard at, no doubt, but it is also something that is God-given. I'm fortunate to be blessed with the ability to make music. But the fact that I can do this well doesn't make me any better than someone else, who perhaps cannot sing as well as I.

Nnenna Freelon, whose family is African-American from the South, is another who feels she doesn't own her gift:

As my gift for music and singing emerged, my grandmother and parents impressed on me that my talent did not belong to me. When I sang in church and people praised me for my voice early on, whatever praise I received was always tempered with the sense that the gift came from a spiritual space and was passing through me, that it wasn't something I owned and could do with as I chose. When I sang at weddings, or for spiritual renewal for a sick person or shut-in, there was never any financial compensation: my talent came with a sense of service, it was community property if you like. Everyone offered whatever they had to the community, and this was my gift. This was a part of our culture, and I think this is a great part of who I am.

I remember one display of humility from a great artist as if it were yesterday, even though it happened more than thirty years ago. I had just played a concert performance of Handel's *Julius Caesar* at the Cincinnati Choral May Festival. Beverly Sills had sung the role of Cleopatra, in a performance that was filled with artistry, grace, and virtuosity. I felt compelled to acknowledge such an obviously brilliant performance, and when

I finally met Ms. Sills backstage, I blurted out something like "I play bass in the orchestra and I'm sure you must have heard this so many times— but I have to tell you that your singing was one of the greatest things I have ever heard in my life!"

Ms. Sills acknowledged this comment as though it were the first time she had ever heard such praise. She thanked me for coming backstage and heaped praise on the Cincinnati Symphony for their performance. I left shaking my head at this remarkable display of humility.

Sills has raised more than $70 million for the March of Dimes and has been honored with the Presidential Medal of Freedom; she is not one to rest on her accomplishments. Reflecting recently on her long and illustrious career, she told the *San Francisco Chronicle*'s Octavio Roca:

> The funny thing is that I have great memories, but I don't stay home
> and play my old records, I never have the time. The day after I retired,
> I was in my office running New York City Opera.

When I decided to use interviews with singers to write this chapter on humility and ego, several friends told me that finding a singer with humility might be like finding a needle in a haystack. My encounters with Beverly Sills, Nnenna Freelon, and Cleo Laine showed me this is far from the case.

Balancing Humility with Healthy Ego

There is no room in this business for humility, a colleague of the British opera singer Sir Thomas Allen's at Covent Garden once told him. Allen said that what a singer is called upon to do is quite extraordinary. You simply cannot stand up in front of thousands of people and sing without a healthy ego. And it may well be the healthiness of your ego that determines how far you go in this field.

> The way that I see it, I am the servant of the music, and the work of
> art is always greater than the artist. You might find it difficult to believe
> at times, and there are some artists who believe that the masterpiece is

there to serve the artist, but that is not the case. On the other hand, in order to survive and do the job we do, and as the chemistry comes into play, the temperament of the artist requires tremendous confidence, self-belief, and sheer ego.

Playing with the Sun Valley Idaho Summer Symphony gave me the chance to meet Lara Nie, a gifted singer of chamber music, opera, and concert works. When she sings onstage, she calls on the pride and presence she needs, while offstage she mingles with colleagues and tends to her newborn baby in a manner that's not at all standoffish and proud. She was the first singer to clue me in to the fact that a healthy ego can really be an essential part of anyone's career. She told me her humility has helped her work with colleagues but it hasn't helped her *get* work. She feels it is really important to be aggressive when you are starting out in your career because of the extreme competition.

There are very few singers I know who can be humble, soft-spoken, and stay on top of their careers. Dawn Upshaw is my favorite exception. She is such a wonderful person.

People like Dawn Upshaw have earned their highly regarded status and don't need to act aggressively to get their roles. But they still have to deliver the goods every time they go onstage. Lara told me she knows some singers in New York with great voices who are very aggressive about getting roles. She envies them for their offstage ego. They will do anything to get a part, sacrifice anything in their lives, demonstrating strength, aggression, and great self-confidence. In this highly competitive field when you don't have an international reputation, this is a common behavior. And it works for a lot of singers.

Cleo Laine believes that all artists have a certain amount of arrogance or ego, especially the ones that are at the "top of their tree," because they wouldn't have gotten there without it.

They work in an atmosphere where there are so many people who would put them down if they possibly could, so they have defended themselves.

Mark Hardy, the Broadway veteran of roles in *Les Misérables, Titanic*, and *Sunset Boulevard*, who also teaches acting and musical theater at the college level, says that some casting directors, producers, and conductors seem to be attracted by artists who are known to be "a little difficult." He believes it gives them the feeling they are dealing with a real star, and that some artists cultivate "difficult" personalities for just this reason. It is all part of creating that distinctive aura.

Kevin Mahogany suggested that the more you're in control of what you're doing, the less ego you need. Some of the greatest artists, he said, simply don't need to put on airs.

> Joe Williams doesn't need an ego because five thousand people turn out to see him. It is the lesser-known artists who need this kind of thing.

Kevin wants to appear larger than life when he's onstage. That's him, he loves being the center of attention. But when he is not onstage he tends to be shy. He hinted to me that sometimes what you do onstage is what you would *like* to do in life. In music, it can help you to bring out sides of yourself that you might not otherwise express. But you wouldn't want to be *on* the entire time.

Ego as Protection

Shirley Verrett told me about a time when she had to protect her voice, her time, and her self-respect. The Metropolitan opera was staging Berlioz's opera *Les Troyens*, and she had been asked to sing the role of Cassandra. She also loved the part of Dido, but that had been given to her wonderful colleague Christa Ludwig. When Christa came down with a cold, however, Shirley was asked to learn Dido and sing it for the dress rehearsal: this would help Christa save her energy, and give her more time to recover. Shirley turned the offer down cold. She explained:

> They wanted me to sing Dido for the dress rehearsal, but Christa was to sing it for all the performances. I asked myself, Why learn a role

that you are never going to sing? This is where the ego comes in. If I take time to learn this part and sing the dress rehearsal, and then two days later it's opening night and Christa sings it, that's not fair—and I said so. And so Rafael Kubelik gave me the role of Dido for opening night.

The story goes that I took the part away from Christa, but it wasn't something that I had asked for: it was just the only fair thing to do, to handle the situation. But I agree that from the outside it may have not looked that way.

This story tells us that there can be good reasons behind actions that appear on the surface to be sheer self-indulgence. In this case, it was a matter of negotiation: Verrett was willing to help the Met out, but not unless it would justify the time she would spend learning the new role, especially since she was already singing the role of Cassandra in that production. She was taking on a lot of responsibility and putting her own voice at risk to learn this new role.

Being Proud of Your Ego

Catherine Keen believes that a healthy ego is no more and no less than a sense of confidence. She recalls the time when she first had the opportunity to sing at the Kennedy Center with Plácido Domingo:

This was my first *Parsifal*, singing the role of Kundry. Here I was, onstage with Plácido Domingo, giggling to myself in sheer disbelief that I was sharing the stage with this guy—but I felt, you know, I belong here. It isn't a matter of I'm better or worse, it's that I'm comfortable with myself. I did the work and I deserve to enjoy it. I am enjoying it. And that is what having a positive sense of ego means to me.

After my performance with Domingo, I took some criticism for seeming "very grand"—all because I was assured of myself. I didn't walk around with my tail between my legs, I just learned that I can put up the goods.

When you have earned your place, there comes a point where you have to own your talent and hard work. This is not a time for doubt, anxiety, or concern about the opinions that others have of you. It is a time for action. It is a time to believe in who you are and what you have to say, and to be proud of it. It is a time for healthy ego, for a healthy sense of self-respect.

FAME VS. ARTISTRY

We have been exploring both good and less good ego. When the ego is unhealthy, it is destructive to others; it leads the performer down a road of self-obsession and into the Outer Game of fame in a way that takes essential concentration away from the making of great music. There are times when a healthy ego can be very effective.

The Effective Ego

Effective ego has to do with confidence, with preparation, with entitlement or ownership. It has integrity of purpose, and that purpose is all about artistry and music making. The effective ego can include standing up for yourself when you deserve to have your chance, and it can include insisting on all the things that will allow you to focus on your work. It is all about art.

Mark Hardy told me about seeing Polly Bergen sing in public for the first time in about twenty-five years. Polly had fabulous success in the sixties with her hit recordings of the Julie Styne songs "The Party's Over" and "Make Someone Happy," but then she left the stage: now, with enormous courage, she wanted to sing again. Watching her sing "The Party's Over" after all those years was like a master class, Mark told me:

What we saw was someone truly pouring her life experience into her art, distilling the essence of a song and putting it across very simply and very truthfully. This wasn't about Ms. Bergen acting as a prima donna—yet it was a diva moment. It was beautiful to watch. Here is this fully mature woman with all kinds of credits to her name, Broadway, major motion pictures, TV, who has been out of the public eye and is making a comeback. It wasn't about her hunger for fame; it was because she missed the work.

All the current pop stars are hungry for this kind of diva moment, but perhaps some of them have forgotten that they have to have something going for them in order to reach it. Barbra Streisand, Bette Midler, Shirley Verrett, and Jessye Norman have that special something going for them. But people who are hungry for stardom often study the effect but miss what causes it. They study all the tricks and techniques, but their work lacks substance. And ultimately their performances ring hollow.

Nnenna Freelon performs for school-age children in the Boston community. The kids are in awe of her fame and success, and many of them envy Nnenna for having made it in the land of neon lights. It was inspiring to hear Nnenna processing this youthful desire for riding in a limousine, wearing designer clothing, and receiving the adulation of total strangers. She said she rarely hears children say "I really want to feel good about who I am through my art, and this is going to make me feel I'm a success"—so she begins to compare the world of artistry to the world of fame. She asks them whether they've ever ridden in a limo, and comments that limos are actually long and low to the ground, and it can be a little hard getting in and out of them:

I ask them, "What is it that's neat about a limo? Do you think it would be exciting getting in a limo if there was no one else around to see you?" Maybe what's neat about getting into a limo is the idea that other people will think of us as special. "Okay," I say, "but tell me this: is it better to have someone think of us as special, or to truly be special?" And as we keep unraveling this ball of yarn, we get to something very interesting, we get to self-esteem.

No matter what the kids say, what they really mean is that they want to feel good about themselves.

It's easy to be confused in this consumer-driven culture that's constantly emphasizing the right jeans, the whitest teeth, the special perfume, or the perfect hairstyle. It's easy to think that fame is going to bring you these good feelings. I try to communicate to my kids that it is my art that has given me these feelings. I love connecting with other people in a unique, spontaneous, and exciting way with my music. It is making that connection that makes me bigger, stronger. The other things, the compensation, the applause, the limousine, the good reviews, are great—but they are not the biggest part of it. I do my best to tell them, but maybe you have to go through this to believe it.

What is your goal? Are you striving for fame, or are you striving for excellence? Is there enough satisfaction in your art, your progress, your music making, to sustain the long hours of dedication that are necessary for a stage career? Or are you pursuing an unrealistic dream?

It is particularly important for young artists to think about these things (and for coaches and role models to talk about them) because music is such a competitive field, and only a few of them will "make it." It is important to let them glimpse the value of the craft of music itself, which is something that can continue to enrich their lives whether they become professionals in the world of music or not.

The pursuit of artistry, and the experience of musical communication with others—these are experiences which are available to anyone willing to invest time and effort and patience into developing these skills.

Competition

We have talked about competition elsewhere in this book, and you know that I think competition can be excellent when it inspires us to access the best we have to give. But it also has its downside.

What is it that drives you as an artist to dig deep into your soul to come up with your best? Is it the wish to match and outdo your own personal best performance? Or is it the shadow of someone else, waiting for you to falter? Is someone else about to take away what you hold dearest—the role, the part, the chair, the position, the award, the fame and attention?

When you use ego to compete against another person rather than striving within yourself, the game changes from an Inner Game of artistry to an Outer Game of "beat the competition"—and that's not a game you can ever really win, because it zaps your energy, it takes your attention away from the music. That's the premise of the Inner Game, and it is something that has been known for thousands of years. Competition can work when it sets a standard for your own work. It works when it inspires you to dig down and work harder. It works when it tells you that you can get more out of yourself. But it isn't about other people. It isn't about them. It's about you.

This brings us to the main point of this chapter: it all comes back to the issue of what is the motivation of the artist? Is it external or is it internal?

It doesn't matter whether you are playing the bassoon in the community band or vying to be the world's greatest tenor: you can only be as good as you can be. Let's accept that. Okay, then what is the most direct path to your own optimal level? Do you assassinate everyone who is competing with you for your coveted chair? What really gives you satisfaction? Is it all in the result? What's the difference between mastering something with integrity and perfection, and getting a favorable press review or limousine ride?

My guess is that when you sort all your different feelings out, it is the music making that will be most satisfying every time.

From Competition to Partnership to Artistry

Many of you may recall a time when two of the world's greatest tenors were bitter rivals: Plácido Domingo and Luciano Pavarotti. They both made their Metropolitan debuts in 1968, only weeks apart. Domingo, living in the New York area, was known for his great work ethic, intellect, and supreme musicianship. He was soft-spoken, and very well liked by his colleagues. Pavarotti was more celebrated than Domingo, and lived in Italy. Less formally schooled in music, he was a very expressive artist with flawless diction and pitch and an exquisite voice. He was known for his irritable, sometimes temperamental behavior and frequent canceled performances. Pavarotti loved attention. Johanna Fiedler wrote of him:

> He saw nothing wrong with feature articles about his struggles with his weight. He loved serving as grand marshal of New York City's Columbus Day Parade, riding in front on a tall chestnut horse: he kissed and hugged every pretty woman in sight; he attended opening-night parties wearing his costume from the performance instead of a tuxedo. In short, he was great copy and the media gobbled him up.

The pursuit was not of excellence: they both had that in plenty. These two great artists battled with agents over billing, engagements, titles, and headlines. Here were two of the world's greatest singers jockeying for the title of "the world's greatest tenor."

At one point Pavarotti engaged Herbert Breslin, the same manager who represented Domingo. When it appeared that Breslin might be playing favorites to Pavarotti, Domingo hired his current press agent, Edgar Vincent, and the two plotted a different strategy. Domingo was known for his superior musicianship and was an accomplished pianist; he took up conducting. He also had the courage to expand the kinds of roles he sang and began exploring the challenges of Wagnerian opera. He had no need to take on new roles, but he still had a desire to grow as an artist—the ultimate goal of this book!

While every great artist is unique, it may be that what allowed these two rival artists to make room for each other under the same sun had something to do with Domingo's personal pursuit of his multiple talents. Then, when the devastating earthquake hit Mexico City in 1985, Domingo suffered terribly: he lost his aunt and uncle and two cousins, and his own parents died shortly after. Perhaps this meant that he had more important things to care about than the headlines garnered by that other tenor. In any case, the competition between the two men finally abated.

In 1972, José Carreras made his debut with the New York City Opera.

Carreras was another fabulously gifted singer, and one who was untouched and unscathed by the competitive threats of the famous Pavarotti/Domingo rivalry. He was humble and respectful of others, and had a great sense of humor about himself. He was also secure in his career and didn't seem to seek publicity or interviews. Tragically, he developed acute lymphocytic leukemia and had to undergo extensive cancer treatment, including a bone-marrow transplant. He made a miraculous comeback to singing after a successful battle with cancer—embodied in a 1989 Barcelona concert for an audience of 150,000.

As Johanna Fiedler tells the tale:

> Both Pavarotti and Domingo had been deeply affected by Carreras's illness, and when Carreras presented the idea of the three of them giving a benefit concert for his Leukemia Foundation at the Italian World Cup, they both agreed.

The rest is history. The *Three Tenors* became the largest commercial and artistic success in the history of classical music.

It seems that Domingo's personal pursuit of artistry with his new manager, Edgar Vincent, his experience of the loss of loved ones in the Mexico earthquake, and his compassion for Carreras's courageous struggle with cancer all conspired and inspired him to join forces with the other two tenors for a higher cause. And with the *Three Tenors*, they have made a contribution to the world of music beyond what any one could have achieved alone.

The circle is complete. It is undoubtedly possible to have both artistry and fame: but the question is, *Which comes first?* What is your motivation? The same rules for getting fulfillment in life that apply to the superstars also apply to aspiring young musicians. It is easy to let your ego run away with fame, jealousy, or material success. And there is nothing wrong with success; it has its benefits. But here's the point: it can never overshadow true artistry. There comes a point where greater fame means nothing, where the only challenge remaining is the challenge to grow and learn something new. And herein lies the ego's true motivation: the pursuit of excellence.

ten

CREATIVITY: THE JOURNEY INTO THE SOUL

(Composers and Improvising Musicians)

What Is Creativity?

Creativity is elusive. It is hard enough to describe, and difficult if not impossible to command. And yet when people tap into it, their thoughts take on a universality that can touch all of our lives. Each one of us possesses creativity. Once we acknowledge its existence, it can reveal itself to us in the most wonderful ways. And perhaps paradoxically, the more relaxed we are, the more readily creativity will flow through us.

It may help if I describe what creativity means to me and how I experience it myself. I have been accused of "thinking differently," for instance, when I plan a bass concert or decide to write a new book. I don't consider myself a particularly creative person, but I know that when I do get an idea, I like to ask the next question, which may lead me down a new path. My curiosity fuels my interest, and when I'm patient and in a very open place, my questions are sometimes answered from within.

To me, this business of looking and listening inside is the key to an exploration of one's own creativity. When we learn where to listen for the answers, we may hear the answers more often. Once we understand the nature of questions being asked and questions being answered, we can put ourselves in situations where our creativity is stimulated, we can put ourselves in places where we can use these tools in our music and in our lives, and we can travel that path deep into the soul.

John Dankworth, the great English jazz saxophonist, told me that creative improvisation is like telling a joke. At the beginning, nobody can think of anything much to say, but if someone kicks things off with a joke and then someone else tells one, within a short time there will be a chain reaction, and jokes will start pouring out. Creativity breeds creativity just as humor breeds humor. Dankworth goes on to say:

> You can pick up cues from the other members of the band. The drummer, the bass, or the guitar can trigger an idea with a filler or a lick. When you are doing your solo, you are mostly concerned with what you are doing yourself, but if things get a little humdrum and you hear something quirky, it can spur you on to new ideas.

Libby Larsen, a wonderfully expressive American composer, thinks of creativity as a living voice within us. She believes that this voice speaks to us all the time, but we have to make ourselves available to hear it: we always have to be in a state of readiness. She told me she is never without ideas, and that she has learned to recognize the moment of inspiration, when an idea articulates itself very clearly. That's the moment when she goes to work on it creatively.

> I do everything I can to feed this moment of inspiration, but I never know where or when I will find it.

Libby tells me that when she feeds her inspiration, she may take a walk outside, go to a museum, or just listen to herself.

> It's a special moment, and you have to be courageous and go with it. You can't stop and analyze things when the moment comes, you need to be ready to discard whatever you are working on, and the decision time may be no more than a millisecond. Most people decide not to go with it.

Not only do people often cut off their own creative inspirations, sometimes we are actually taught by our teachers or others *not* to tap our creative potential. Sir Peter Maxwell Davies, one of the United Kingdom's most distinguished composers, used to work with young children, and he told me:

> It is so easy to eliminate creativity from people's lives. You are told that you have to play this and that, and you aren't allowed to write consecutive fifths (principles that were used in Bach's time), and all that nonsense. For a lot of people, creativity just doesn't exist.
>
> One has to be open to the creative process and not be regimented. I found that most children can compose and improvise perfectly well. You have to give them the tools whereby they can liberate what they have, rather than inhibit it. The impact of liberation is that the kid's whole life becomes more meaningful. There is no doubt about it. If they do well with their creativity, all of a sudden all of their other school subjects suddenly become much better.

New York Philharmonic bassist/composer Jon Deak, whose music I have admired and performed for more than thirty years, has been working recently with school-age children in New York, Denver, Chicago, and Vermont, helping them to translate their ideas into music. Fourteen of his students from ages eight to eleven have heard their works played by the New York Philharmonic.

If the barriers to creativity can be minimized for these children to the point where they can compose music as easily as they paint pictures, it may be time to examine more closely some of the structures that have limited or discouraged the creative process in adults. The creative process can be made more accessible to everyone, not just children. Unlocking the barriers to creativity not only allows our dreams to be fulfilled but also builds self-esteem and confidence in people of all ages.

Whether you are composing, improvising, planning a program, rehearsing, playing with a computer, engaging in sports or business, your life will be enriched by learning how to nurture your creative side.

The Importance of Structure

It's a truism that creative ideas can "emerge" quite spontaneously, but it can take a great deal of work to bring them to life. Once our ideas become conscious, we must also find a form or structure that allows us to translate them into some kind of music. If you are improvising, you don't have much time to think: your playing channels the idea into melodies, grooves, and licks. If you're composing, then you will bring structural considerations to bear on melodic and harmonic ideas.

Stravinsky once said that if you commissioned him to write a piece of any length in any style he preferred for any instrumentation he might choose, he wouldn't know where to begin. But give him the commission and then ask him to write a three-minute piece for percussion, tuba, and three trombones to accompany four male dancers performing a ritual around a fire—and he will have a piece for you in no time!

I spoke with the great improvising pianist Fred Hersch about the importance of structure in music, and he used the analogy of a glass fish bowl to explain his view:

> Let's say you're playing some jazz: in one chorus, you can fill the bowl with M&Ms, in the next you can use it as a goldfish bowl, in the third you can use it to mix cookie dough, and in a fourth chorus you can use it to keep your loose change. The point I'm making is that you keep putting different things in it, but the structure stays the same. And if you're a gifted improviser, you can even improvise the form a bit.

Then Fred let slip what I believe is one of the great artistic secrets of all time:

> There's a freedom that comes from having constraints.

Wasn't that what Stravinsky was hinting at, too, with his story about percussion, tuba, and three trombones?

Allowing Creativity to Flow

Once we have tapped into our creative current and found a structure to work with, we need to iron out the details. This can be the point where frustration or anxiety come in. Self I may want to take over our attention and mess things up. The mind wants to analyze, paralyze, remind you of success, predict failure, and in general throw doubt on your insights and intuitive direction. Christian McBride is one of the world's most sensational jazz bassists, and also writes a lot of his own music. He told me about the extraordinary fluency of ideas he had back when he was in the eleventh grade:

> The ideas were just flowing. In retrospect, I think back to why that was. At the time, I didn't have any ideas of how music was supposed to sound. I just wrote, I had an open mind. I didn't think, This sounds too much like Wayne Shorter or Chick Corea. I just let it happen, and it felt natural and magical.
>
> I don't think I have ever been able to write music with that ease. Now when I write music, it is difficult for me to just let it flow.

Christian's experience supports the importance of creating for the sake of creating, while avoiding critical judgments from Self I. Bringing in too many outside ideas about what to do can block your internal inspiration.

The Soul in Creativity

We each have our own unique DNA, fingerprints, voice pattern, and so forth, and our minds are every bit as diverse as our physical characteristics. Our creative ideas emerge from the cauldron of our imagination, memories of past experiences, contacts with other individuals and their creative works, cultural upbringing and education, interests and intuitive feelings.

David Balakrishnan is the founder, violinist, and celebrated composer for the Turtle Island String Quartet, whose music is a fusion of jazz and many ethnic styles. David's father is Indian and his mother American. Not surprisingly, perhaps, his own music is influenced by his exposure to his father's Indian culture while growing up to the sounds of both classical and rock music in the sixties. He told me that his love of music comes from many inspirations:

> The elements that go into my own creative thinking come from my love of various styles of music, and my interest in finding out where they meet. I feel the same passionate love listening to Mozart as I do an Indian raga, so I figure there must be something that is the same in the music as well. My teacher Allaudin Mathieu in Sonoma County helped me to combine the styles that I love, so my music wouldn't sound like Indian music or jazz as such, it would just sound like beautiful music.

Turtle Island's music brings creative and refreshing elements to the string quartet, but that freshness stems from a foundation of playing established styles. David says he wants the audience to feel the same joy and beauty that he felt when he wrote a piece.

> If we are looking for something new, it is to reexperience that timeless moment of connection. It doesn't have to be a new sound that no one has ever heard before. Where is the soul in that? The soul has always been there, it cannot be new.

When Fred Hersch was only seventeen, he learned an important lesson from Cincinnati jazz musician Jimmy McGary. Fred had joined the local jazz legend in a "sit-in," and after they played "Autumn Leaves," McGary told Fred that he was being too ambitious. Jimmy took him backstage and put on a record of tenor saxophonist Paul Gonsalves playing twenty-seven choruses of the blues on the album *Ellington at Newport* with the Duke Ellington Orchestra.

The next day, Fred went to a used-record store and bought every album he could find that had "Autumn Leaves" on it. There were at least a dozen, including versions by Oscar Peterson, Sarah Vaughan, Miles Davis, Bill Evans, and Chet Baker.

I bought them all, and listened to every track. They were all great. There was no definitive version. Each person was basically giving the listener his or her point of view on this particular tune. The idea was to be personal. If I was going to play this song, I had to find my own way of playing it. Being personal—bringing my own voice and sensibilities into everything I do—has become the foundation of my playing.

Creativity is a matter of translating messages of passion, excitement, and soul into our own musical language through structure, harmony, rhythm, and style. We ourselves are made up of everything to which we have ever been exposed. Even the study of one style of music may involve a blend of many cultures, and the broader our exposure and the more sensitive our inner listening, the richer our unique voice will be.

The Roots of Creativity

Most people don't enjoy eating the same food, viewing the same movie, or wearing the same clothes every day. Creativity seems to be inspired by a human desire for variety, uniqueness, and personal expression. While the creative process is always going on within the souls of everyone, sometimes we need a specific inspiration to bring these impulses to an artistic form.

Over the centuries, many great masterworks have been inspired by the loss of loved ones or the contemplation of human mortality. The creative process is often activated by the circumstances of loss, grief, or death. When I joined the Cincinnati Symphony in 1967, the guest artist for our first pops concert was Dave Brubeck, and we performed the world premiere of his oratorio for vocal soloists, chorus orchestra, and jazz improvisations, *The Light in the Wilderness*.

Dave told me how he got into writing sacred works in his unique jazz and classical style. His first sacred piece was dedicated to his brother Howard and called *Let Not Your Heart Be Troubled—Ye Believe in God*, which was later incorporated into *The Light in the Wilderness*.

Howard's sixteen-year-old son had just died, and he wrote it to comfort him. When Ernie Farmer at Shawnee Press saw that first piece he said, "Dave, you have some talent in this choral field—why don't you write an oratorio?" A little later Erich Kunzel came to Brubeck's house to talk over his first pops concert, and asked him about this new oratorio Dave was working on. Erich said, "When you finish, I'd like to do it with the Cincinnati Symphony."

When I asked Dave what inspired his unique approach to jazz rhythms he told me a fascinating story about his childhood. He was raised on a 45,000-acre cattle ranch, twenty-five miles across. Every day, his father would send him to pump water for the cattle, and the engine that was used to pump the water had a tremendous clanking sound that created rhythms that were never the same. Dave would have to stay there for hours in the hot summer heat to make sure the engine didn't fail.

> There was nobody to talk to, nobody to see, nothing to do, except wait for hours for that engine to fill the tank. I would lie down on the wood planks supporting the tank and just feel that whole vibration in my body, and then I'd put other rhythms against it. All you have with you is your mind. There is nobody you could even see in the distance. Then again I would put rhythms against the walking or trotting gait of my horse as I rode out to the pump. This is how I would occupy my time. Even walking down the street, I would put 5/4 or 3/4 rhythm against my walking. My tune "The Duke" was inspired by the rhythm of the windshield wipers on my car.

Ralph Towner, composer, guitarist, and pianist with the world music group Oregon, said that his musical ideas come from the entire range of his emotional experiences. Having fully valued those sometimes difficult or stressful life experiences himself, he captures the intensity of these times in his music.

> I like things that are a little enigmatic, subjects that have conflicting emotions like happy/sad, bitter/sweet—these things are like life itself.

I remember snow blowing through the windows in Vienna when I was twenty-four years old and studying classical guitar eighteen hours a day. I ate rice and tea for a year while I was practicing. Art is boundlessly fascinating.

Composer and bassist Frank Proto was one of my closest colleagues in the Cincinnati Symphony. Frank's music is a blend of classical, twelve-tone, and jazz styles, and he has written for such diverse artists as Gerry Mulligan, Doc Severinsen, and Eddie Daniels. Like Ralph Towner's, Frank's music borders on many worlds and varied emotions.

Proto believes he has an obligation as an artist to reflect on our times, and four of his recent major symphonic works present this kind of commentary: Proto's *Ghost in the Machine* was inspired by the Rodney King incident in Los Angeles, and Frank wanted a narrator and a singer working together to address the racial inequality we find around us. The second work, *Four Scenes After Picasso* is based on four of Picasso's paintings from World War II, which set the tone for the four movements of a bass concerto written for François Rabbath. The third piece is a violin concerto called *Can This Be Man*. It is a Holocaust piece, written on the sixtieth anniversary of Kristallnacht for Alex Kerr, co-concertmaster of the Concertgebouw Orchestra. And the final piece is *My Name Is Citizen Soldier,* which commemorates D-Day and honors the soldiers who fought in World War II.

It's not surprising, perhaps, that Frank is motivated by the great themes of life and death as they take shape in the world around us: Beethoven, after all, originally dedicated the *Eroica* Symphony to Napoleon.

Gunther Schuller, the great American composer, educator, scholar, and conductor, was the principal horn player of the Cincinnati Symphony and the Metropolitan Opera and often played under Arturo Toscanini. As a child, he was very gifted as a painter, but then he switched to music. One of Schuller's best-known works, *Seven Studies on Themes of Paul Klee*, was based on Klee's art, and he was inspired to write his entire quartet for four double bass players by the final chord of the fourth movement from Schoenberg's *Five Pieces for Orchestra.*

World renowned flutist/composer Robert Dick is a wonderful example of someone who listens carefully to his inner voice and *goes when it calls* rather than ignoring it. He expanded the traditional sounds of the flute beyond what others ever dreamed possible through his creative listening and unlimited persistent exploration. He is known especially for the innovative techniques he has devised to expand the sonic possibilities of the flute. If he was not satisfied with finding a new sound, he would just keep working at it until the solution came. Robert tells me he has been influenced by pop artists like Jimi Hendrix and Janis Joplin, singers like Nina Simone, and musicians from other world traditions like the Indian sarod master and composer Ali Akbar Khan.

When he heard Nina Simone singing "Don't Let Me Be Misunderstood," he noticed a four-note percussion break that could be played with key clicks on the alto or C flute. He started reading snare drum books, translating the rhythms to his flutes.

> I used my embouchure as a resonator to color the sounds. I discovered I could energize the flute by firing my tongue into the embouchure hole, which gives an amazingly effective sound. After I duplicated the sounds of drums on the flute, I asked myself how I could make the sound of cymbals. I created the sound of double-pitched cymbals by blowing air into multiphonics. I developed the "glissando head joint" when I saw the "whammy bars" that electric guitar players use—it's like a telescope, but it does the same thing. And I love to listen to birdcalls and the sounds of water. Animals and insects do some really exciting rhythmic jams.

Creativity can also foster the spiritual and healthful benefits of music. When the distinguished New Age composer Steven Halpern was introduced to the ancient tradition of sound healing in books about Pythagoras and Edgar Cayce, he intuitively recognized that music could be used in today's world to help him and others reduce their stress and amplify their connection to the spiritual dimension of life. In the late sixties, he began the explorations and experiments that were to inspire the unique form of meditative New Age music for which he is famous. At that time, however, employing music as a healing art was virtually unknown to modern practitioners of both music and healing.

The ancients understood that we have both a physical anatomy and an energetic or spiritual anatomy. The terminology and approach of modern science is different from that of classical yoga, of course, but yoga texts describe seven chakras or vital energy centers in the body, which correspond pretty closely with the glands of the endocrine system. Because everything in the universe vibrates at a specific frequency, it is possible to resonate these energy centers with sound. If you play the right frequencies, you can literally tune the electromagnetic energy fields of the body.

The compositional structure of Steven's award-winning first album, *Spectrum Suite*, is based on a series of seven ascending tonal centers that relate to the seven chakras. And so the path the creative energy takes continues from one discovery to the next.

Absolute Music—Inspired from the Abstract

While much music has been inspired by the human condition, or by dance, poems, stories, nature, celebrations, or works of art, there is also a large body of "abstract" or "absolute" music composed without any specific program. The music is not intended to sound like anything in particular or to represent any kind of activity. It just exists as it is, as pure sound.

Where does the inspiration for this "absolute" music come from? According to Gunther Schuller:

Music is the most powerful artistic creation that we humans have invented, precisely because of its inability to say anything specific unless we add words to it or give it a title. The power of music resides in the fact that it can say anything and everything. What would we have if

Strauss had never used the title *Till Eulenspiegel*? If you play this music to someone from northern Japan who has never heard it before, there is no way that person will say "Oh yes, that's about Till Eulenspiegel." When you take away titles, descriptive scenarios, and program notes, you have "absolute" music. Every listener will have his or her own unique reaction to the same music, and these responses will all be valid.

This is how music differs from all other art forms. Literature and paintings communicate more easily—oratorios and songs express something more specific, because they have texts. Music communicates feeling and emotion, but nothing concrete. So in a sense everything is abstract. The wonder of music is that it can express anything and everything for anybody.

Absolute Music Still Has Inspiration

Even absolute music springs from some form of creative seed. Sometimes a composer may go to great creative lengths to compose music and hide the structure or creative inspiration of that music. It may be the composer's intention to communicate an idea or feeling, but without their audience being able to name what the music expresses. Gunther Schuller believes that many composers, including Beethoven, Mahler, Brahms, and Berg, have had "secret scenarios" that have inspired their "absolute" pieces. Some have involved love affairs, and that's why their specific inspiration has been kept secret. The *Lyric Suite* of Alban Berg, for example, was written as a gigantic love letter to a woman Berg was in love with, even though he was married to Helene. After Berg died in 1935, Helene spent much of her life trying to suppress this secret scenario. Schuller told me:

> I happen to know of probably some fifty of these secret scenarios myself, so there have to be many more than that! Musicologists have done research on Beethoven, exploring the inspirations of his work, but Beethoven probably felt or thought, "That's my secret." Bach was known to have been a member of a secret society of mathematicians. As a result of his interest in mathematics, he wrote many works based on number systems. There are about forty so-called mathematical

fugues in which a strict number process is applied to the construction of the fugue—and yet it is such great music!

Absolute music draws its creative inspiration from concrete secret or less conscious places, but it does seem to have specific inspirations—yet what is communicated through this creative surge of sound can touch people in unlimited ways. What is important is that it comes from a place of inspiration and feeling. And this is the one thing that *must* come through to the listener. It may lack a program, but it can be felt and experienced.

Frank Proto wants his music to engage the imagination and touch his listeners—with or without a program. He said:

> I also want to stretch myself as a composer and I want it to challenge the performer, be fun and enjoyable. It is the difference between watching a real mystery, when you don't know what is happening until the end, and watching a straightforward chase story where the cop catches the bad guy. You have to pay attention, because if you miss something, you will get lost. This means a repeat hearing. When you hear Bach, you hear something different every time.

The composer wants to *lead* musicians somewhere with those tensions, challenges, and unexpected resolutions and he wants the performers to learn and be challenged by his music. And then, too, the audience needs to be engaged, so they too can experience the unexpected resolution of sounds and feelings. We all leave having learned something from the creative experience: we are enriched, and inspired to go back for more.

This is how creativity inspires and perpetuates human development.

INSPIRING YOUR OWN CREATIVITY

Composers and improvising musicians quickly become adept at listening to their intuition and hearing what Libby Larsen calls *the voice of go!* They pick up on cues, and rather than analyzing, criticizing, or ignoring them, they follow them. The difference between creative musicians and uncreative ones has a great deal to do with the creative musician's willingness to listen to and act upon that *voice of go!* And recognizing the mental barriers we've set up between that voice and the way we live our lives is usually the first step toward increasing our own creativity.

Exploring this subject of creativity with my colleagues has taught me a great deal about writing, as well as about playing my bass. When I heard musicians as diverse as David Balakrishnan, Ralph Towner, and Libby Larsen giving my readers the same kinds of advice, I began paying more attention to it myself. The first suggestion that rang loud and clear for me was the idea of being willing to start over, to put early attempts (and even favorite paragraphs) in the trash can.

Libby Larsen put it like this:

> You have to let go, start over, go on, and know it is going to be good. In our culture, people think it's a radical change when you leave your previous work behind you and begin afresh—but if you look at the music of Bach or Beethoven, every piece is about that moment of change. Innovation and change frighten us, but the necessity to change course is what brings us creativity. A major theme of Rollo May's wonderful book *The Courage to Create* is the need to let go.

When I am writing, working away on one particular passage, and a new idea comes to me, I tend to bat it away unless it's directly related to the topic I'm working on. And often it isn't. It takes courage and humility to set aside the work I've been doing and explore a new direction; but I've found that when I let myself do it, I sometimes come up with some great writing that has nothing to do with my current chapter. Igor Stravinsky used to say you have to commit little murders and kill some of your favorite ideas in order to find the best solutions.

John Dankworth told me that different instrumentalists have many myths about what they should and shouldn't do when improvising. He finds that when we sidestep these myths, creativity flows more smoothly. It is perfectly okay to keep things simple and go with what feels right.

So often the important consideration isn't *what to do* so much as *what not to do*. Many musicians seem to feel obliged to use all the skills they've ever developed at once, now—whereas I feel it's a sure sign of mature artistry when someone knows when to back off, and when to play.

At times he has told jazz pianists not to be afraid to just sit there with their hands in their laps while their colleagues play on: they might not play for a long time, and just find a few bars to fill in with something that is really interesting, but that's all right. He reminds drummers that being able to swing has nothing to do with the volume. Trombone players often feel obliged to articulate their notes as cleanly as a trumpet player, and ignore their ability to move more smoothly between notes, and exploit what they do best—using their slide!

There are times that when we really want to do well, we feel compelled to be more complex and creative. Christian McBride learned a lesson in "less is more" and "more is less" when he felt nervous about writing a song for singer Dianne Reeves. Christian knew Herbie Hancock would be playing piano in the session. Herbie loves to rearrange other people's music when he doesn't like it, and Christian was afraid that he might find the piece too simple. But then Christian asked himself, What's wrong with simplicity?

I left it simple, and sent it to Dianne and she dug it. When I got to the studio, it turned out that Herbie liked it too, and said, "It's all laid out." He didn't want to touch it. I didn't have to change a note.

Creativity Through Spontaneity

When Fred Hersch is working out an idea, there are times when he stops thinking about it and just puts his hands down on the keys:

I don't think. Thinking is the enemy. I like to screw around. When kids learn, they make a mess. Parents don't teach children to walk—kids see their parents walking, and feel a strong desire to do it themselves. They fall over, they crawl, hold on to the table and cruise a bit, then try it again. They fall down a lot. And eventually they are able to stand up and walk. Picasso said that if you want to create art, you have to make a mess. You have to take the time to experiment. You can't get side-tracked by perfection issues if you want to be a great artist. You have to take chances—and a certain percentage of them are *not* going to bake. But over time, your batting average will get higher. Sometimes in a middle of an improvisation I'll hit an absolute clam. Over the years, I have learned to say, "Hmmm, this is interesting, I'll have to see where this goes."

We've seen that such things as dispelling myths, using the trash can, keeping it simple, and letting yourself make a mess can all help to remove barriers to creativity, but there are still times when we need to stimulate the mind into a state of creative momentum—when we need that first joke to bring on the next one and start the ball rolling.

Robert Dick told me about a useful technique when you have the germ of an idea and you don't quite know where to go with it: learning to amplify an image with your imagination. He's talking about images that you can hear and see. Can you make them bigger? Creative ideas are usually accompanied by creative energy—can you tap into that energy? Can you tap into the emotion of the piece before you begin to play?

Imagine the first note of your piece is buried half a mile underground, and imagine it drilling its way up towards you, accelerating as it goes—until it's coming to you at a thousand feet a second and BOOM here it is! The sound itself, the picture in your mind's eye, and the rush of expectation can all help you tap into the emotion and release your pent-up energies. If the piece is lyrical, you need to think of something very sensual. Imagine a marvelous food, sense its texture on your tongue. If the piece is about love or loss or joy, I believe you need to go inside yourself to find these places, the way actors find love or grief within their own resources when playing Romeo or Juliet.

We need to welcome all kinds of ideas—and the only time to welcome an idea is when it pops up. Fred Hersch is a great believer in the spontaneity of improvisation. He says that nothing in the world compares with the freshness and immediacy of hearing something that is not planned in advance. In his book *The Poetics of Music*, Stravinsky tells us that *composition is selective improvisation*. Bach knew this too. If you want to be a composer, constant improvisation is the way to go.

Each year for the past few years, Fred has spent some time at the MacDowell Colony. It's a place where composers, writers, and visual artists can work undisturbed in private cottages on the estate. Fred brings a kitchen timer and a baseball cap with him. He cuts an index card into twelve chips and puts the name of one of the twelve musical notes on each chip. He puts them into the baseball cap and shakes them up. Then he pulls out a pitch, which becomes the pitch of the day. He sets his kitchen timer for forty-five minutes—and has to write a tune based on the pitch he drew within that time limit.

This really helps me generate some great material. I wrote a lot of my *Songs Without Words* this way. I don't have time to sit around waiting for the great idea to strike, I have to grab something and work with it. The idea is to really finish something in forty-five minutes. It's almost like speed writing of the sort that writers do. And the fact that you've completed something gives you energy to continue working. And if you don't come up with anything great, hey, you only wasted forty-five minutes.

Fred has come up with his own creative way to harness the energy that comes from facing a deadline, and to work spontaneously while still giving himself a limited opportunity to refine his material. It's also an example of Stravinsky's concept of *selective improvising*.

The creative process is something that will go on as long as our hearts are beating. Composers have had some of their most wonderful musical ideas in dreams, in the shower, while traveling, in some especially serene and beautiful setting—or while preoccupied with other things in the busiest of places. And they were willing to follow these insights.

Settings for Creativity

We may have some control over where and when we like to work, but we cannot always control where and when we are going to get creative ideas. My British composer friend and colleague Tony Osborne told me he has found ideas for writing pieces in a train, in a school common room, on the motorway, on a walk in the park, in front of the television, and so on. Over time, though, he has become more sensitive to distraction and finds that when he's composing he has to give it his full attention. What do you do when your ideas come at you while you're on the motorway, and you can't work with them until you've arrived? Tony finds that when he gets an idea, he can put creativity on hold while he goes about the tasks of daily life and leaves some of the processing to the unconscious:

Things seem to keep on going at a subconscious level until I get a space to write. Then, I find I can switch my attention back on, and the ideas just flow—I go in and out of composing mode—and this turns out to be a far more productive and creative way for me to work. I still keep manuscript paper and pencils at hand, because ideas still come to me in unlikely places, and there have been times when I've woken up from a dream with a fragment of music looping through my head.

Solitude is certainly important!

Dave Brubeck was inspired to write a piece by a celebrated speech that's often attributed to Chief Sealth (also known as Chief Seattle):

How can you buy or sell the sky, or the land? The idea is strange to us. If we do not own the freshness of the air and sparkle of the water, how can you buy them? Every part of this earth is sacred to my people. Every shining pine needle, every sandy shore, every mist in the dark woods, every clearing and humming insect is holy in the memory and experience of my people. The sap which courses through the trees carries the memories of the red man.

Dave told me he wrote the piece on a little island pond at his home, with ducks, geese, muskrats, and fish—and eagles overhead.

It was the perfect place to write this particular piece. It's about one hundred yards from my house, and I don't have anything to interfere with my process, no phones, nothing. But I don't always get the opportunity to choose where I shall work. I have learned to write in all circumstances—in airplanes, trains, cars, hotel rooms, park benches, wherever I happen to be—and my oratorio *The Light of the Wilderness* was partly written while working in Las Vegas!

After composers have received an inspiration for a work, they often like to work at their craft in a pleasant environment.

Composer Sir Peter Maxwell Davies actually goes to a special place for his inspiration, then returns home to work out the details. He lives in a small community on the island of Sanday in the Orkney Islands of Scotland. When he is composing, he prepares himself by walking at least five miles every day along the beach. The waves and tides in that part of the world can be very tricky, and he views the sea around him as a dangerous place where two worlds meet. He spoke movingly of "the deep, extraordinary land you think you know so well, and of course you don't," and said, "It is like walking on a knife edge. I love it."

Maybe Davies likes to give his creative ideas a sense of urgency. Perhaps his dangerous beach walks infuse some adrenaline into his creative juices as he works out his musical forms and pieces.

What is most remarkable is that Peter Maxwell Davies actually composes his music while he walks along the coastal waters. He describes pacing a piece on the beach by walking back and forth:

I'll compose in that place over there where there is a little hill or group of rocks. I'll walk "inside the piece" as if it is physically around me in three dimensions. I can shove the notes around in different places and try out an instrumentation. Then I'll go back and walk it through with a different instrumentation. It is like it is happening around me—I'm actually listening to it. People think I'm just walking back and forth, but I'm not. I'm actually pacing it out and composing in my head. I have to be quite alone to work this out, in a very big space. The birds or otters don't bother me. By the time I have walked a piece out, I go to my desk and I already have a good idea of what it is going to look and sound like.

Different artists seem to need stimulation, background noise, silence, or seclusion. Each one of us must find what suits us. Creative ideas will be at work in us as long as we keep on breathing, as long as we keep on living. And the composers and improvising musicians we have met in this chapter can offer us some fresh choices as to where we want to be, while we work to transform our creative hunches and insights into reality.

Entering the Creative State

Is there a way to bring both body and mind into an optimal state to receive creative messages?

Previously, I have mentioned the importance of having the body rested, free of tension, and free of drugs, alcohol, and stimulants, and many musicians find this in itself helps them to achieve a quiet, meditative state in which to listen for the creative voice. Once the body is ready and available, it is also important for us to clear the mind of the travails of the day. It is scientifically proven that our receptivity to creative energy is best when our brain is in a low-frequency alpha or theta state, and there are several techniques we can use to help us slip into a state of relaxed consciousness.

I like to jog when I'm thinking about problems and waiting for answers. When I begin my run, I pose the questions to myself, and then forget about them. After a few minutes, the mind quiets down. After about thirty minutes, in a way that I find constantly amazing, things begin to happen, answers come. Many times when I've had questions while writing this book, they have been answered while I was either running or doing some form of meditation. Picking up my bass and just playing some very pure tones can also help. In the morning before I get out of bed, I love to stare at the trees through the window for a long time. This helps me to get away from the everyday humdrum concerns that tend to clutter up my mind. And when I'm writing, I have to have complete silence.

Steven Halpern believes that hearing arpeggios, drones, or repeated *ostinato* rhythmic figures makes it easier for him to get in a creative mood. The brain reacts to repeated stimuli, and that can help catapult you into an alpha or theta state. The most ancient use of rhythm was to entrain whole tribes, and drumming circles can have a similar effect on the brain and bring entire groups into a state of creative energy. Steve said:

> I have learned that when I enter a deeply relaxed meditative state, I enter "the zone" where creativity flows more freely. I enjoy watching the motion of branches swaying in a gentle breeze, or the flickering leaves in afternoon sunlight—it has an almost hypnotic effect. There are times when I hear an audible click inside my brain as I shift into this altered state. When I'm in the studio recording, I re-create that experience in my mind. Then I play from within that place of peace, and the music seems to play itself. I become the instrument of the instrument.

Terry Riley is widely considered one of the most influential figures in minimalist music. He is a noted pianist, composer, improviser, and master of tabla and Indian chanting. During his earlier years studying more traditional harmony at Berkeley, Riley was influenced by his classmate LaMonte Young. LaMonte and Terry wrote many pieces in which each tone would last twenty to thirty seconds. This allowed them to experience music in a different way.

Terry's study of Buddhism and Hinduism also contributed to his music, which is something of a personal synthesis of Indian and Western cultures. Like the Vedic seers, for instance, Terry believes in the power of chant as a technique for focusing attention and entering a creative state:

The repetition of a mantra focuses the mind and has a steadying, peace-giving effect. All cultures have their own distinct ways of doing this: meditation and chanting are examples. I practice raga-singing every day, like a yoga that involves using my voice. This is my main practice, and it can take me one or two hours a day. In turn, this technique fine-tunes my hearing and enables me to hear microtones and play tambura. All of this requires a lot of deep listening.

For those who are on a spiritual path of some kind, this kind of exercise can be an offering to a higher being—but even if someone isn't interested in that aspect, it still gives you a sense of balance and peace.

What seems clear is that both mind and body need to be alone and available, and that some kind of repetitive calming activity can be of help.

Creativity Coming from the Walls

The Salzburg Mozarteum is a beautiful place with very strong musical associations, a place where musicians can study composition, and where ideas flow—but is that all? Some of my musical colleagues believe there may be more to creativity than we can easily understand. There may be, as Hamlet put it, more things in heaven and earth than are dreamt of in our philosophy.

In what sense can we say that Mozart "inspires" the students at the Mozarteum? Some would suggest that a twenty-first-century musician could "channel" the spirit of Mozart, others that his influence subtly pervades the place. What's fascinating is that musicians will often glean inspiration or creativity from within the walls of a magical place, whether it is a historic landmark or a simple red church.

Steven Halpern referred me to the work of British scientist Rupert Sheldrake. Sheldrake's theory of morphogenetic resonance holds that there may be tappable, quasi-physical "fields" which retain the mental pathways of the human race in such a way that once one person has made a creative breakthrough, others can "follow the same path" with greater ease—even if they don't know of the earlier breakthrough. Sheldrake's theory is highly controversial, as is the "hundredth monkey" story which describes a similar phenomenon.

Is there some principle of resonance at work in the world that allows musicians to tap into the same source of music that Mozart tapped?

Terry Riley doesn't know if we can ever explain the seemingly miraculous ways of creation, but he does feel that in some sense music resides in a universal spirit or consciousness.

> If you believe that there's a field of consciousness which somehow connects the whole universe including ourselves in one seamless web, it follows that everything arises from that consciousness—and we call the place where things arise in consciousness within us our own consciousness, or awareness, or intuition. Someone like Mozart has a very fine-tuned antenna for this kind of thing, so he can pick up signals from the "consciousness" station much better than others—but we can tune in to that station too. And since consciousness is infinite and we are finite, we won't all hear the same music.

Terry believes that a public performance is a very important event in which the musician passes creative energy to the listener, and the listener gives it back to the performer: music as a form of shared consciousness. He also believes that a universal spirit is guiding humanity and giving us knowledge. There are many examples of a creative spiritual influence in what some might call smaller "wonders of the world." He points to the pyramids, saying they were built more than four thousand years ago, yet we still don't know how the ancients pulled off such feats of engineering. We still cannot figure out the secret of the varnish on Stradivarius violins. We cannot build the perfect concert hall; acoustics is not a perfect science. And even Leonard Bernstein could only write one *West Side Story!*

So where does inspiration come from? Gunther Schuller pondered.

> I somehow feel and think that there are forces out there which we don't understand and may never understand, which generate in us human be-

ings some need to pick up on their vibrations and use them in our artistic expression. I cannot deny that this is a possibility. These are the real deep mysteries that we may never be able to understand.

Terry Riley puts it like this:

We cannot really know, because it happens beyond the realm of our experience—but people have always believed that we are somehow connected beyond space and time, that knowledge is somehow sitting there, and on occasion we manage to tap into it. And very occasionally, when we have an inspiration, we do know—because the inspiration comes to us so strongly that we are convinced by the experience. This isn't a matter of belief but of experience—an experience that's filled with awareness and truth and love.

Perhaps the Bible says it best: *The wind bloweth where it listeth, and thou hearest the sound thereof, but canst not tell whence it cometh, and whither it goeth.* (John 3:8)

Whether you call it the wind, or the spirit, or the breath, whether you think of it as God, whether you call it consciousness or the field of being, is not the point. The important thing is that music *does* well up inside us where and when it wants and not where and when we'd necessarily choose—and we can indeed *hear the sound thereof*, but can't exactly explain *whence it cometh, and whither it goeth.*

If we could—if creativity and inspiration were genuinely within human control—Bernstein would have written a second masterpiece like *West Side Story*, borrowing his plot from Shakespeare's *King Lear* this time perhaps. But inspiration isn't something we control. Beethoven couldn't just finish the Ninth Symphony one week and cap it with a Tenth the next. Inspiration exists, it is within us, and at times we can tap into it. It does have the power to communicate, and we do have the power to listen to it. And it inspires us and reminds us what a joy it is to be alive.

Let's avoid the theological thickets and just call it the spirit of music. It is our greatest joy to continue to reexperience this spirit—to appreciate it, to acknowledge its existence, to get to know it better, to polish it through the study and practice of art, and to share it with the world, which Mozart so clearly did.

Mozart's Mozart Within

On the final page of *The Inner Game of Music*, I quoted Mozart's description of his own creative process. I'd like to quote it again here, and I think that as you read it, you'll be amazed at how many of the themes we've touched on in this chapter can be found right in Mozart's words: the need for solitude; maintaining a positive attitude; riding in a car, train, or carriage; walking or jogging; not knowing "whence and how" the ideas come (the wind that "bloweth where it listeth"); the idea that creativity is not within our control—it just *is*.

When I am, as it were, completely myself, entirely alone, and of good cheer—say traveling in a carriage, or walking after a good meal, or during the night when I cannot sleep; it is on such occasions that my ideas flow best and most abundantly. Whence and how they come, I know not; nor can I force them. Those ideas that please me I retain in memory, and am accustomed, as I have been told, to hum them to myself.

All this fires my soul, and provided I am not disturbed, my subject enlarges itself, becomes methodized and defined, and the whole, though it be long, stands almost completed and finished in my mind, so that I can survey it, like a fine picture or a beautiful statue, at a glance.

Nor do I hear in my imagination the parts successively, but I hear them, as it were, all at once. What a delight this is I cannot tell! All this inventing, this producing takes place in a pleasing lively dream. Still the actual hearing of the tout ensemble is after all the best. What has been thus produced I do not easily forget, and this is perhaps the best gift I have my Divine Maker to thank for.

We call those whose music touches us most deeply *gifted*, and in Mozart's words, we may be able to catch an echo of the origin of that word. When we open ourselves and our souls, by practice and inspiration, but also by listening and letting go, music comes to us not as something we command, but as a gift. It is as a gift, too, that we should pass the gift of music along.

FINALE: INSPIRATIONS FOR STAYING ON THE PATH

(Teachers, Choirs, Adversity)

nd so we come to the finale of our work: *inspiration.*

Inspiration is the key to everything we've been discussing in this book, because inspiration is the engine that can power all the rest. If we feel inspired, we will find the passion, discipline, and courage to go forward: we will play together, we will practice, we will gain the technical skills we need, we will inspire others, and we will be inspired to continue on our own path of personal growth toward true artistry.

It is notoriously difficult to describe inspiration, but we can all sense the magic when it's present in a performance. It can power the flight of a jazz soloist in fiery response to a shift in drum rhythm, the trance of a Balinese dancer, or the mathematical pyrotechnics of a Bach fugue. Inspiration is closely related to the *flow* state which psychologist Mihaly Csikszentmihalyi describes, in which we respond to a challenge that is neither so great that it paralyzes us nor so easily accomplished that we take it for granted and slip imperceptibly into boredom. It pushes the limits of what we can understand, of what we can expect, of what we can hope. It goes beyond best into something better. It is the core of musical mastery.

There will be times when we feel stagnant. There will be times when we are not motivated to practice or learn. There will be times when the music we so dearly love does not speak its magic to us. In these times of conflict when we are discouraged, scared, intolerant, and unable to connect with others or the music, or stuck in our own tracks, we need to look at those things that can pull us back to the road of true artistry.

How can we find inspiration?

In this chapter we will explore how people, music, and even the adversities of life can inspire us in our own pursuit of artistry.

INSPIRATIONS FROM OTHERS

People we interact with in our lives on a daily basis can bring us tremendous inspiration. When I think of those who have inspired me to grow and learn to play the bass as a performer and teacher, I realize their influence had a tremendous impact, not just on my musicianship but on my character and soul. The great violin teacher Josef Gingold gave me generous and unsolicited encouragement while I was at Indiana University, and his faith in me continues to inspire me to practice and develop my skills after more than thirty years. In the past two decades, too, I have enjoyed the deep friendship of a gifted colleague who motivates and inspires others to be their best: Dr. Tim Lautzenheiser.

Tim is known to millions of music students, teachers, and booster-parents as an enthusiastic advocate of quality music education as it relates to the development of human potential, and he has certainly been like a guardian angel and cheerleader to me, always encouraging me to go forward with my dreams.

Tim teaches that the messenger is as important as the message, that the attitude of teachers or leaders is the key to unlocking the value of their message when all's said and done.

Successful people can all play the part—that is a given just to get into the game. I've found that what catapults people beyond that into true greatness has to do with the messenger, not just the message: it's their vision, their communication skills, their people skills, their understanding of others that makes people great. The real heroes are people who are always looking for ways to empower the people around them.

Akin Cook currently teaches voice at the Harlem Boys Choir public school. He is an alumnus of the Boys Choir himself and a living testament to Tim Lautzenheiser's belief that messengers are even more important than the messages they bring.

Akin joined the Harlem Boys Choir when he was eleven. He lived with his mother in Harlem on 135th and Fifth Avenue, behind Harlem Hospital, and his father was active in his upbringing. He discovered his talent and love for singing when he won a part in a school play singing the Michael Jackson song "Ben."

> People just told me that singing is what I should do. I have a learning disability—I'm dyslexic—and school life was difficult for me. There was rap and hip-hop around me, but it didn't appeal to me. I was in a basketball club, I never felt too comfortable there—but I did know how to hustle with the guys. Music was my escape. My grandmother would put me in the back room and give me records to play. My mom really encouraged me to join the Boys Choir. And singing just clicked for me.

Music provided the stage on which Akin learned many of the ten pathways to artistry, but he gladly acknowledges the inspiration of those whose words, example, and music taught him so many of these qualities.

Akin told me that at first he didn't realize how important it was to be present at all the rehearsals. He cared about being in the choir, to be sure, but he had no idea how important the choir had become in everyone's life. The choir was learning a difficult contemporary piece by George Walker, and Akin had to learn extended vocal techniques like gargling and making clicks and other sounds. All this required lots of rehearsal time—and when Akin didn't show, the directors called him on it:

> They would call my home. I had missed some rehearsals because I was hanging out with friends after school. I'm very human—I liked to

watch TV and play hooky. And sometimes I felt I could never attain the standard of some of the other marvelous singers in the choir—it felt like I couldn't keep up. But they'd call and say *I want you in these rehearsals*, and then I felt I'd better meet this challenge. They actually wanted to *know* where I was! They really cared about me—and they are passionate about their music.

The feeling that he was truly *cared for* translated into a fierce loyalty, and Akin made their PASSION for music his own.

The legendary director of the Boys Choir, Dr. Walter Turnbull, is known for his extraordinary presence and personal rapport with every kid. Akin told me Turnbull was aware of the boys' strengths and weaknesses, and knew how to get each one to perform at his best. Akin said he would never forget his second performance with the choir. It was a pops show, there weren't many rehearsals, and he had to get the dance steps and harmonies down in just two days. Needless to say, Akin was extremely nervous, and the performance didn't go that well for him.

After the performance I apologized and said to Dr. Turnbull, "I really can do better." He just said, "Don't worry about it." I was really taken aback by his understanding. He was like a father to me. After that experience, I just worked with a vengeance to get just what he wanted.

Akin credits Dr. Turnbull with teaching him the responsibility to prepare his music with integrity and DISCIPLINE. Dr. Turnbull would make the boys sing whatever repertoire they were doing for that season in solo quartets (one soprano, alto, tenor, and bass), in front of the large choir. Performing your own part with just three other singers means that each person is the only one singing his own part. Doing this gave Akin tremendous self-confidence.

We had to know this music cold. Dr. Turnbull would go through everybody in the choir, all sixty kids, and wait until everybody was heard—so nobody could hide. You really had to know your part, or you would be ridiculed about it. When I went to graduate school at the

Manhattan School of Music, I always took learning my part very seriously. Tenors are often considered to be weak on musicianship and slow to learn music, and I have been hired for a lot of gigs because I read and learn music quickly. I really give credit for that to the Harlem Boys Choir.

Warren Wilson was another inspirational teacher with the Harlem Boys Choir, and Akin says he learned about CONCENTRATION and focus by watching Wilson conduct the choir's galas.

It wasn't enough to sing the notes on the page. Mr. Wilson would get into dynamics. He was unrelenting. Sometimes we would be in rehearsals for over two hours just working on *one note* or *one phrase* to get that certain dynamic level, with everyone perfect. I just hated him for it—but I had never seen that kind of focus or attention to the music before.

Touring is part of life with the Harlem Boys Choir. Akin's first national tour lasted three weeks and involved a lot of one-night stands— you travel all day on a bus, arrive in a new city, drop off your suitcase in a hotel, rehearse, perform, go to sleep, then get up and do it again the next day. This can be quite a feat of endurance and can test your ability to eat, sleep, and perform at your best with fellow choir members. Akin said that by the third week the boys started to get on each other's nerves, so he began to realize he needed some people skills to get along.

This whole experience taught me a lot about TOLERANCE. Spending this amount of time together brought us very close, like a family. I learned a lot about brotherhood from these tours. If someone got sick, we learned to bring up the slack. We learned to work together. And I think these things had a big impact on the musical quality of our performances.

What Akin learned about CONFIDENCE in the Harlem Boys Choir has stayed with him to this day. He explained to me that everyone in the choir has to earn his place by accepting the assignments he is given. Dr. Turnbull asked him to learn "Lean on Me" by Bill Withers as a solo. Akin didn't want to do it, and didn't take the assignment seriously. At the first rehearsal, Dr. Turnbull pointed to him and said, "Okay, Akin, you sing it," but Akin wasn't prepared. He was very embarrassed, and it was a moment he will never forget:

> Oh, he let me have it. Dr. Turnbull *really* let me have it. He said, "You had better learn this piece by tomorrow." At that moment I didn't see this as an opportunity—I had no choice. I learned it, and I learned it well. There's nothing like the confidence you get when you know you can stand up in front of hundreds of people and sing a solo. When I got to Manhattan, some things just clicked for me because I had been forced to do these things with the choir.

Confidence comes from being prepared, and when Akin took responsibility for always knowing his music, he benefited from the confidence skills that accompany this state of readiness. While Akin learned many of these pathways to true artistry in his time with the Harlem Boys Choir, these same lessons are played out in school and community music programs throughout the world.

But it's not just the teachers and peers and ensembles that provide this inspirational environment for positively motivating people. For the past ten years, the Harlem Boys Choir has also been a year-round public school, with over 560 students, boys and girls, from the fourth through the twelfth grade. Director Walter Turnbull says that music is a major tool they use to enhance and develop the children's lives—but he stresses the many other forces in the child's life that all work together to make each child a success.

> When we audition children, we interview the parents as well as former schoolteachers, and when they come into the choir, they go to the two-week Summer Institute, which is a live-away camp at Skidmore College. Our developmental process sets a tone for them to learn our values. During the year, they work with their theory teachers, choral teachers,

and counselors as well as with their academic teachers, and as they progress through the system, they see role models that look just like them and are right where they are.

Dr. Turnbull says there's a special quality to the student-teacher relationships that's possible at the Harlem Boys Choir because of their focus on music, a quality that addresses not just the children's minds but their hearts and deepest values. Similarly, there's an integrated quality to the curriculum, which is designed to show the relationship of history, science, math, and other disciplines to music.

Dr. Turnbull explained with pride:

One of the reasons the Boys Choir developed into a full school is that we found we could have a greater influence on our students' social development and the quality of music they can make. When a bunch of children come together with the same interest and the same sense of purpose, it makes a big difference. They learn respect for art. They learn a musical worldview that becomes very important to them. They learn how important music is for everything in life. And their music experiences help them to understand the process of success. Ninety-eight percent of our kids graduate high school, and the vast majority go on to college.

Music programs build winners. Music students make up a large proportion of the nonmajors who are admitted into graduate schools for law or medicine, and they are so highly valued because of their training. There are few fields like music in which 99 percent accuracy is unacceptable, and any performing ensemble from a trio to an orchestra inevitably demands discipline, concentration, passion, and people skills from its members.

Tim Lautzenheiser echoed these sentiments:

I don't think people should be in music just to develop life skills, they should be in music for the sake of music—but I'm certain that the life skills music teaches them explain why musicians are so successful in all aspects of life. It's not that all the smart students are in music, it's more that students of music develop the skills to negotiate life at a more intelligent level. They are playing, listening, blending, and multitasking in every facet of their journey.

In music, each person is an integral part of the tapestry the entire ensemble is putting together. I don't know of any other discipline where you have to bring so many skills together for the common goal of success. Music ensembles offer a microcosm of life, and a blueprint for high-level achievement. There has to be a freedom to agree to disagree, and an acceptance of people for what they are rather than for what you want them to be. And people don't say, "I play the trumpet." They say, "I'm in the band." There is a sense of family.

Music teachers and colleagues can inspire us to make music and live life more richly and fully—and as we've seen, many of the lessons that musicianship brings are applicable to life even if we leave the world of music. But there's a point where music itself becomes our way of life as well as a source of our growth and development as a human being, and there is a whole other level of inspiration that comes strictly from contact with artistic greatness. Each one of us, whether student, performer, teacher, or member of an audience, is enriched when we come in contact with great performers and great works of art. The greatness of art and artistic expression can be the fuel that inspires us to continue our journey. Music is one of the most powerful sources of truth we have: it has the power to change lives.

INSPIRATION FROM MUSIC

There are few things quite so inspiring as a multitude of human voices singing together.

Craig Jessop, the music director of the Mormon Tabernacle Choir, speaks of the human voice as the first art: before there were drums to beat, before we picked up conch shells or hollowed out reeds to blow through them, we lifted our voices together and sang. When the choir of Westminster Abbey in London lifts hearts and voices to sing Handel's anthem "Zadok the Priest" at the coronation of an English monarch, when an American family passes the time on a long interstate car ride singing rounds and spirituals, when the monks of the Tibetan Gyuto Choir produce their haunting recordings in which each monk sings all three notes of a chord at once, or when a prison chain gang smashes rock to the sound of Leadbelly's "Take This Hammer," or the U.S. Marines march and sing "The Marines Hymn," a very special thing takes place. I said earlier that the human voice is the only musical instrument that can catch cold or feel grief; it is also the first great instrument of harmony among humankind.

We come together, the great choral director Robert Shaw told Craig Jessop, *so that we can collectively create something of more lasting value and beauty than we could ever manage as individuals.* Joseph Jennings, the music director of the internationally acclaimed male vocal ensemble Chanticleer, points to the sense of kinship that this builds:

> When you sing with others and the vibrations and harmonies start to link up, you realize you aren't in this world alone. There are common experiences you are all having at that moment and there is a sharing that happens.

The voice is the most intimately human of all instruments, and the most universal. Most everyone has sung at some time or another, whether at sports events or in music productions, at births, weddings, and funerals or at a party, to comfort a child, in a bus with other vacationers, or in the shower. Many of us have sung in choirs in our spiritual communities. There are educators who believe that every one of us should sing every day, and physicians who recommend singing as a means of achieving good health!

Joseph Flummerfelt, artistic director of the New York Choral Singers and the Westminster Choir, has been at the forefront of professional, collegiate, and amateur choirs for decades. He emphasized the power of inspiration that choral work can bring:

When singers come together through the intense listening that the ensemble necessitates, there is a power and a sound that emerges which I believe changes the singers' lives—and it has an impact on those who listen, too. Even though an audience member may not be able to verbalize it, I believe that something deep and profound is touched in this experience.

Everyone enjoys experiencing and participating in great choral masterpieces. In Cincinnati we have the longest-running choral festival in America, called the May Festival. Our concert hall was built to accommodate the more than five thousand people who all participate in the singing festival. In New York, there is an annual public singing of Handel's *Messiah*. Three thousand or more people buy tickets to come with their scores and sing through this great masterwork—and this can have a great impact on people who do not spend their lives immersed in music.

Dr. Flummerfelt also directs an amateur chorus at the Berkshire Music Institute, where doctors, lawyers, computer programmers, and schoolkids rehearse all week before performing a great work with the Springfield Symphony. For many of them, this week is their cherished family vacation. Singing the Bach B Minor Mass or Mozart's Requiem is a joyful experience, and for many participants this is the highlight of their year.

Dr. Flummerfelt believes that what gives a great work of music its continuing relevance is the composer's deep connection to some power beyond the confines of the ego, a connection which allows the composer to tap into some kind of musical truth.

This is what we are digging for and probing for: some deeper connection with the sense of an eternal truth that we are all hungry for—some truth within the notes, within the composer's voice. People want to make contact with that voice and bring it to life.

Most people who sing in a choral ensemble will tell you they feel an inspiration that goes way beyond the notes and rhythms. Joseph Jennings told me that people often feel the inspiration while sidestepping the theological side of sacred choral music: *Some people tell me, "I love your music. I don't believe in God, but this music is so spiritual I feel it."*

Jennings points out that while Chanticleer indeed performs a great deal in churches, its concerts are geared to provide a moving aesthetic experience, but not necessarily a religious or spiritual experience.

When we are inspired and touched by greatness in music, what's important is for us to feel it as deeply as we can. We don't have to put words to it, or try to manipulate the religious text to fit in with our own opinions, whether we're believers or nonbelievers. The music just is, we feel it, and we experience its greatness. It is best when the essence of the music connects with the essence of our selves. Jennings reminded me of a classic Inner Game truth when he said that when we escape our analytical self and allow the music to move us, we can come into a new awareness of our human existence:

> This is what is so great about live music: when we leave, we see the world in a whole different way. The green looks different; we realize how vast the sky is, what a wonder the trees are. We realize how different we each are as human beings, but at the same time recognize that we are all the same.

The inspiration, clearly, doesn't stop with the music itself, it extends out into our lives. And once we have been touched by it, what are we to do with it? Are we kinder to those we meet? More confident in our ability to share ourselves and our music? Are we more humble in our respect for humanity, more open to differences, more tolerant of other people? Are we more passionate and in love with life, perhaps, because of this experience? Inspiration and joy that music brings can be a potent force for good—if we allow it to empower ourselves, our lives, and our relations with the world around us.

INSPIRATION THROUGH ADVERSITY

I said at the beginning of this chapter that people, great art, and adversity are three great means to achieve inspiration. I can recommend great art with a fair amount of confidence, and people too, most of the time—but adversity is a bit of a special case, because I don't believe anyone should go out actively seeking it, with the intention of developing inspiration.

Inspiration is something you can make of adversity when it befalls you, but you shouldn't lie in wait for it! And having given you that warning . . .

Artistic expression has historically been a reflection of the human condition. Adversity, loss, and tragedy have at times inspired great inventions, great masterpieces, and peaks of human achievement. The Renaissance composer Josquin des Pres's greatest motets were born out of the hardships of the Plague. Slavery gave rise to the African-American spirituals. Beethoven's Third Symphony, *Eroica*, was inspired by Napoleon. Mahler's great music was inspired by his own struggle with issues of life and death. And Britten's *War Requiem* expresses his anguish at the world wars of the past century. So it goes.

Today, too, there are events which history will deem tragic, but working artists are also influenced by personal problems and the adversities of their daily lives. Like many other professionals, musicians are subject to the approval of peers and superiors, and at times have to compete for their livelihood. They compete for grades, awards, roles, and jobs. Their performance is on public display for all to see and hear. All artists must deal with failure, rejection, embarrassment, disappointment, and professional loss—yet a physical or emotional failure can ruin the career of any artist. All musicians have had bad days, and the emotional pressures performers are under and the sacrifices artists have to make are regular components of the life of music.

In sports, they have a saying: *From Worst to First*. Often it's the game after a team goes down in a humiliating defeat that crowns them with glory. As an advocate of the Inner Game, I discourage the mental attachment to winning that often comes with competition—but the feeling that comes from defeat can certainly be a catapult to success.

Tim Lautzenheiser has been working in the field of competition for several decades. Here's how he explains it:

Those who say that competition itself is bad are missing the point. It is the way we so often interpret competition that can be detrimental. If we sit down to play a game of cards together, I'm going to play to win. I'm going to enjoy the process of two intelligent minds working together to challenge and strengthen each other. That's a win-win situation—you win if you win, and you win if you lose, too. When I watch basketball, I am most interested in the last four minutes of the game when it is still a close call—because we are going to see the players at their best. I need you to win so that I can dig deeper and play better. In a sense, it is the COOPERATION of the competition that offers growth to everyone involved.

I've always felt that competition is only good when it inspires you to work harder, but it wasn't until I talked to Tim that I realized that we really need people to set standards for us to shoot for. When we are pressed to do better because of the competition, we somehow find a way to dig deeper.

Life-and-death issues too can be inspiring. Fred Hersch, whom we met in the chapter on creativity, is one of the world's greatest improvising pianists. He is also HIV-positive. Fred told me that the best musical experience of his life came right on the heels of his hospitalization with HIV.

Three and a half years ago, I was hospitalized with complications of HIV. This was the first time since 1986 that I had been under direct threat, and it was a wake-up call. I was in the hospital during May 1998, then took the following summer off, rethinking and putting myself back together. It was a time when I was scared out of my mind, and it was a period of intense personal growth as well.

That fall, I rejoined the New England Conservatory faculty and booked a concert at Jordan Hall, one of the great halls in the country. There was a certain energy generated by my first solo concert in this newly renovated hall, on a piano that I really loved. And this time I wanted to do some things that I had never done. I wanted to play some pieces I decided on the night before. I didn't want to play it safe, I really wanted to put the pedal to the metal and push this one. I wanted to see what would happen, I wanted to shake it up. And from the first moment, I felt I was in a different kind of zone.

About a week later, I was preparing a recording for the Nonesuch label. When the tape of that New England Conservatory concert arrived, I went to Bob Hurwitz and told him, "Bob, the record is done—here it is. I can't play any better than this." The sound was fine, and he agreed. He released that performance as *Let Yourself Go: Fred Hersch at Jordan Hall.*

Was this concert a testimony to the fragility of life? Fred had a brush with death: it inspired him to take chances that he never took, to go deeper than he ever dreamed possible. And that in turn unleashed the performance of a lifetime.

September 11, 2001

The terrible events in New York and Washington on September 11, 2001, have affected us all, and the ripple effects will no doubt be felt for years to come. Catastrophic events of this magnitude change lives and alter the course of history. And as with the two world wars, the dropping of the atomic bomb, and the Holocaust, our first response may be to say, *Never again!* At the least, those who survive such events are shocked into a new sense of reality or truth—and this is often accompanied by a *need for human expression.*

We met Craig Jessop earlier in this chapter. In 1992, I had the honor of meeting and working with Craig during an Inner Game of Music demonstration for the Iowa Bandmasters Association. Craig was the director of the regional Air Force Band, which served as my "demonstrating ensemble." I could tell right away that Craig intuitively grasped the Inner Game concepts even before reading my book! He was already incorporating the Inner Game principles in his leadership and musical directorship. After receiving his doctorate in choral music from Stanford, he returned to his native Utah in 1995 as artistic director of the world-famous Mormon Tabernacle Choir.

On September 11, 2001, the Tabernacle Choir was scheduled to perform at the National Insurance Underwriters convention. Many of those attending were from New York and the East Coast, and Craig didn't know whether he should proceed with the concert. The question was put to the senior officer of the Church of Latter-Day Saints, President Gordon B. Hinckley, and he asked whether it would be possible to change the program and make it a memorial concert. The time was two-thirty in the afternoon of September 11. Craig said, "By all means we can."

The president asked me to submit a program, and I met the choir at seven p.m. and told them, "This will now be a memorial concert, and here are the things we are going to do." I passed out new music that we didn't have time to rehearse.

The entire First Presidency of the church was in attendance. President Hinckley introduced himself and said, "I know this was to have been a gala concert for your convention, but obviously things have changed dramatically because of the events of the day. We would like to proceed, and to make this concert a memorial concert for those who lost their lives and those who are grieving, and to provide comfort for those in mourning." And we proceeded without applause.

We played for ninety minutes and offered a concluding prayer, but no one would leave. I had intentionally left "The Battle Hymn of the Republic" off the program, although this is one of our signature pieces. But then President Hinckley asked that we sing "The Battle Hymn." Well, the place just erupted, we had to do five encore bows—and still they wouldn't leave. We sang "God Be with You Till We Meet Again," and then sang it again. The audience just laughed, and would not leave. They just wanted to stay in the building, to stay in that space.

Two women from the Salt Lake community had been on the plane from Boston: a mother and grandmother had put their daughter and granddaughter in school and were returning home when their plane slammed into the WTC. Their families were present for this program.

It remains a great mystery to me how the inhumane actions of a few evil people can bring such an abrupt ending to the lives of thousands of innocent victims. Joseph Flummerfelt suggests the September 11 experience forces us all back to some sense of fundamental truth: it shows us the triviality of our concerns, and highlights the profundity of our deeper resources, causing us all to stop and ask ourselves what is really important.

Craig Jessop said:

> After 9/11 I'm much more respectful of how fragile our institutions are, and how fragile human life is. We are not invulnerable, either as a nation or as individuals. There is a tenuous quality to life that requires our utmost vigilance and care. We mourn for all people. I think we are all changed. This has made me much more appreciative of the mystery of life, of the need for kindness and tolerance.

One young Juilliard violin student expressed for many musicians the firsthand impact that this tragedy had on his life, his music, and his soul. William Harvey tells his powerful story as a violinist who volunteered to play for the rescue workers of the Fighting 69th. His letter describing this was initially sent to a few friends back home in Indiana, but soon found its way via the Internet to millions of readers throughout the world. It is another story of quiet heroism, reminiscent in its way of the story of Vedran Smailovic, the cellist who played the Albinoni Adagio for twenty-two days on the streets of Sarajevo—another story of the compassion and strength that music can inspire and convey. It is reprinted here with William Harvey's permission.

PLAYING FOR THE FIGHTING 69TH

Yesterday, Sept. 15, I had probably the most incredible and moving experience of my life. Juilliard organized a quartet to go play at the Armory. The Armory is a huge military building where families of people missing from Tuesday's disaster go to wait for news of their loved ones.

Entering the building was very difficult emotionally, because the entire building (the size of a city block) was covered with missing persons posters. Thousands of posters, spread out up to eight feet above the ground, each featuring a different, smiling, face.

I made my way into the huge central room and found my Juilliard buddies. For two hours we sight-read quartets (with only three people!), and I don't think I will forget the grief counselor from the Connecticut State Police who listened the entire time, or the woman who listened to "Memory" from the play *Cats*, crying the whole time.

At 7 p.m., the other two players had to leave; they had been playing at the Armory for six hours and simply couldn't play any more. I volunteered to stay and play solo, since I had just gotten there.

I soon realized that the evening had just begun for me. A man in fatigues who introduced himself as Sergeant Major asked me if I'd mind playing for his soldiers as they came back from digging through the rubble at Ground Zero. Masseuses had volunteered to give his men massages, he said, and he didn't think anything would be more soothing than getting a massage and listening to violin music at the same time.

So at 9 p.m., I headed up to the second floor as the first men were arriving. From then until 11:30 p.m., I played everything I could do from memory: Bach B Minor Partita, Tchaikovsky's violin concerto, the Dvořák concerto, Paganini Caprices 1 and 17, Vivaldi "Winter" and "Spring," the theme from *Schindler's List*, Tchaikovsky's "Melodie," "Meditation" from *Thaïs*, "Amazing Grace," "My Country 'Tis of Thee," "Turkey in the Straw," "Bile Them Cabbages Down."

Never have I played for a more grateful audience. Somehow it didn't matter that by the end, my intonation was shot and I had no bow control. I would have lost any competition I was playing in, but it didn't matter. The men would come up the stairs in full gear, remove their helmets, look at me, and smile. At 11:20, I was introduced to Col. Slack, head of the division. After thanking me, he said to his friends, "Boy, today was the toughest day yet. I made the mistake of going back into the pit, and I'll never do that again."

Eager to hear a firsthand account, I asked, "What did you see?" He stopped, swallowed hard, and said, "What you'd expect to see." The colonel stood there as I played a lengthy rendition of "Amazing Grace," which he claimed was the best he'd ever heard. By this time it was 11:30, and I didn't think I could play anymore. I asked Sergeant Major if it would be appropriate if I played the national anthem. He shouted above the chaos of the milling soldiers to call them to attention, and I played "The Star-Spangled Banner" as the 300 men of the 69th Division saluted an invisible flag.

After shaking a few hands and packing up, I was prepared to leave when one of the privates accosted me and told me the colonel wanted to see me again. He took me down to the War Room, but we couldn't find the colonel, so he gave me a tour of the War Room. It turns out that the division I played for is the famous Fighting 69th, the most decorated division in the U.S. Army. He pointed out a letter from Abraham Lincoln offering his condolences after the Battle of Antietam—the 69th suffered the most casualties of any division at that historic battle.

Finally, we located the colonel. After thanking me again, he presented me with the coin of the regiment. "We only give these to someone who's done something special for the 69th," he informed me. He called over the division's historian to tell me the significance of all the symbols on the coin.

As I rode the taxi back to Juilliard—free, of course, since taxi service is free in New York right now—I was numb. Not only was this evening the proudest I've ever felt to be an American, it was my most meaningful as a musician and a person as well. At Juilliard, kids are hypercritical of each other and very competitive. The teachers expect, and in most cases get, technical perfection. But this wasn't about that. The soldiers didn't care that I had so many memory slips I lost count. They didn't care that when I forgot how the second movement of the Tchaikovsky went, I had to come up with my own insipid improvisation until I somehow (and I still don't know how) got to a cadence.

I've never seen a more appreciative audience, and I've never understood so fully what it means to communicate music to other people. So how did it change me as a person?

Let's just say that, next time I want to get into a petty argument about whether Richter or Horowitz was better, I'll remember that when I asked the colonel to describe the pit formed by the tumbling of the towers, he couldn't. Words only go so far, and even music can only go a little further from there.

Your friend,

William Harvey

William's letter made me very proud to be a musician. He represents so many people who have the gift of music to give. His compassion and generosity express the true spirit of most of humanity. We are all grateful to him.

I asked William to share how the impact of this experience continues to shape his life and musical goals, and he said:

Aside from the general emotional impact I felt, it has had the very specific effect of making me more open to alternate career paths. Before I played for the Fighting 69th, I was dead set on being a soloist. Gotta go to Juilliard, gotta be a soloist, gotta be the next Joshua Bell or I'm worthless, that whole mentality. But now I would like a large part of my career to involve presenting music outside the concert hall, to people who can benefit from the emotional solace it can provide.

William's response reminds me of Dale Clevenger's expression of gratitude to his heart surgeon. You'll recall from the second chapter that Dale's doctor told him, "Dale, we physicians deal with muscle tissue and bones . . . but what you do affects our souls," to which Dale responded:

To me, playing music is a very high calling: it is a responsibility, and a sacred trust. Making music may sometimes be difficult and sometimes fun—but for me at least, it is first, last, and always an honor and a joy.

THE CONTINUING PATH TO TRUE ARTISTRY

I began this book with the promise that the mastery of music would not be about what we do as musicians, but rather who we are as people. Now that we have heard from so many wonderful musical artists, I believe that what they have shown us is even more profound: that what we do as musicians and who we are as people cannot be separated, that life and music are interwoven in ways that language cannot match.

There is this gift we have, which is also the inspiration we crave, and a technique that we can learn ourselves and teach to others: we call it music. It is uniquely human. To those who grieve, it can offer solace, to those fatigued, laughter, and to those who are in love, the sweetest and most intimate communication.

Music is the voice of our humanity, the voice of truth and beauty, the inner voice of the soul. The mastery of music comes from within the human spirit—this is the pathway of a true artist.

One of life's joys is to fully experience our connection to this inner voice that inspires us to continue to grow and learn as human beings. It is a rushing crystalline current that is available to anyone who chooses to acknowledge its existence. The song that Mozart captured without having to change a note, the song that Beethoven heard with a relentless desire to clarify and perfect, the song that we glimpse and keep returning for more—this song is alive in us, this voice will never stop singing. These are the masters. This was their path. It's a journey we can all travel. It is our privilege to be inspired by it, in our silences, in our music making, and in our life on earth.

Let us travel the pathway to mastery together. *The road goes ever on....*

CODA: ACKNOWLEDGMENTS AND THANKS

It all started in the summer of 1998 when I was hiking with my wife, Mary, in Sun Valley, Idaho. I was playing with the Sun Valley Summer Symphony at the time; it had been sixteen years since I had written *The Inner Game of Music*. I had been thinking for a couple years about taking a new tack in my work. Mary was already on her own path of self-discovery. She had enrolled in a master's program in Culture and Spirituality at Holy Names College in Oakland, California. She wanted to leave her stressful professional counseling work in alcohol and drug addiction and explore some other "disciplines of the heart." She was writing, dancing, creating art works, and evolving—and I wasn't. I guess that part of my desire to grow and learn came from the envy I felt as I watched my wife proceeding along this path.

I presented the idea of writing a novel to Mary on this mountain walk. I had an idea for a story about a lost traveler looking for the "keys to his soul"; he would run into groups of musicians, and each instrumental group would present him with another lesson to learn, another station on his quest. Mary listened to me in such a way that I felt inspired to stay with the idea. Six months later, on a car ride from Los Angeles to San

Francisco, we talked some more—and the book began to take shape. We made a list of the qualities I wanted to explore, and wrote it down while driving. There was an energy there that Mary nurtured; she encouraged me. When I get on an idea, I really don't think about whether it is possible or what it will take to make it happen. After that car ride, I was on my journey—officially. And it continues today.

Thank you, Mary Tarbell-Green, for your acknowledgment and support. This book all started with you.

When I think further back, I remember my parents teaching me as a child that I should make a contribution while I'm on this earth, that I needed to *do something* with my life. I want to make them proud of me. Their support has been and remains invaluable to me, and their expectation constantly reminds me that I need to continue to learn and to give. My oldest son, Zachary, has taught me much and inspired me more, through his community service, his sense of humor and compassion for others. My stepson Rich is a gifted actor and poet; he reminds me that creativity is there for those who want to listen. I cannot describe the pride and thrill of playing music together with one's own blood: playing with my musician percussionist son Adam has fueled my love and passion. I thank you all for being an inspiration in my life, and in this journey into my own pursuit of artistry.

During the first several months of writing this book, I had the privilege and pleasure of working with the editor of our *International Society of Bassists Journal,* my bassist colleague Joelle Morton. When I saw how she edited my "bass column" for our double bass journal, I begged her to help me with this book. She nurtured me through the first couple of chapters, helping me to learn about writing until it became obvious that she didn't have the time to both help me and still earn a living! Then I was reunited with my *Inner Game of Music* partner and private editor Charles Cameron. He has served as the spokesperson for everyone who doesn't play the double bass! Charles takes what I write and rephrases it with a touch of Mozart. He is a master poet and has a gift of words that allows him to make a technical subject readable and engaging—for other musicians, educators, amateurs, critics, skeptics, believers, nonbelievers, and nonmusicians. Charles, you are the voice behind my voice, and know what I mean better than I know myself! Thank you!

My gratitude to Timothy Gallwey is unending. This book would not have been possible had I not written *The Inner Game of Music* with Tim. He gave me the opportunity to develop the Inner Game for musicians, which nurtured my curiosity to learn more about what goes on in the soul of the musician. This pathway opened endless doors that made it possible for me to embark on this current journey exploring true artistry with all these great musicians.

A special thank-you to Mark Stryker, the music critic for the *Detroit Free Press*, for taking the time and interest to write the Prelude.

I had the help of many experts who gave me names to contact about each of the instruments or disciplines I explored. Tim Janof not only helped line up some of the world's great cellists, but as the experienced editor of the Internet Cello Society, he gave me critical feedback on every chapter. Jeffrey Snedeker was my horn contact. My percussionist son Adam Green suggested the percussionists I should speak to. Linda Gilbert helped me with the wind players. The trumpet heros came from my friend at A&G Music who knows everyone in the business, Dick Akright. My English colleague the composer Tony Osborne made recommendations as to the violists, some composers, and other U.K. personalities, and other violist contacts came from my Indiana University classmate Alan DeVeritch. Tuba contacts were assisted by Carol Nowicke. Ron Gallman, my dear friend and boss at the San Francisco Symphony Education Department, suggested management and musical colleagues. My friend the fabulous singer Catherine Keen arranged all the opera interviews. Jane Wenstrup and Jim Ferguson brought me pop and theater contacts. A special thanks to Jeffrey Kahane for help and support. And choral contacts came from Alec Harris at GIA Music, who also publishes the Inner Game of Music workbooks.

Talking to some of the artists involved going through managers, agents, or publicists. If some of these "behind the scenes" people hadn't trusted very early on that this was a worthwhile project which would be in the best interests of their clients, many of these interviews would not have been possible. I want to thank the following individuals for trusting me, making these decisions, and setting up the interviews with their clients: Judy Arnold, Jane Covner, Sharon Devol, Michele Eaton, Linda Goldstein, Ed Keane, George Moore, David Sholemson, and Tommy Wilson.

I'd like to thank my book agent Judith Weber of Sobel/Weber Associates and Abner Stein in Europe for securing the publication rights with my editor Charles Conrad at Doubleday Broadway. I'd like to thank Claire Johnson at Doubleday Broadway for her invaluable editorial suggestions. Special thanks to the copy editors, marketing department, and sales force at Doubleday Broadway and Morven Knowles and her entire staff at Pan Macmillan in the U.K.

I'd like to thank my young private bass students in California, who continue to challenge me as their teacher. These young people aged eleven to eighteen are pleasantly unimpressed with my past musical experiences and accomplishments, which frankly don't mean a thing to them. And while they may like me as a person, all they really care about is that I keep giving them great music to play, and they keep having fun learning and performing. It is my sacred trust to keep feeding their souls the food of music. I feel honored to be in this position, and I'm grateful to these young bassists for giving me the opportunity to develop these skills for them—and for myself.

In 1992 I began to study with my longtime bass idol, the virtuoso bassist François Rabbath. I had sponsored Rabbath in courses and taught his method to my pupils during the eighties, but I had been too involved with my Inner Game of Music work to actually physically study with him. The study I began with him in the nineties was intended to be short-term: I wanted to learn his technique and sound, and capture some of his spirit in performance. At first he told me this would only take a few years of commuting to Paris, but as my studies progressed it became clear that I was learning the lesson of this book. Once I had solved one problem, I found more problems to solve. . . .

François Rabbath, approaching seventy, was continuing to make *new* technical discoveries on the bass and sharing them with me. And he practiced like a young student. The more I learned, the more I realized I didn't know. Soon I was getting the sense that this three-year journey was going to take a lot longer than three years. But I was enjoying the learning, and realizing that when I opened one new door, it led me down a new path that often contained pleasant surprises. Asking myself one question, I started to find two answers. And this led to more questions.

This journey with Rabbath was not something, I realized, that could be completed in a few years: it is endless, it continues to this day. So thank you, François, for, in addition to so much else, convincing me that there is no reason to complete any journey on the road to artistry—it just keeps going.

Now I am finally willing to accept that I'll never finish this journey. I invite you to accompany me. The journey continues.

FURTHER READING

Books for Staying on the Pathway and Leading to Others

Benzon, William L. *Beethoven's Anvil: Music in Mind and Culture.* New York: Basic Books, 2001.

Berger, Dorita S. *Toward the Zen of Performance.* St. Louis: MMB Music, 1999.

Blum, David. *Casals and the Art of Interpretation.* Berkeley: University of California Press, 1977.

Cameron, Julia, with Mark Bryan. *The Artist's Way.* New York: Tarcher/Putnam Book, 1992.

Campbell, Don G. *Introduction to the Musical Brain.* St. Louis: MMB Music, 1984.

Campbell, Don G. *The Mozart Effect.* New York: Avon Books, 1997.

Campbell, Don G. *Music and Miracles.* Wheaton Ill.: Quest Books, 1993.

Casals, Pablo. *Joys and Sorrows.* London: Macdonald, 1970.

Csikszentmihalyi, Mihaly. *Flow: The Psychology of Optimal Experience.* New York: HarperCollins, 1991.

Feldenkrais, Moshe. *Awareness Through Movement.* New York: Harper & Row, 1977.

Fiedler, Johanna. *Molto Agitato.* New York: Nan A. Talese/Doubleday, 2001.

Gallwey, W. Timothy. *The Inner Game of Tennis.* New York: Random House, 1974, 1997.

Gallwey, W. Timothy. *Inner Tennis: Playing the Game.* New York: Random House, 1976.

Gallwey, W. Timothy, with Robert Kreigle. *The Inner Game of Skiing.* New York: Random House, 1977.

Gallwey, W. Timothy. *The Inner Game of Golf.* New York: Random House, 1981, 1998.

Gallwey, W. Timothy. *The Inner Game of Work.* New York: Random House, 1999.

Gendlin, Eugene. *Focusing.* New York: Bantam Books, 1981.

Gorden, Edwin. *Learning Sequences in Music.* Chicago: GIA Publications, 1980, 1984, 1988, 1993.

Green, Barry, with W. Timothy Gallwey. *The Inner Game of Music.* New York: Doubleday, 1986.

Green, Barry, with Eugene Corporon. *The Inner Game of Music Workbook for Band.* Chicago: GIA Publications, 1991.

Green, Barry, with Margery Deutch. *The Inner Game of Music Workbook for Orchestra.* Chicago: GIA Publications, 1992.

Green, Barry, with Gerald Doan. *The Inner Game of Music Workbook for Strings.* Chicago: GIA Publications, 1992.

Green, Barry. *The Inner Game of Music Workbook for Solo Instruments.* 2 vols. Chicago: GIA Publications, 1993.

Green, Barry, with Donna Loewy. *The Inner Game of Music Workbook for Voice.* Chicago: GIA Publications, 1994.

Green, Barry, with Phyllis Lehrer. *The Inner Game of Music Workbook for Piano.* Chicago: GIA Publications, 1994.

Green, Barry, with Greg Lyne and Larry Ajer. *The Inner Game of Music Workbook for Men's and Women's Barbershop Quartets, Choruses and Classrooms.* Kenosha, Wis.: SPEBSQSA Inc., 1996.

Green, Barry, with Eugene Corporon. *The Inner Game of Music Video.* Madison: University of Wisconsin, Clinics on Cassette, 1990.

Greene, Don, Ph.D. *Fight Your Fear and Win.* New York: Broadway Books/ Doubleday, 2001.

Havas, Kato. *Stage Fright: Its Causes and Cures.* London: Bosworth, 1973.

Jordan, James. *The Musician's Soul.* Chicago: GIA Publications, 1999.

Kemp, Anthony E. *The Musical Temperment.* New York: Oxford University Press, 1996.

Lamott, Anne. *Bird by Bird.* New York: Anchor Books/Random House, 1994.

Lautzenheiser, Tim. *The Art of Successful Teaching*. Chicago: GIA Publications, 1992.

Lautzenheiser, Tim. *The Joy of Inspired Teaching*. Chicago: GIA Publications, 1993.

Lehrer, Paul, and Robert Woolfolk. *Principles and Practices of Stress Management*. New York: Guilford Press, 1984.

Leonard, George. *The Silent Pulse*. New York: Dutton, 1978.

Littlehales, Lillian. *Pablo Casals*. Westport, Conn.: Greenwood Press, 1970.

May, Rollo. *The Courage to Create*. New York: Norton, 1975, 1995.

Nachmanovitch, Stephen. *Free Play*. New York: Jeremy P. Tarcher/Perigee Books, 1990.

Nierenberg, Gerard I. *The Art of Creative Thinking*. New York: Simon & Schuster, 1982.

Palmer, Helen. *The Enneagram*. San Francisco: Harper, 1991.

Pirsig, Robert M. *Zen and the Art of Motorcycle Maintenance*. New York: Bantam, 1974.

Pleeth, William. *Cello*. London: Macdonald, 1982.

Redfield, James. *The Celestine Prophecy*. New York: Warner Books, 1993.

Ristad, Eloise. *A Soprano on Her Head*. Moab, Utah: Real People Press, 1982.

Schickele, Prof. Peter. *The Definitive Biography of P.D.Q. Bach*. New York: Random House, 1976.

Schuller, Gunther. *The Compleat Conductor*. New York: Oxford University Press, 1997.

Schuller, Gunther. *Musings: The Musical Worlds of Gunther Schuller*. New York: Oxford University Press, 1986.

Stewart, M. Dee. *Arnold Jacobs: The Legacy of a Master*. Chicago: Instrumentalist, 1987.

Storr, Anthony. *Music and the Mind*. New York: Free Press/Macmillan, 1992.

Sullivan, J.W.N. *Beethoven: His Spiritual Development*. New York: Random House, 1960.

Suzuki, Shimichi. *Nurtured by Love*. New York: Exposition Press, 1969.

Tame, David. *The Secret Power of Music*. New York: Destiny Books, 1984.

Triplett, Robert. *Stage Fright*. Chicago: Nelson-Hall, 1983.

Werner, Kenny. *Effortless Mastery*. New Albany, Indiana: Jamey Abersold, 1996.

Wilson, Elizabeth. *Jacqueline du Pré—Her Life, Her Music, Her Legend*. New York: Arcade Publishing, 1999.

Wilson, Frank R. *Tone Deaf and All Thumbs*. New York: Viking Penguin, 1986.

© Paul Haggard

A B O U T   T H E   A U T H O R

Barry Green served as principal bassist of the Cincinnati Symphony for twenty-eight years, and more recently principal bassist of the California Symphony and the Sun Valley, Idaho Summer Symphony. He is currently active as a bass soloist, clinician and teaches bass at the University of California, Santa Cruz, and for the young bassist program of the San Francisco Symphony Education Department. Green has been performing for young audiences in schools in the Bay Area, as well as performing bass concerts and clinics on tour. He is also the author of the Inner Game of Music, with W. Timothy Gallwey and has written seven Inner Game of Music workbooks for keyboard, voice, instruments, and ensembles. He conducts seminars throughout the world on principles of his Inner Game and Mastery of Music books that also include his current work in the field of creativity and inprovisation.

For information on Green's personal appearances and publications, please contact his website at www.innergameofmusic.com and www.themasteryofmusic.com.